Object Oriented Design and Programming

OBJECT ORIENTED DESIGN AND PROGRAMMING

Anju Bhati

CENTRUM PRESS
NEW DELHI-110002 (INDIA)

CENTRUM PRESS
H.O.: 4360/4, Ansari Road, Daryaganj,
New Delhi-110002 (India)
Tel: 23278000, 23261597, 23255577, 23286875
B.O.: No. 1015, Ist Main Road, BSK IIIrd Stage,
IIIrd Phase, IIIrd Block, Bangalore-560085 (INDIA)
Tel: 080-41723429
Email: centrumpress@gmail.com
Visit us at: www.centrumpress.com

Object Oriented Design and Programming

First Edition, 2011

PRINTED IN INDIA

Printed at Tarun Offset Printers, Delhi-110053

Contents

Preface

Object oriented programming (OOP) is a programming paradigm "objects" data structures consisting of data fields and methods together with their interactions - to design applications and computer programs. Programming techniques may include features such as data abstraction, encapsulation, messaging, modularity, polymorphism, and inheritance. Many modern programming languages now support OOP. Object oriented programming is a method of programming based on a hierarchy of classes, and well-defined and cooperating objects.

Object oriented programming, like most interesting new developments, builds on some old ideas, extends them, and puts them together in novel ways. The result is many-faceted and a clear step forward for the art of programming. An object-oriented approach makes programs more intuitive to design, faster to develop, more amenable to modifications, and easier to understand. It leads not only to new ways of constructing programs, but also to new ways of conceiving the programming task.

Nevertheless, object oriented programming presents some formidable obstacles to those who would like to understand what it's all about or begin trying it out. It introduces a new way of doing things that may seem strange at first, and it comes with an extensive terminology that can take some getting used to. The terminology will help in the end, but it's not always easy to learn. Moreover, there are as yet few full-fledged object oriented development environments available to try out. It can be difficult to get started.

Author

1

Concept of Programming

OVERVIEW

The awk, also called nawk, provides additional capabilities. Every modern Unix system comes with a version of new awk, and its use is recommended over old awk. Different systems vary in what the two versions are called. Some have oawk and awk, for the old and new versions, respectively.

With original awk, *you can*:

- Think of a text file as made up of records and fields in a textual database.
- Perform arithmetic and string operations.
- Use programming constructs such as loops and conditionals.
- Produce formatted reports.

With nawk, *you can also*:

- Define your own functions.
- Execute Unix commands from a script.
- Process the results of Unix commands.
- Process command-line arguments more gracefully.
- Work more easily with multiple input streams.
- Flush open output files and pipes.

In addition, with GNU awk (gawk), *you can*:

- Use regular expressions to separate records, as well as fields.
- Skip to the start of the next file, not just the next record.
- Perform more powerful string substitutions.
- Retrieve and format system time values.

COMMAND-LINE SYNTAX

The syntax for invoking awk has two forms:

```
awk [options] 'script' var=value file(s)
awk [options] -f scriptfile var=value file(s)
```

You can specify a *script* directly on the command line, or you can store a script in a *scriptfile* and specify it with *-f*. nawk allows multiple *-f* scripts. Variables can be assigned a value on the command line. The value can be a literal, a shell variable (*$name*), or a command substitution ('cmd'), but the value is available only after the BEGIN statement is executed. awk operates on one or more *files*. If none are specified (or if - is specified), awk reads from the standard input.

The recognized options are:

-Ffs

Set the field separator to *fs*. This is the same as setting the system variable FS. Original awk allows the field separator to be only a single character. Nawk allows *fs* to be a regular expression. Each input line, or record, is divided into fields by whitespace (blanks or tabs) or by some other user-definable record separator. Fields are referred to by the variables $1, $2..., $n. $0 refers to the entire record.

`-v var=value`

Assign a *value* to variable *var*. This allows assignment before the script begins execution (available in nawk only). To print the first three (colon-separated) fields of each record on separate lines:

```
awk -F: '{print $1; print $2; print $3}'/
etc/passwd
```

PATTERNS AND PROCEDURES

awk scripts consist of patterns and procedures:

```
pattern {procedure}
```

Both are optional. If *pattern* is missing, {*procedure*} is applied to all lines; if {*procedure*} is missing, the matched line is printed.

Patterns

A pattern can be any of the following:

```
/regular expression/
```

```
relational expression
pattern-matching expression
BEGIN
END
```

- Expressions can be composed of quoted strings, numbers, operators, functions, defined variables, or any of the predefined variables described later under "Awk System Variables.
- In addition, ^ and $ refer to the beginning and end of a string (such as the fields), respectively, rather than the beginning and end of a line.
- Relational expressions use the relational operators listed under "Operators" later in this section. Comparisons can be either string or numeric. For example, **2 > 1** selects lines for which the second field is greater than the first.
- Pattern-matching expressions use the operators ~ (match) and !~ (don't match).
- The **BEGIN** pattern lets you specify procedures that take place *before* the first input line is processed.
- The **END** pattern lets you specify procedures that take place *after* the last input record is read.

Except for BEGIN and END, patterns can be combined with the Boolean operators || (or), && (and), and ! (not). A range of lines can also be specified using comma-separated patterns:

```
pattern,pattern
```

BUILT-IN VARIABLES

Version	Variable	Description
awk	FILENAME	Current filename
	FS	Field separator (a space)
	NF	Number of fields in current record
	NR	Number of the current record
	OFMT	Output format for numbers ("%.6g") and for conversion to string
	OFS	Output field separator (a space)
	ORS	Output record separator (a newline)

	RS	Record separator (a newline)
	$0	Entire input record
	$*n*	*n*th field in current record; fields are separated by FS
nawk	ARGC	Number of arguments on command line
	ARGV	An array containing the command-line arguments, indexed from 0 to ARGC - 1
	CONVFMT	String conversion format for numbers ("%.6g") (POSIX)
	ENVIRON	An associative array of environment variables
	FNR	Like NR, but relative to the current file
	RLENGTH	Length of the string matched by match() function
	RSTART	First position in the string matched by match() function
	SUBSEP	Separator character for array subscripts ("\034")
gawk	ARGIND	Index in ARGV of current input file
	ERRNO	A string indicating the error when a redirection fails for getline or if close() fails
	FIELDWIDTHS	A space-separated list of field widths to use for splitting up the record, instead of FS
	IGNORECASE	When true, all regular expression matches, string comparisons, and calls to index()s ignore case
	RT	The text matched by RS, which can be a regular expression in gawk

OPERATORS

The following table lists the operators, in order of increasing precedence, that are available in awk.

The table below lists the operators, in order of increasing precedence, that are available in awk.

Symbol	Meaning
= += -= *=/= %= ^= **=	Assignment
?:	C conditional expression (nawk only)
||	Logical OR (short-circuit)
&&	Logical AND (short-circuit)
in	Array membership (nawk only)
~ !~	Match regular expression and negation
< ⇐ > ⇒ != ==	Relational operators
(blank)	Concatenation
+ –	Addition, subtraction
*/ %	Multiplication, division, and modulus (remainder)
+ – !	Unary plus and minus, and logical negation
^ **	Exponentiation
++ —	Increment and decrement, either prefix or postfix
$	Field reference

ARRAY ASSIGNMENTS

Variables can be assigned a value with an = sign.

For example:

```
FS = ","
```

Expressions using the operators +, –,/, and % (modulo) can be assigned to variables. Arrays can be created with the split() function (see below), or they can simply be named in an assignment statement. Array elements can be subscripted with numbers (*array*..., *array*[*n*]) or with strings. Arrays subscripted by strings are called *associative arrays*. For example, to count the number of widgets you have, you could use the following script: In fact, all arrays in awk are associative; numeric subscripts are converted to strings before using them as array subscripts. Associative arrays are one of awk's most powerful features.

```
/widget/{count["widget"]++}  Count widgets
END {print count["widget"]}  Print the count
```

You can use the special for loop to read all the elements of an associative array:

```
for (item in array)
    process array[item]
```

The index of the array is available as item, while the value of an element of the array can be referenced as array[item]. You can use the operator in to see if an element exists by testing to see if its index exists (nawk only):

```
if (index in array)
```

This sequence tests that array[index] exists, but you cannot use it to test the value of the element referenced by array[index]. You can also delete individual elements of the array using the delete statement (nawk only).

Escape Sequences

Within string and regular expression constants, the following escape sequences may be used. The \x escape sequence is a common extension; it is not part of POSIX awk.

Sequence	Meaning	Sequence	Meaning
\a	Alert (bell)	\v	Vertical tab
\b	Backspace	\\	Literal backslash
\f	Form feed	*nnn*	Octal value *nnn*
\n	Newline	\x*nn*	Hexadecimal value *nn*
\r	Carriage return	\"	Literal double quote (in strings)
\t	Tab	\/	Literal slash (in regular expressions)

USER-DEFINED FUNCTIONS

Nawk allows you to define your own functions. This makes it easy to encapsulate sequences of steps that need to be repeated into a single place, and reuse the code from anywhere in your program.

Note: for user-defined functions, no space is allowed

between the function name and the left parenthesis when the function is called. The following function capitalizes each word in a string. It has one parameter, named input, and five local variables, which are written as extra parameters.

```
# capitalize each word in a string
function capitalize(input, result, words, n,
i, w)
{
        result = ""
        n = split(input, words, " ")
        for (i = 1; i <= n; i++) {
              w = words[i]
              w = toupper(substr(w, 1, 1))
                    substr(w, 2)
              if (i > 1)
                      result = result " "
              result = result w
        }
        return result
    }
    # main program, for testing
    {print capitalize($0)}
```

With this input data:

```
A test line with words and numbers like 12 on it.
```

This program produces:

```
A Test Line With Words And Numbers Like 12 On It.
```

FUNCTIONS AND COMMANDS

The following alphabetical list of keywords and functions includes all that are available in awk, nawk, and gawk. nawk includes all old awk functions and keywords, plus some additional ones (marked as {N}). gawk includes all nawk functions and keywords, plus some additional ones (marked as {G}). Items marked with {B} are available in the Bell Labs awk. Items that aren't marked with a symbol are available in all versions.

atan2

```
atan2(y, x)
```

Return the arctangent of *y/x* in radians. {N}

break

```
break
```

Exit from a while, for, or do loop.

close

```
close(filename-expr)
close(command-expr)
```

In most implementations of awk, you can have only 10 files open simultaneously and one pipe. Therefore, nawk provides a close function that allows you to close a file or a pipe. It takes as an argument the same expression that opened the pipe or file.

This expression must be identical, character by character, to the one that opened the file or pipe; even whitespace is significant. {N}

continue

```
continue
```

Begin next iteration of while, for, or do loop.

cos

cos(*x*)

Return the cosine of *x*, an angle in radians. {N}

delete

```
delete array[element]
delete array
```

Delete *element* from *array*. The brackets are typed literally. The second form is a common extension, which deletes *all* elements of the array at one shot. {N}

do

```
do
  statement
while (expr)
```

Looping statement. Execute *statement*, then evaluate *expr* and, if true, execute *statement* again. A series of statements must be put within braces. {N}

exit

```
exit [expr]
```

Exit from script, reading no new input. The END procedure, if it exists, will be executed. An optional *expr* becomes awk's return value.

exp

```
exp(x)
```

Return exponential of x (e^x).

fflush

```
fflush([output-expr])
```

Flush any buffers associated with open output file or pipe *output-expr*. {B} gawk extends this function. If no *output-expr* is supplied, it flushes standard output. If *output-expr* is the null string (""), it flushes all open files and pipes. {G}

for

```
for (init-expr; test-expr; incr-expr)
      statement
```

C-style looping construct. *init-expr* assigns the initial value of a counter variable. *test-expr* is a relational expression that is evaluated each time before executing the *statement*. When *test-expr* is false, the loop is exited. *incr-expr* increments the counter variable after each pass. All the expressions are optional. A missing *test-expr* is considered to be true. A series of statements must be put within braces.

for

```
for (item in array)
      statement
```

Special loop designed for reading associative arrays. For each element of the array, the *statement* is executed; the element can be referenced by*array*[*item*]. A series of statements must be put within braces.

function

```
function name(parameter-list) {
statements
}
```

Create *name* as a user-defined function consisting of awk *statements* that apply to the specified list of parameters. No space is allowed between *name*and the left paren when the function is called. {N}

getline

```
getline [var] [< file]
   or
command | getline [var]
```

Read next line of input. Original awk doesn't support the syntax to open multiple input streams. The first form reads input from *file*; the second form reads the output of *command*. Both forms read one record at a time, and each time the statement is executed, it gets the next record of input. The record is assigned to $0 and is parsed into fields, setting NF, NR and FNR. If *var* is specified, the result is assigned to *var*, and $0 and NF aren't changed. Thus, if the result is assigned to a variable, the current record doesn't change. getline is actually a function and returns 1 if it reads a record successfully, 0 if end-of-file is encountered, and –1 if it's otherwise unsuccessful. {N}

gensub

```
gensub(r, s, h [, t])
```

General substitution function. Substitute *s* for matches of the regular expression *r* in the string *t*. If *h* is a number, replace the *h*th match.

If it is "g" or"G", substitute globally. If *t* is not supplied, $0 is used. Return the new string value. The original *t* is *not* modified. (Compare gsub and sub.) {G}

gsub

```
gsub(r, s [, t])
```

Globally substitute *s* for each match of the regular expression *r* in the string *t*. If *t* is not supplied, defaults to $0. Return the number of substitutions. {N}

if

```
if (condition)
  statement
[else
    statement]
```

If *condition* is true, do *statement(s)*; otherwise do *statement* in the optional else clause. The *condition* can be an expression using any of the relational operators <, ⇐, ==, !=, ⇒, or >, as well as the array membership operator in, and the pattern-matching operators ~ and !~ (*e.g.*, if ($1 ~/[Aa].*/)).

A series of statements must be put within braces. Another if can directly follow an else in order to produce a chain of tests or decisions.

index

```
index(str, substr)
```

Return the position (starting at 1) of *substr* in *str*, or zero if *substr* is not present in *str*.

int

```
int(x)
```

Return integer value of *x* by truncating any fractional part.

length

```
length([arg])
```

Return length of *arg*, or the length of $0 if no argument.

log

```
log(x)
```

Return the natural logarithm (base *e*) of *x*.

match

```
match(s, r)
```

Function that matches the pattern, specified by the regular expression *r*, in the string *s*, and returns either the position in *s*, where the match begins, or 0 if no occurrences are found. Sets the values of RSTART and RLENGTH to the start and length of the match, respectively. {N}

next

`next`

Read next input line and start new cycle through pattern/procedures statements.

nextfile

`nextfile`

Stop processing the current input file and start new cycle through pattern/procedures statements, beginning with the first record of the next file. {B} {G}

print

`print [output-expr[...]] [dest-expr]`

Evaluate the *output-expr* and direct it to standard output, followed by the value of ORS. Each comma-separated *output-expr* is separated in the output by the value of OFS. With no *output-expr*, print $0.

Output Redirections

dest-expr is an optional expression that directs the output to a file or pipe.

`> file`

Directs the output to a file, overwriting its previous contents.

`>> file`

Appends the output to a file, preserving its previous contents. In both cases, the file is created if it does not already exist.

`| command`

Directs the output as the input to a Unix command. Be careful not to mix > and >> for the same file. Once a file has been opened with >, subsequent output statements continue to append to the file until it is closed.

Remember to call close() when you have finished with a file or pipe.

If you don't, eventually you will hit the system limit on the number of simultaneously open files.

printf

```
printf(format [, expr-list]) [dest-expr]
```

An alternative output statement borrowed from the C language. It can produce formatted output and also output data without automatically producing a newline. *format* is a string of format specifications and constants. *expr-list* is a list of arguments corresponding to format specifiers. *Format* follows the conventions of the C-language *printf*(3S) library function.

Here are a few of the most common formats:

%s	A string.
%d	A decimal number.
%*n.m*f	A floating-point number; *n* = total number of digits. *m* = number of digits after decimal point.
%[–]*nc*	*n* specifies minimum field length for format type *c*, while - left-justifies value in field; otherwise, value is right-justified.

Like any string, *format* can also contain embedded escape sequences: \n (newline) or \t (tab) being the most common. Spaces and literal text can be placed in the *format* argument by quoting the entire argument. If there are multiple expressions to be printed, there should be multiple formats specified

Example

Using the script.

```
{printf("The sum on line %d is %.0f.\n", NR,
$1+$2)}
```

The following input line:

```
5    5
```

Produces this output, followed by a newline:

```
The sum on line 1 is 10.
```

rand

`rand()`

Generate a random number between 0 and 1. This function returns the same series of numbers each time the script is executed, unless the random number generator is seeded using srand(). {N}

return

`return [expr]`

Used within a user-defined function to exit the function, returning value of *expr*. The return value of a function is undefined if *expr* is not provided. {N}

sin

`sin(x)`

Return the sine of *x*, an angle in radians. {N}

split

`split(string, array [, sep])`

Split *string* into elements of array *array*[1]...,*array*[*n*]. The string is split at each occurrence of separator *sep*. If *sep* is not specified, FS is used. The number of array elements created is returned.

sprintf

`sprintf(format [, expressions])`

Return the formatted value of one or more *expressions*, using the specified *format* (see printf). Data is formatted but not printed. {N}

sqrt

`sqrt(arg)`

Return square root of *arg*.

srand

`srand([expr])`

Use optional *expr* to set a new seed for the random number generator. Default is the time of day. Return value is the old seed. {N}

strftime

`strftime([format [,timestamp]])`

Format *timestamp* according to *format*. Return the formatted string. The *timestamp* is a time-of-day value in seconds since midnight, January 1, 1970, UTC. The *format* string is similar to that of sprintf. (See the Example for systime.) If *timestamp* is omitted, it defaults to the current time. If *format*is omitted, it defaults to a value that produces output similar to that of date. {G}

sub

`sub(r, s [, t])`

Substitute *s* for first match of the regular expression *r* in the string *t*. If *t* is not supplied, defaults to $0. Return 1 if successful; 0 otherwise. {N}

substr

`substr(string, beg [, len])`

Return substring of *string* at beginning position *beg* and the characters that follow to maximum specified length *len*. If no length is given, use the rest of the string.

system

`system(command)`

Function that executes the specified *command* and returns its status. The status of the executed command typically indicates success or failure. A value of 0 means that the command executed successfully. A nonzero value indicates a failure of some sort. The documentation for the command you're running will give you the details. The output of the command is *not* available for processing within the awk script. Use *command* | getline to read the output of a command into the script. {N}

systime

`systime()`

Return a time-of-day value in seconds since midnight, January 1, 1970, UTC. {G}

Example: Log the start and end times of a data-processing program:

```
BEGIN {
        now = systime()
        mesg = strftime("Started at %m/%d/%Y
        %H:%M:%S", now)
        print mesg
}
process data...
END {
        now = systime()
        mesg = strftime("Ended at %m/%d/%Y
        %H:%M:%S", now)
        print mesg
}
```

Tolower

`tolower(`*`str`*`)`

Translate all uppercase characters in *str* to lowercase and return the new string.[6] {N}. [6] Very early versions of nawk don't support tolower() and toupper(). However, they are now part of the POSIX specification forawk, and are included in the SVR4 nawk.

toupper

`toupper(`*`str`*`)`

Translate all lowercase characters in *str* to uppercase and return the new string. {N}

while

```
while (condition)
statement
```

Do *statement* while *condition* is true (see if for a description of allowable conditions). A series of statements must be put within braces.

Printf Formats

Format specifiers for printf and sprintf have the following form:

`%[flag][width][.precision]letter`

The control letter is required. The format conversion control letters are as follows.

Character	Description
c	ASCII character
d	Decimal integer
i	Decimal integer (added in POSIX)
e	Floating-point format ([–]*d.precision*e[+–]*dd*)
E	Floating-point format ([–]*d.precision*E[+–]*dd*)
f	Floating-point format ([–]*ddd.precision*)
g	e or f conversion, whichever is shortest, with trailing zeros removed
G	E or f conversion, whichever is shortest, with trailing zeros removed
o	Unsigned octal value
s	String
x	Unsigned hexadecimal number; uses a-f for 10 to 15
X	Unsigned hexadecimal number; uses A-F for 10 to 15
%	Literal %

The optional flag is one of the following:

Character	Description
–	Left-justify the formatted value within the field.
space	Prefix positive values with a space and negative values with a minus.
+	Always prefix numeric values with a sign, even if the value is positive.
#	Use an alternate form: %**o** has a preceding 0; %x and %X are prefixed with 0x and 0X, respectively; %e, %E, and %f always have a decimal point in the result; and %g and %G do not have trailing zeros removed.
0	Pad output with zeros, not spaces. This happens only when the field width is wider than the converted result.

The optional *width* is the minimum number of characters to output. The result will be padded to this size if it is smaller. The 0 flag causes padding with zeros; otherwise, padding is with spaces.

The *precision* is optional. Its meaning varies by control letter, as shown in this table.

Conversion	**Precision Means**
%d, %i, %o %u, %x, %X	The minimum number of digits to print
%e, %E, %f	The number of digits to the right of the decimal point
%g, %G	The maximum number of significant digits
%s	The maximum number of characters to print

2

Imperative Programming Language

INTRODUCTION

THE LANGUAGE

ABC is an imperative language originally designed as a replacement for BASIC: interactive, very easy to learn, but structured, high-level, and easy to use. ABC has been designed iteratively, and the present version is the 4th iteration. It is suitable for general everyday programming, the sort of programming that you would use BASIC, Pascal, or AWK for. It is not a systems-programming language. It is an excellent teaching language, and because it is interactive, excellent for prototyping. It is much faster than Unix 'bc' for doing quick calculations. ABC programs are typically very compact, around a quarter to a fifth the size of the equivalent Pascal or C program. However, this is not at the cost of readability, on the contrary in fact. ABC is simple to learn due to the small number of types in the language (five). If you already know Pascal or something similar you can learn the whole language in an hour or so. It is easy to use because the data-types are very high-level.

The five types are:

- *Numbers*: Unbounded length, with exact arithmetic the rule
- *Texts (strings)*: Also unbounded length
- *Compounds*: Records without field names
- *Lists*: Sorted collections of any one type of items (bags or multi-sets)

- *Tables*: Generalised arrays with any one type of keys, any one type of items (finite mappings).

THE ENVIRONMENT

The implementation includes a programming environment that makes producing programs very much easier, since it knows a lot about the language, and can therefore do much of the work for you. For instance, if you type a W, the system suggests a command completion for you:

```
W?RITE ?
```

If that is what you want, you press [tab], and carry on typing the expression; if you wanted WHILE, you type an H, and the system changes the suggestion to match:

```
WH?ILE ?:
```

This mechanism works for commands you define yourself too. Similarly, if you type an open bracket or quote, you get the closing bracket or quote for free. You can ignore the suggestions if you want, and just type the commands full out.

There is support for workspaces for developing different programs. Within each workspace variables are persistent, so that if you stop using ABC and come back later, your variables are still there as you left them. This obviates the need for file-handling facilities: there is no conceptual difference between a variable and a file in ABC.

PROGRAM

These source files were produced by using the 'abc -p' option for packing a workspace. To unpack it in your own workspaces, save the file as F, choose the name of your new workspace W, and say:

```
abc -u -w W F
```

(you may freely choose the names W and F, but avoid using an existing workspace name for W).

A Telephone List

This uses the table data-type. In use, tables resemble arrays:

```
>>> PUT {} IN tel
```

```
>>> PUT 4054 IN tel["Jennifer"]
>>> PUT 4098 IN tel["Timo"]
>>> PUT 4134 IN tel["Guido"]
>>> WRITE tel["Jennifer"]
4054
```

You can write all ABC values out. Tables are kept sorted on the keys:

```
>>> WRITE tel
{["Guido"]: 4134; ["Jennifer"]: 4054; ["Timo"]:
4098}
```

The *keys* function returns a list:

```
>>> WRITE keys tel
{"Guido"; "Jennifer"; "Timo"}
>>> FOR name IN keys tel:
        WRITE name, ":", tel[name]/
Guido: 4134
Jennifer: 4054
Timo: 4098
```

You can define your own commands:

```
HOW TO DISPLAY t:
    FOR name IN keys t:
        WRITE name<<10, t[name]/
>>> DISPLAY tel
Guido 4134
Jennifer 4054
Timo 4098
```

To find the user of a given number, you can use a quantifier:

```
>>> IF SOME name IN keys tel HAS tel[name]
= 4054:
WRITE name
Jennifer
```

Or create the inverse table:

```
>>> PUT {} IN subscriber
>>> FOR name IN keys tel:
        PUT name IN subscriber[tel[name]]
>>> WRITE subscriber[4054]
Jennifer
>>> WRITE subscriber
```

```
{[4054]: "Jennifer"; [4098]: "Timo"; [4134]:
"Guido"}
```

Commands and functions are polymorphic:

```
>>> DISPLAY subscriber
4054        Jennifer
4098        Timo
4134        Guido
```

Functions may return any type. Note that indentation is significant - there are no BEGIN-END's or {}'s:

```
HOW TO RETURN inverse t:
   PUT {} IN inv
 FOR k IN keys t:
   PUT k IN inv[t[k]]
 RETURN inv
>>> WRITE inverse tel
{[4054]: "Jennifer"; [4098]: "Timo"; [4134]:
"Guido"}
>>> DISPLAY inverse inverse tel
Guido 4134
```

A Cross-reference Indexer

Text files' are represented as tables of numbers to strings:

```
HOW TO DISPLAY t:
   FOR name IN keys t:
     WRITE name<<10, t[name]/
>>> DISPLAY poem
1          I've never seen a purple cow
2          I hope I never see one
3          But I can tell you anyhow
4          I'd rather see than be one
```

The following function takes such a document, and returns the cross-reference index of the document.

A table from words to lists of line-numbers:

```
HOW TO RETURN index doc:
    PUT {} IN where
    FOR line.no IN keys doc:
         TREAT LINE
    RETURN where
```

```
TREAT LINE:
    FOR word IN split doc[line.no]:
        IF word not.in keys where:
           PUT {} IN where[word]
          INSERT line.no IN where[word]
```

Logic Programming

The program uses backtracking, and in the way it is formulated takes advantage of the fact that functions in *B* have no side-effects, in effect doing the backtracking automatically for you. However, the program does have the 'side effect' of writing the results out as it goes along, rather than returning the result. When pointing this out, Tim says:

In other words, if the effect you want to have is more than just writing your answer out, bad luck. The purpose of this article is to show that it is not at all difficult to write such a program, both using ABC's automatic backtracking*and* returning a result. Just for interest's sake, I shall also modify some other aspects of Tim's program, to compare how different approaches to data-structures affect the program, but this in no way affects the main point of the article, which is to demonstrate returning results in a backtracking program.

Rather than represent north and south by 1 and 0, I shall use the texts "N" and "S". For the text representation, we have to alter the definition of the function *opposite*:

```
HOW TO RETURN opposite position:
RETURN {["N"]: "S"; ["S"]: "N"}[position]
```

Just to test it:

```
WRITE opposite "N"
S
WRITE opposite "S"
N
```

(Alternatively, a global target could contain the above table, and be SHAREd wherever needed.)

Now a more explicit data-structure can be used to represent the positions, such as a table:

```
{["cabbage"]: "N"; ["farmer"]: "N"; ["goat"]:
"N"; ["wolf"]: "N"}.
```

Next we need an easy method of altering the set of positions when a boat-load goes to the opposite bank. If we represent a boat-load by a list of who is in the boat, for instance {"farmer"; "goat"} then we can use the following function to take a position and a list of travellers and return the new position:

```
HOW TO RETURN position altered.for occupants:
  FOR occupant IN occupants:
    PUT opposite position[occupant] IN
      position[occupant]
    RETURN position
>>> PUT {} IN start
>>> FOR participant IN {"farmer"; "goat";
"wolf"; "cabbage"}:
      PUT "N" IN start[participant]
>>> WRITE start altered.for {"farmer"; "goat"}
{["cabbage"]: "N"; ["farmer"]: "S"; ["goat"]:
"S"; ["wolf"]: "N"}
```

We also need a way to see if a given position is 'safe', that is to say that the goat is not left alone with the cabbage, and that the wolf is not left alone with the goat:

```
HOW TO REPORT safe pos:
  REPORT farmer.with.goat OR
  goat.out.of.mischief
farmer.with.goat:
  REPORT pos["farmer"] = pos["goat"]
goat.out.of.mischief:
  REPORT pos["cabbage"] <> pos["goat"] <>
    pos["wolf"]
```

(Notice the shorthand c<>g<>w instead of c<>g AND g<>w. Another way of writing the same is g not.in {c; w}.)

Now, the new version of the program to solve the river problem, instead of printing out its results as it goes along, will return the answer as a value. This result is a sequence of boat-loads necessary to solve the problem. Sequences are typically represented in ABC as tables with the elements of the sequence as items, and integers as keys. Elements are then added to the sequence with a command such as,

```
PUT element IN sequence[#sequence]
```

so that the first element is stored at key [0], the second at [1], and so on. In this program, the result is a sequence of boat-loads and so it will be represented as a table with integers as indexes, and boat-loads as elements.

The only difference is that the boat-loads are produced by the program in reverse order to how they will be printed out, and so the elements will be added at the *head* of the sequence.

This can be done with the command PUT element IN path[-#path], which we can make into a function:

```
HOW TO RETURN path with element:
    PUT element IN path[-#path]
    RETURN path
```

An example of a sequence of boat-loads is:

```
{[-2]: {"farmer"; "goat"}; [-1]: {"farmer"};
[0]: {"wolf"; "farmer"}}
```

representing the farmer taking the goat across the river, returning alone, and then taking the wolf.

The program either succeeds, and produces such a path, or the (sub-)problem has no solution, and so it should fail. To represent these two cases, the program returns a compound, consisting of a text, either "success" or "failure" indicating whether it has succeeded or not, and then the path, empty for failure, and the solution for success. (At first I had the program only return a path, and used an `impossible' path, such as {[1]: {}} to represent failure. I quickly saw this as a typical programmer's kludge, and replaced it with the cleaner solution here.).

To make life easier, let's have a command to print out the result (this is just a simple version, it could be made prettier):

```
HOW TO PRINT result.and.path:
  PUT result.and.path IN result, path
SELECT:
    result = "failure":
      WRITE "No solution"/
ELSE:
  FOR move IN path:
```

```
WRITE "Move", move/
```

The original program took as parameter the target position of the four, and then searched *backwards* to see if there was a way that that position could be reached from the start position (which was 'hard-wired' in the program). It was necessary to search backwards, because, like the new version, it produced its answers backwards, and so the two backwardses cancelled each other out. Another change I have made to the original program is to make both the start and the target positions parameters, and to make the program search from the start position for a path to the target position. As I have already said, it produces its answers backwards, but stores them in the result backwards, so that they still come out the right way round. The final change is that now 'allowable' boat-loads are not hard-wired in the program, but represented as a list: a maximum of two can fit in the boat (it's a very large cabbage), and furthermore only the farmer can row:

```
>>> PUT {} IN allowable
>>> INSERT {"farmer"} IN allowable
>>> FOR other IN {"cabbage"; "goat"; "wolf"}:
        INSERT {"farmer"; other} IN allowable
```

We can now write a function that returns which boat-loads are possible from the current position:

```
HOW TO RETURN possible.from position:
  SHARE allowable
  PUT {} IN result
  FOR boat.load IN allowable:
    IF EACH occupant IN boat.load HAS
    on.same.side:
        INSERT boat.load IN result
    RETURN result
  on.same.side:
    REPORT position[occupant] = position[min
    boat.load]
```

So now, after that introduction to the data-types, we can see the program proper. You'll notice comparing it with Tim's original, that the main body is more or less the same, except that results are being returned rather than tests being reported.

The main difference is in the refinement to try the next move. Tim's program tried each of four refinements until one succeeded. The new version tries each of the allowable boat-loads until one succeeds. If none succeeds, it fails. A marginal issue is how to treat the case where the aim is reachable, but not safe in itself. Tim's version accepted it, and printed the result; this version by reversing the order of the first two IF commands, does not accept it.

```
HOW TO RETURN position path.to aim:
  SHARE looking
  IF position in looking OR NOT safe position:
  RETURN failure
  IF position = aim: RETURN success
  INSERT position IN looking
  RETURN next.move
next.move:
  FOR boat.load IN possible.from position:
    PUT new.position path.to aim IN result,
    path'
    IF result <> "failure": RETURN result,
    path' with boat.load
    RETURN failure
new.position: RETURN position altered.for
  boat.load
success: RETURN "success", {}
failure: RETURN "failure", {}
```

(Remember that *looking* is used to prevent the program searching for a solution to a position it is already trying to solve — otherwise you can get an infinite loop.)

Now to try it out:

```
>>> PUT {}, {} IN start, aim
>>> FOR occupant IN {"farmer"; "goat"; "wolf";
"cabbage"}:
   PUT "N", "S" IN start[occupant], aim
   [occupant]
>>> PUT {} IN looking
>>> PRINT start path.to aim
Move {"farmer"; "goat"}
```

```
Move {"farmer"}
Move {"cabbage"; "farmer"}
Move {"farmer"; "goat"}
Move {"farmer"; "wolf"}
Move {"farmer"}
Move {"farmer"; "goat"}
```

Now to try it with a different aim: the farmer has to get the cabbage to the other side (to sell it to the hungry computer programmer who lives there):

```
>>> PUT start IN aim
>>> PUT "S" IN aim["cabbage"]
>>> PRINT start path.to aim
Move {"farmer"; "goat"}
Move {"farmer"}
Move {"cabbage"; "farmer"}
Move {"farmer"; "goat"}
```

Now, finally, the farmer is fed up with goats, cabbages and wolves, and wants to be alone on the other side:

```
>>> PUT start IN aim
>>> PUT "S" IN aim["farmer"]
>>> PRINT start path.to aim
No solution
```

APPROXIMATE NUMBERS

Exact numbers are held internally as a fraction of two (unbounded-length) integers, reduced to their lowest common multiple. You can retuen the two numerator and denominator of these fractions with the operators */and/*. You can convert exact numbers to approximate ones with the operator ~ and vice versa with round, floor and ceiling. Exact numbers are the result of computations where the result can be computed exactly: addition, subtraction, multiplication, division, and some exponentiations. However, some operations, such as taking the square root, can't deliver an exact result in general, and deliver an approximate number instead. Of course, some exact numbers (like 4), have exact square roots, but if you want exact results in these cases you have to write your own function to calculate them, something like:

```
HOW TO RETURN xroot x:
    IF exact x:
        PUT root */x, root/*x IN a, b
        PUT (round a)/(round b) IN r
        IF r*r = x: RETURN r
RETURN root x
```

For approximate numbers, the ABC implementations use the hardware representation of floating-point, and this is the only place where ABC programs can deliver different results on different machines (apart from the workings of the random generator): some machines have greater floating-point accuracy than others.

Machines hold floating-point numbers as an encoding of a pair of numbers *(f, e)*, where *f*, the fraction, has a fixed number of digits to some base *b*. Such a pair then represents the number $f \times b^{e}$. To find out how much accuracy your machine has, you can use the following command to find the base and number of significant digits used on your machine:

```
HOW TO PRINT ACCURACY:
    PRINT BASE
    PRINT FRACTION
PRINT BASE:
    PUT ~2, ~2, ~0 IN a, b, base
    WHILE a+1-a-1 = ~0: PUT a+a IN a
    WHILE base = ~0: PUT a+b-a, b+b IN base,b
    WRITE "Base =", base/
PRINT FRACTION:
    PUT 1, base IN sig, b
    WHILE b+1-b-1 = ~0: PUT sig+1, b*base IN
    sig, b
    WRITE "Significant digits =", sig/
    WRITE "This is about `decimal` decimal
    digits"/
decimal:
    RETURN 1 round (sig/(base log 10))
```

It works by first looking for a whole number that doesn't produce a different number when you add 1 to it. For instance, suppose the representation we are examining has 4 digits to base 10. Then you can add 1 to all 4 digit numbers, but not to 5 digit numbers, so it will try in turn 2, 4, 8, 16, 32, 64, 128, 256, 512, 1024, 2048, 4096, and 8192. Finally it will try 16384, which is only representable as 1638×10^{1}, which is 16380.

The routine then searches for a number that can be added to it which does produce a different number. Exactly which number it finds depends on whether the machine rounds the last digit of a calculation, or just chops excess digits off. So it tries to add 2, 4, and 8. If the machine rounds then 16380 + 8 = 16388, which rounded to 4 places is 16390. However, if the machine chops, then 16388 chopped is 16380, so then it tries to add 16, which gives 16396, and chopped this gives 16390, so in either case we get the same result from the two types of machine.

Now subtracting these two values, 16390 - 16380, gives the base used, in this case 10.

Having found the base, the routine then goes on to find the number of significant digits by repeatedly multiplying by the base until again 1 cannot be added. In our case, it will try 1, 10, 100, 1000, and finally 10000 to which 1 cannot be added. From the number of times that the multiplication is done, the number of significant digits can be deduced.

Here is an example of its output, for a VAX:

```
>>> PRINT ACCURACY
Base = 2
Significant digits = 56
This is about 16.9 decimal digits
```

The Consequences of Approximate Numbers

The advantage of using approximate numbers in ABC is that for large numbers they are generally faster to calculate than the equivalent exact numbers. The big disadvantage is of course that your results are only approximately correct. But how approximate is that?

To give an example, consider the value 1/((sqrt x) - (sqrt (x–1))). This is the same as (sqrt x) + (sqrt (x–1)) (you just multiply all through by ((sqrt x) + (sqrt (x–1)))/((sqrt x) + (sqrt (x–1)))).

However, if you calculate these using approximate numbers, you will get different results.

For instance:

```
HOW TO COMPARE VALUES FOR x:
    PUT root x, root (x-1) IN r, r1
    PUT 1/(r-r1), r+r1 IN u, v
    WRITE "1/((root x)-(root (x-1)))=", u/
    WRITE "(root x)+(root (x-1))= ", v/
    WRITE "Difference =", u-v/
>>> COMPARE VALUES FOR 10**12
1/((root x)-(root (x-1)))= 2000042.97959778
(root x)+(root (x-1))= 1999999.9999995
Difference = 42.9795982764044
>>> COMPARE VALUES FOR 10**15
1/((root x)-(root (x-1)))= 63161283.7647059
(root x)+(root (x-1))= 63245553.2033676
Difference = -84269.4386616889
```

This is on a machine with nearly 17 decimal digits of accuracy, and yet the two results differ already in the third digit in the second example! The explanation for this is that if you subtract two very close numbers, you lose a lot of accuracy. Try doing it for $x = 256$ with 4 digits of accuracy: root 256 = 16.00, and root 255 = 15.97. Subtracting these two gives 0.03, leaving only one digit of accuracy where before you had four. The inverse of this is 33.33, while the sum of the two is 31.97, a very different value (and as close as you can get to the real value with 4 digits).

So the question arises, in a given program, how can you tell how close a result is to the *real* answer? The rest of this article presents a package to help answer this question.

Range Arithmetic

This package simulates approximate arithmetic, and keeps for each arithmetic value an upper and lower bound on its real value. For instance, using 4 digits, *pi* lies between 3.141 and 3.142. Then for each operation, it calculates the upper and lower bounds of the result. For instance, when adding two values $(l\ , u)$ and $(l'\ , u')$, the result is (rounded.down(l +

l'), rounded.up(*u* + *u'*)). For *pi* + *pi*, this would give (6.282, 6.284).

In ABC:

```
HOW TO RETURN a plus b:
    PUT a, b IN (la, ua), (lb, ub)
    RETURN down (la + lb), up (ua + ub)
```

or shorter yet:

```
HOW TO RETURN (la, ua) plus (lb, ub)
    RETURN down (la + lb), up (ua + ub)
```

Since we want to simulate approximate arithmetic using a fixed number of digits of accuracy, the functions up and down take a number and remove excess digits, rounding either up or down.

The contents of the shared location accuracy specify how many digits of accuracy *we are interested in*:

```
HOW TO RETURN up x:
    SHARE accuracy
    IF x=0: RETURN 0
    PUT 0, 10**accuracy IN shift, limit
    WHILE abs x < limit: PUT x*10, shift - 1
    IN x, shift
    WHILE abs x > limit: PUT x/10, shift + 1
    IN x, shift
    RETURN (ceiling x) * 10**shift
```

This takes a number like 3.14159265, and multiplies or divides it so that its integral part has accuracy digits, also calculating the number of digits it has been shifted. So for accuracy = 4, x ends up as 3141.59265, with shift = -3. It then applies ceiling, which gives 3142, and multiplies this by 10 –3 to shift it back to give 3.142. The function to round down is the same, except it uses floor instead of ceiling.

```
>>> PUT 4 IN accuracy
>>> WRITE down pi, up pi
3.141 3.142
>>> WRITE down 123, up 123
123 123
>>> WRITE down 12345, up 12345
12340 12350
```

Because exact arithmetic is being used, any value for accuracy can be used. Calculating to 100 places will only take more time.

Subtraction is similar to addition:

```
HOW TO RETURN (la, ua) minus (lb, ub):
   RETURN down (la-ub), up (ua-lb)
```

Multiplication is slightly harder, mainly because of problems caused when multiplying values whose upper and lower bounds have different signs.

Here we take the easy way out, and calculate all possible values and identify the maximum and minimum:

```
HOW TO RETURN (la, ua) times (lb, ub):
   RETURN minmax {la*lb; la*ub; ua*lb; ua*ub}
```

where minmax returns the minimum and maximum values from a list: *HOW TO RETURN minmax list*: RETURN down min list, up max list.

We can do the same for division, but additionally we have to check for division by zero:

```
HOW TO RETURN (la, ua) over (lb, ub):
  CHECK NOT (lb <= 0 <= ub) \Division by zero
  RETURN minmax {la/lb; la/ub; ua/lb; ua/ub}
```

To use the package, a method is needed for converting an ABC number like pi into a range: HOW TO RETURN range v: RETURN down v, up v.

Just to show it works:

```
>>> WRITE range pi
3.141 3.142
>>> WRITE range 123
123 123
>>> WRITE range 12345
12340 12350
```

Also useful is a way of printing ranges more visibly as ranges:

```
HOW TO RETURN bounds (l, u): RETURN
  "[`l`:`u`] "
>>> WRITE bounds range pi
[3.141:3.142]
>>> WRITE bounds range 123
[123:123]
```

Now finally to define a function for square root. This uses the Newton-Raphson method, which repeatedly calculates for argument*a*, r = half ({a ÷ r} + r), until two consecutive *r*'s are sufficiently close:

```
HOW TO RETURN sq.root (l, u):
    RETURN down sq.root' l, up sq.root' u
HOW TO RETURN sq.root' f:
    IF f=0: RETURN 0
PUT f, (f+1)/2 IN r, r'
    WHILE converging: PUT r', (f/r' + r')/2
IN r, r'
    RETURN r
converging:
    REPORT down r <> down r'
```

The definition of closeness is whether the two approximations differ only in digits outside the accuracy we are interested in.

```
>>> WRITE bounds sq.root range 256
[16:16.01]
>>> WRITE bounds sq.root range 2
[1.414:1.415]
```

(Actually sq.root' can be speeded up by adding at the beginning

```
SHARE accuracy
PUT accuracy+1 IN accuracy
```

and replacing (f/r' + r')/2 by up((f/r' + r')/2). In that way, intermediate calculations don't get calculated with too great an accuracy.)

Now, finally back to our original problem:

```
>>> PUT range 1 IN one
>>> PUT sq.root range 256 IN r256
>>> PUT sq.root range 255 IN r255
>>> WRITE bounds (r256 plus r255)
[31.96:31.98]
>>> WRITE bounds (one over (r256 minus r255))
[20:33.34]
```

This makes it quite clear which of the two results is more accurate. This last result is both shocking and sobreing. But if you work it out, root 256 is [16:16.01] and root 255 is

[15.96:15.97]. The difference of these two is [0.03:0.05], so obviously the inverse is [20:33.34].

Even if we use range 16 *instead of* r256, *we still get a wide range*:

```
WRITE bounds (range 16) minus    r255)
[25:33.34]
```

OBJECT-ORIENTATION

While the exact definition of the term is highly variable depending upon who you ask, there are several qualities that most will agree an Object-Oriented language should have:

- Encapsulation/Information Hiding.
- Inheritance.
- Polymorphism/Dynamic Binding.
- All pre-defined types are Objects.
- All operations performed by sending messages to Objects.
- All user-defined types are Objects.

For the purposes of this discussion, a language is considered to be a "pure" Object-Oriented languages if it satisfies all of these qualities. A "hybrid" language may support some of these qualities, but not all. In particular, many languages support the first three qualities, but not the final three.

C++ is considered to be a multi-paradigm language, of which one paradigm it supports is Object-Orientation. Thus, C++ is not (nor does it contend to be) a pure Object-Oriented language.

Python is often heralded as an Object-Oriented language, but its support for Object-Orientation seems to have been tacked on. Some operations are implemented as methods, while others are implemented as global functions. Also, the need for an explicit "self" parameter for methods is awkward. Some complain about Python's lack of "private" or "hidden" attributes, which goes against the Encapsulation/Information Hiding principle, while others feel that Python's "privateness is by convention" approach offers all of the practical benefits as language-enforced encapsulation without the hassle. The

Ruby language, on the other hand, was created in part as a reaction to Python.

TYPES OF TYPING

The debate between static and dynamic typing has raged in Object-Oriented circles for many years with no clear conclusion. Proponents of dynamic typing contend that it is more flexible and allows for increased productivity. Those who prefer static typing argue that it enforces safer, more reliable code, and increases efficiency of the resulting product.

It is futile to attempt to settle this debate here except to say that a statically-typed language requires a very well-defined type system in order to remain as flexible as its dynamically-typed counterparts. Without the presence of genericity (templates, to use the C++ patois) and multiple type inheritance (not necessarily the same as multiple implementation inheritance), a static type system may severely inhibit the flexibility of a language. In addition, the presence of "casts" in a language can undermine the ability of the compiler to enforce type constraints.

A dynamic type system doesn't require variables to be declared as a specific type. Any variable can contain any value or object. Smalltalk and Ruby are two pure Object-Oriented languages that use dynamic typing. In many cases this can make the software more flexible and amenable to change. However, care must be taken that variables hold the expected kind of object. Typically, if a variable contains an object of a different type than a user of the object expects, some sort of "message not understood" error is raised at run-time. Users of dynamically-typed languages claim that this type of error is infrequent in practice.

Statically-typed languages require that all variables are declared with a specific type. The compiler will then ensure that at any given time the variable contains only an object compatible with that type. (We say "compatible with that type" rather than "exactly that type" since the inheritance relationship enables subtyping, in which a class that inherits from another class is said to have an IS-A relationship with the class from which it inherits, meaning that instances of the inheriting class can be considered to be of a compatible type with instances of the inherited class.)

By enforcing the type constraint on objects contained or referred to by the variable, the compiler can ensure a "message not understood" error can never occur at run-time. On the other hand, a static type system can hinder evolution of software in some circumstances. For example, if a method takes an object as a parameter, changing the type of the object requires changing the signature of the method so that it is compatible with the new type of the object being passed.

If this same object is passed to many such methods, all of them must be updated accordingly, which could potentially be an arduous task. One must remember, though, that this ripple effect could occur even a dynamically-typed language.

If the type of the object is not what it was originally expected to be, it may not understand the messages being sent to it. Perhaps even worse is that it could understand the message but interpret it in a way not compatible with the semantics of the calling method. A statically-typed language can flag these errors at compilation-time, pointing out the precise locations of potential errors. A user of a dynamically-typed language must rely on extensive testing to ensure that all improper uses of the object are tracked down.

Eiffel is a statically-typed language that manages to remain nearly as flexible as its dynamic counterparts. Eiffel's generic classes and unprecedentedly flexible inheritance model allow it to achieve the safety and reliability of a static type system while still remaining nearly as flexible as a dynamic type system, all without requiring (nor allowing) the use of type casts. C++ also offers generic classes (known as "templates" in the C++ parlance), as well as multiple inheritance. Unfortunately, the presence of type casts and implicit type conversions can sometimes undermine the work of the compiler by allowing type errors to go undetected until run-time. Java is seriously hindered by a lack of generic classes.

This is alleviated to a degree by Java's singly-rooted type hierarchy (*i.e.* every class descends directly or indirectly from

from the class Object), but this scheme leaves much to be desired in terms of type-safety. Forthcoming versions of Java will address this shortcoming when generic classes are introduced in Java 1.5 or later.

GENERIC CLASSES

Generic classes, and more generally parametric type facilities, refer to the ability to parameterize a class with specific data types. A common example is a stack class that is parameterized by the type of elements it contains. This allows the stack to simultaneously be compile-time type safe and yet generic enough to handle any type of elements.

The primary benefit of parameterized types is that it allows statically typed languages to retain their compile-time type safety yet remain nearly as flexible as dynamically typed languages. Eiffel in particular uses generics extensively as a mechanism for type safe generic containers and algorithms. C++ templates are even more flexible, having many uses apart from simple generic containers, but also much more complex.

As already mentioned in the previous section, Java's lack of generic classes is a severe hole in the Java type system. When one considers that most living objects in a program are stored in container classes, and that containers in Java are untyped due to lack of generics, it is questionable whether Java's type system provides any benefit over the more flexible dynamic counterparts. See also this article by Dave Thomas for a discussion of Java's type system in regards to its lack of generics.

Dynamically typed languages do not need parameterized types in order to support generic programming. Types are checked at run-time and thus dynamically typed languages support generic programming inherently.

INHERITANCE

Inheritance is the ability for a class or object to be defined as an extension or specialization of another class or object. Most object-oriented languages support class-based inheritance, while others such as SELF and JavaScript support object-based inheritance. A few languages, notably Python and Ruby, support both class- and object-based inheritance, in which a class can inherit from another class and individual objects can be extended at run time with the capabilities of other objects. For the remainder of this discussion, we'll be dealing primarily with class-based inheritance since it is by far the most common model.

Although commonly thought of as simple subtyping mechanism, there are actually many different uses of inheritance. In his landmark book *Object-Oriented Software Construction,* Bertrand Meyer identified and classified as many as 17 different forms of inheritance. Even so, most languages provide only a few syntactic constructs for inheritance which are general enough to allow inheritance to be used in many different ways.

The most important distinction that can be made between various languages' support for inheritance is whether it supports single or multiple inheritance. Multiple inheritance is the ability for a class to inherit from more than one super (or base) class. For example, an application object called Persistent Shape might inherit from both Graphical Object and Persistent Object in order to be used as both a graphical object that can be displayed on the screen as well as a persistent object that can be stored in a database.

Multiple inheritance would appear to be an essential feature for a language to support for cases such as the above when two or more distinct hierarchies must be merged into one application domain. However, there are other issues to consider before making such an assertion.

First, we must consider that multiple inheritance introduces some complications into a programming language supporting it. Issues such as name clashes and ambiguities introduced in the object model must be resolved by the language in order for multiple inheritance and this leads to additional complexity in the language. Eiffel is known for its carefully and thoroughly well-designed support for multiple inheritance, which features feature renaming and fine-grained control over the manner in which multiply-inherited features are selected and applied to the inheriting class. The mechanisms C++ provides for multiple inheritance are more complicated and less flexible leading many people to (mistakenly) believe that multiple inheritance is inherently ill-conceived and complex.

Next, we must distinguish between implementation inheritance and interface/subtype inheritance. Subtype inheritance (also known loosely as interface inheritance) is the most common form of inheritance, in which a subclass is considered to be a subtype of its super class, commonly referred to as an IS-A relationship. What this means is that the language considers an object to conform to the type of its class *or any of its super classes*. For example, a Circle IS-A Shape, so anywhere a Shape is used in a program, a Circle may be used as well. This conformance notion is only applicable to statically typed languages since it is a feature used by the compiler to determine type correctness.

Implementation inheritance is the ability for a class to inherit part or all of its implementation from another class. For example, a Stack class that is implemented using an array might inherit from an Array class in order to define the Stack in terms of the Array. In this way, the Stack class could use any features from the Array to support its own implementation. With pure implementation inheritance, the fact that the Stack inherits its implementation from Array would not be visible to code using the Stack; the inheritance would be strictly an implementation matter. C++ supports this notion directly with "private inheritance", in which methods from the base class are made private in the derived class. Recent versions of Eiffel also support this form ot pure implementation inheritance using what is known as non-conforming inheritance. Most languages, on the other hand, do not support pure implementation inheritance so a class that inherits from another class is always considered to be a subtype of its super class(es).

Returning to the issue of multiple inheritance, we can see that a language's support for multiple inheritance is not a boolean condition; a language can support one or more different forms of multiple inheritance in the same way it can support different forms of single inheritance (*e.g.* implementation and subtype inheritance). We've already seen that C++ and Eiffel independently support pure implementation inheritance as well as subtype inheritance. Both of these languages also support multiple inheritance in both forms. Java, while it does not support *pure* implementation inheritance, provides two separate inheritance mechanisms. The extends keyword is used for a combination of implementation and subtype inheritance while the implements keyword is used for pure subtype (interface) inheritance.

Subtype inheritance is less important in dynamic languages since type conformance is not generally an issue, so multiple implementation inheritance is preferred over multiple subtype inheritance (although most languages still consider any class inheriting from another to be a subtype). Smalltalk supports only a single notion of inheritance: single inheritance of both interface and implementation. This means that a class may only inherit from one other class and it inherits both implementation and interface.

Python similarly supports one form of inheritance (both implementation and subtype) but allows multiple inheritance and is thus more flexible in this regard than Smalltalk. Ruby lies somewhere in between the two approaches by allowing a class to inherit from only one class but also allowing a class to "mix in" the implementation of an arbitrary number of modules. This model is a slightly restricted version of the model provided by Python, but the restrictions can be overcome by Ruby's ability to support a prototype-based approach using object-based inheritance.

FEATURE RENAMING

Feature renaming is the ability for a class or object to rename one of its features (a term we'll use to collectively refer to attributes and methods) that it inherited from a super class.

There are two important ways in which this can be put to use:

- Provide a feature with a more natural name for its new context

- Resolve naming ambiguities when a name is inherited from multiple inheritance paths

As an example of the first use, consider again a stack implemented by inheriting from an array. The array might provide an operation called remove_last to remove the last element of the array. In the stack, this operation is more appropriately named pop.

Eiffel and Ruby both provide support for feature renaming. Ruby provides an alias method that allows you to alias any arbitrary method. Eiffel also provides support for feature renaming, although it is slightly more limited than in Ruby because you can only rename a feature in an inheritance clause.

METHOD OVERLOADING

Method overloading (also referred to as parametric polymorphism) is the ability for a class, module, or other scope to have two or more methods with the same name. Calls to these methods are disambiguated by the number and/or type of arguments passed to the method at the call site. For example, a class may have multiple print methods, one for each type of thing to be printed. The alternative to overloading in this scenario is to have a different name for each print method, such asprint_string and print_integer.

Java and C++ both support method overloading in a similar fashion. Complexities in the mechanism to disambiguate calls to overloaded methods have lead some language designers to avoid overloading in their languages. None of the other languages under consideration support method overloading. Default argument values provide a subset of the behaviour for which method overloading is used, and some languages such as Ruby and Python have chosen this route instead.

OPERATOR OVERLOADING

Operator overloading is the ability for a programmer to define an operator (such as +, or *) for user-defined types. This allows the operator to be used in infix, prefix, or postfix form, rather than the standard functional form. For example, a user-defined Matrix type might provide a * infix operator to perform matrix multiplication with the familiar notation: matrix1 * matrix2.

Some (correctly) consider operator overloading to be mere syntactic "sugar" rather than an essential feature, while others (also correctly) point to the need for such syntactic sugar in numerical and other applications. Both points are valid, but it is clear that, when used appropriately, operator overloading can lead to much more readable programs. When abused, it can lead to cryptic, obfuscated code. Consider that in the presence of operator overloading, it may not be clear whether a given operator is built in to the language or defined by the user.

For any language that supports operator overloading, two things are necessary to alleviate such obfuscation:

- All operations must be messages to objects, and thus all operators are always method calls.
- Operators must have an equivalent functional form, so that using the operator as a method call will behave precisely the same as using it in infix, prefix, or postfix form.

This second point is subtle. It means that given any operator, it must be possible to invoke that operator in functional form. For example, the following two expressions should be equivalent: 1 + 2 and 1.+(2). This ensures that no implicit behaviour is taking place that may not be immediately obvious from examining the source text.

HIGH ORDER FUNCTIONS

Higher order functions are, in the simplest sense, functions that can be treated as if they were data objects. In other words, they can be bound to variables (including the ability to be stored in collections), they can be passed to other functions as parameters, and they can be returned as the result of other functions. Due to this ability, higher order functions may be viewed as a form of deferred execution, wherein a function may be defined in one context, passed to another context, and then later invoked by the second context. This is different from standard functions in that higher order functions represent anonymous lambda functions, so that the invoking context need not know the name of the function being invoked.

Lexical closures (also known as static closures, or simply closures) take this one step further by bundling up the lexical (static) scope surrounding the function with the function itself, so that the function carries its surrounding environment around with it wherever it may be used. This means that the closure can access local variables or parameters, or attributes of the object in which it is defined, and will continue to have access to them even if it is passed to another module outside of its scope.

Among the languages we're considering, Smalltalk and Ruby have supported both higher order functions and lexical closures from the beginning in the form of blocks. A block is an anonymous function that may be treated as any other data object, and is also a lexical closure. Eiffel has recently added support for higher order functions using the "agent" mechanism. The inline variant of Eiffel agents forms a lexical closure. Python, which has long supported higher order functions in the form of lambda expressions, has recently added support for closures using its improved support for nested static scopes.

While neither Java nor C++ support higher order functions directly, both provide mechanisms for mimicking their behaviour. Java's anonymous classes allow a function to be bundled with an object that can be treated much as a higher order function can. It can be bound to variables, passed to other functions as an argument, and can be returned as the result of a function. However, the function itself is named and thus cannot be treated in a generic fashion as true higher order functions can. C++ similarly provides partial support for higher order functions using function objects (or "functors"), and add the further benefit that the function call operator may be overloaded so that functors may be treated generically. Neither C++ nor Java, however, provide any support for lexical closures.

LANGUAGE IMPLEMENTATION

Garbage collection is a mechanism allowing a language implementation to free memory of unused objects on behalf of the programmer, thus relieving the burden on the programmer to do so. The alternative is for the programmer to explicitly free any memory that is no longer needed. There are several strategies for garbage collection that exist in various language implementations.

Reference counting is the simplest scheme and involves the language keeping track of how many references there are to a particular object in memory, and deleting that object when that reference count becomes zero. This scheme, although it is simple and deterministic, is not without its drawbacks, the most important being its inability to handle cycles. Cycles occur when two objects reference each other, and thus there reference counts will never become zero even if neither object is referenced by any other part of the program. This is the scheme that is utilized by Python and Visual Basic, although in the case of Python an extra step is taken to ensure that cycles are handled appropriately.

"Mark and sweep" garbage collection is another scheme that overcomes this limitation. A mark and sweep garbage collector works in a two phase process, not surprisingly known as the mark phase and the sweep phase. The mark phase works by first starting at the "root" objects (objects on the stack, global objects, etc.), marking them as live, and recursively marking any objects referenced from them. These marked objects are the set of live objects in program, and any objects that were not marked in this phase are unreferenced and therefore candidates for collection. In the sweep phase, any objects in memory that were not marked as live by the mark phase are deleted from memory.

The primary drawback of mark and sweep collection is that it is non-deterministic, meaning that objects are deleted at an unspecified time during the execution of the program. This is the most common form of garbage collection, and the one that is supported by most implementations of Eiffel, Smalltalk, Ruby, and Java.

Generational garbage collection works in a similar fashion to mark and sweep garbage collection, except it capitalizes on the statistical probability that objects that have been alive the longest tend to stay alive longer than objects that were newly created. Thus a generational garbage collector will divide objects into "generations" based upon how long they've been alive. This division can be used to reduce the time spent in the mark and sweep phases because the oldest generation of objects will not need to be collected as frequently. Generational garbage collectors are not as common as the other forms but may be found in some implementations of Eiffel, Smalltalk, Ruby, and Java.

C++ does not provide any sort of garbage collection, the reasons for which are discussed at length in Bjarne Stroustrup's *The Design and Evolution of C++*. It is possible, however, with some effort to layer reference counting garbage collection onto C++ using smart pointers. In addition there exist garbage collectors that can be integrated into C++ programs, though their use has not caught on to any great degree within the C++ community.

NORMAL ACCESS

The Uniform Access Principle seeks to eliminate this needless coupling. A language supporting the Uniform Access Principle does not exhibit any notational differences between accessing a feature regardless of whether it is an attribute or a function. Thus, in our earlier example, access to bar would always be in the form of foo.bar, regardless of how bar is implemented. This makes clients of Foo more resilient to change.

Among our languages, only Eiffel and Ruby directly support the Uniform Access Principle, although Smalltalk renders the distinction moot by not allowing any access to attributes from clients.

CLASS VARIABLES/METHODS

Class variables and methods are owned by a class, and not any particular instance of a class. This means that for however many instances of a class exist at any given point in time, only one copy of each class variable/method exists and is shared by every instance of the class.

Smalltalk and Ruby support the most advanced notion of class variables and methods, due to their use of meta-classes and the fact that even classes are objects in these languages. Java and C++ provide "static" members which are effectively the same thing, yet more limited since they cannot be inherited. Python, surprisingly, does not support class methods or variables, but its advanced notion of a module allows workarounds for this limitation. Eiffel also does not provide direct support for class variables or methods, but it does provide similar, but limited, functionality in the form of "once" functions. Once functions are evaluated once only, and subsequent uses use a cached result.

REFLECTION

Reflection is the ability for a program to determine various pieces of information about an object at run-time. This includes the ability to determine the type of the object, its inheritance structure, and the methods it contains, including the number and types of parameters and return types. It might also include the ability for determining the names and types of attributes of the object. Most object-oriented languages support some form of reflection. Smalltalk, Ruby, and Python in particular have very powerful and flexible reflection mechanisms. Java also supports reflection, but not in as flexible and dynamic fashion as the others. C++ does not support reflection as we've defined it here, but it does supported a limited form of run-time type information that allows a program to determine the type of an object at run-time. Eiffel also has support for a limited form of reflection, although it is much improved in the most recent versions of Eiffel, including the ability to determine the features contained in an object.

ACCESS CONTROL

Access control refers to the ability for a modules implementation to remain hidden behind its public interface.

Access control is closely related to the encapsulation/ information hiding principle of object-oriented languages. For example, a class Person may have methods such as name and e-mail, that return the person's name and e-mail address respectively. How these methods work is an implementation detail that should not be available to users of the Person class. These methods may, for example, connect to a database to retrieve the values. The database connection code that is used to do this is not relevant to client code and should not be exposed. Language-enforced access control allows us to enforce this.

Most object-oriented languages provide at least two levels of access control: public and protected. Protected features are not available outside of the class in which they are contained, except for subclasses. This is the scheme supported by Smalltalk, in which all methods are public and all attributes are protected. There are no protected methods in Smalltalk, so Smalltalk programmers resort to the convention of placing methods that should be protected into a "private protocol" of the class. See this discussion for the benefits and drawbacks of this approach. Visual Basic also supports these two levels of access control, although since there is no inheritance in Visual Basic, protected features are effectively private to the class in which they are declared. Some languages, notably Java and C++, provide a third level of access control known as "private". Private features are not available outside of the class in which they are declared, even for subclasses. Note, however, that this means that objects of a particular class can access the private features of other objects of that same class.

Ruby also provides these three levels of access control, but they work slightly differently. Private in Ruby means that the feature cannot be accessed through a receiver, meaning that the feature will be available to subclasses, but not other instances of the same class. Java provides a fourth level of, known as "package private" access control which allows other classes in the same package to access such features.

Eiffel provides the most powerful and flexible access control scheme of any of these languages with what is known as "selective export". All features of an Eiffel class are by default public. However, any feature in an Eiffel class may specify an export clause which lists explicitly what other classes may access that feature.

The special class NONE may be used to indicate that *no* other class may access that feature. This includes attributes, but even public attributes are read only so an attribute can never be written to directly in Eiffel. In order to better support the Open-Closed principle, all features of a class are always available to subclasses in Eiffel, so there is no notion of private as there is in Java and C++.

Python, curiously, does not provide any enforced access control. Instead, it provides a mechanism of name mangling: any feature that begins with underscores will have its name mangled by the Python interpreter. Although this does not prevent client code from using such features, it is a clear indicator that the feature is not intended for use outside the class and convention dictates that these features are "use at your own risk".

FEATURES OF DBC

- *Pre-conditions*: Which are conditions that must be true before a method is invoked
- *Post-conditions*: Which are conditions guaranteed to be true after the invocation of a method
- *Invariants*: Which are conditions guaranteed to be true at any stable point during the lifetime of an object

There is much more to DBC than these simple facilities, including the manner in which pre-conditions, post-conditions, and invariants are inherited in compliance with the Liskov Substitution Principle. However, at least these facilities must be present to support the central notions of DBC.

MULTITHREADING

Multithreading is the ability for a single process to process two or more tasks concurrently. (We say concurrently rather than simultaneously because, in the absence of multiple processors, the tasks cannot run simultaneously but rather are interleaved in very small time slices and thus exhibit the appearance and semantics of concurrent execution.) The use of multithreading is becoming increasingly more common as operating system support for threads has become near ubiquitous.

Among the languages under discussion, nearly all support multithreading either directly within the language or through libraries. Ruby is somewhat unique in that its threading capabilities are built in to the interpreter itself, rather than wrappers around the operating system threading operations. This has the disadvantage that any operating system calls will block the entire interpreter, but has the advantage of being completely portable even to systems that do not support multithreading, such as MS-DOS.

REGULAR EXPRESSIONS

Regular expressions are pattern matching constructs capable of recognizing the class of languages known as regular languages. They are frequently used for text processing systems as well as for general applications that must use pattern recognition for other purposes. Libraries with regular expression support exist for nearly every language, but ever since the advent of Perl it has become increasingly important for a language to support regular expressions natively. This allows tighter integration with the rest of the language and allows more convenient syntax for use of regular expressions. Perl was the model for this kind of built-in support and Ruby, a close descendant of Perl, continues the tradition. Python, and recently Java, have included regular expression libraries as part of the standard base library distributed with the language implementation.

POINTER ARITHMETIC

Pointer arithmetic is the ability for a language to directly manipulate memory addresses and their contents. While, due to the inherent unsafety of direct memory manipulation, this ability is not often considered appropriate for high-level languages, it is essential for low-level systems applications. Thus, while object-oriented languages strive to remain at a fairly high level of abstraction, to be suitable for systems programming a language must provide such features or relegate such low-level tasks to a language with which it can interact. Most object-oriented languages have foregone support of pointer arithmetic in favour of providing integration with C. This allows low-level routines to be implemented in C while the majority of the application is written in the higher level language.

C++ on the other hand provides direct support for pointer arithmetic, both for compatibility with C and to allow C++ to be used for systems programming without the need to drop down to a lower level language. This is the source both of C++'s great flexibility as well as much of its complexity.

LANGUAGE INTEGRATION

For various reasons, including integration with existing systems, the need to interact with low level modules, or for sheer speed, it is important for a high level language (particularly interpreted languages) to be able to integrate seamlessly with other languages. Nearly every language to come along since C was first introduced provides such integration with C. This allows high level languages to remain free of the low level constructs that make C great for systems programming, but add much complexity.

All of the languages under discussion integrate tightly with C, except for Visual Basic, which can only do so through DCOM. Eiffel and Ruby provide particularly easy-to-use interfaces to C as well as callbacks to the language runtime. Python, Perl, Java, and Smalltalk provide similar interfaces, though they aren't quite as easy to use. C++, naturally, integrates quite transparently with C.

BUILT-IN SECURITY

Built-in security refers to a language implementation's ability to determine whether or not a piece of code comes from a "trusted" source (such as the user's hard disk), limiting the permissions of the code if it does not. For example, Java applets are considered untrusted, and thus they are limited in the actions they can perform when executed from a user's browser. They may not, for example, read or write from or to the user's hard disk, and they may not open a network connection to anywhere but the originating host.

Several languages, including Java, Ruby, and Perl, provide this ability "out of the box". Most languages defer this protection to the user's operating environment.

CAPERS JONES LANGUAGE LEVEL

The Capers Jones Language Level is a study that attempts to identify the number of source lines of code is necessary in a given language to implement a single function point. The higher the language level, the fewer lines of code it takes to implement a function point, and thus presumably is an indicator of the productivity levels achievable using the language.

3

Designing of Program

INTRODUCTION

The single most important skill for a computer scientist is problem solving. Problem solving means the ability to formulate problems, think creatively about solutions, and express a solution clearly and accurately. As it turns out, the process of learning to program is an excellent opportunity to practice problem-solving skills. On another level, you will use programming as a means to an end. As we go along, that end will become clearer.

PROGRAMMING LANGUAGE

The programming language you will be learning is Python. Python is an example of a high-level language; other high-level languages you might have heard of are C, C++, Perl, and Java. As you might infer from the name "high-level language," there are also low-level languages, sometimes referred to as "machine languages" or "assembly languages." Loosely speaking, computers can only execute programs written in low-level languages. Thus, programs written in a high-level language have to be processed before they can run. This extra processing takes some time, which is a small disadvantage of high-level languages.

But the advantages are enormous. First, it is much easier to program in a high-level language. Programs written in a high-level language take less time to write, they are shorter and easier to read, and they are more likely to be correct. Second, high-level languages are portable, meaning that they can run on different kinds of computers with few or no modifications. Low-level programs can run on only one kind of computer and have to be rewritten to run on another.

Due to these advantages, almost all programs are written in high-level languages. Low-level languages are used only for a few specialized applications.

Two kinds of programs process high-level languages into low-level languages:interpreters and compilers. An interpreter reads a high-level program and executes it, meaning that it does what the program says. It processes the program a little at a time, alternately reading lines and performing computations.

A compiler reads the program and translates it completely before the program starts running. In this case, the high-level program is called the source code, and the translated program is called the object code or the executable. Once a program is compiled, you can execute it repeatedly without further translation.

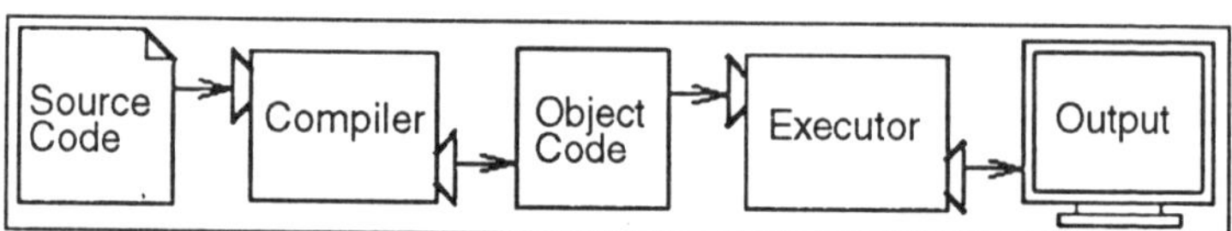

It is considered an interpreted language because Python programs are executed by an interpreter. There are two ways to use the interpreter: command-line mode and script mode.

In command-line mode, you type Python programs and the interpreter prints the result:

```
$ python
Python 2.4.1 (#1, Apr 29 2005, 00:28:56)
Type "help", "copyright", "credits" or
"license" for more information.
>>> print 1 + 1
2
```

The first line of this example is the command that starts the Python interpreter. The next two lines are messages from the interpreter. The third line starts with >>>, which is the prompt the interpreter uses to indicate that it is ready. We typed print 1 + 1, and the interpreter replied 2.

In other development environments, the details of executing programs may differ. Also, most programs are more interesting than this one.

Most of the examples in this book are executed on the command line. Working on the command line is convenient for program development and testing, because you can type programs and execute them immediately. Once you have a working program, you should store it in a script so you can execute or modify it in the future.

PROGRAM

A program is a sequence of instructions that specifies how to perform a computation. The computation might be something mathematical, such as solving a system of equations or finding the roots of a polynomial, but it can also be a symbolic computation, such as searching and replacing text in a document or (strangely enough) compiling a program.

- *Input*: Get data from the keyboard, a file, or some other device.
- *Output*: Display data on the screen or send data to a file or other device.
- *Math*: Perform basic mathematical operations like addition and multiplication.
- *Conditional execution*: Check for certain conditions and execute the appropriate sequence of statements.
- *Repetition*: Believe it or not, that's pretty much all there is to it. Every program you've ever used, no matter how complicated, is made up of instructions that look more or less like these. Thus, we can describe programming as the process of breaking a large, complex task into smaller and smaller subtasks until the subtasks are simple enough to be performed with one of these basic instructions.

That may be a little vague, but we will come back to this topic later when we talk aboutalgorithms.

DEBUGGING?

Programming is a complex process, and because it is done by human beings, it often leads to errors. For whimsical reasons, programming errors are called bugs and the process of tracking them down and correcting them is called debugging. Three kinds of errors can occur in a program: syntax errors, runtime errors, and semantic errors. It is useful to distinguish between them in order to track them down more quickly.

Syntax Errors

Python can only execute a program if the program is syntactically correct; otherwise, the process fails and returns an error message. Syntax refers to the structure of a program and the rules about that structure. For example, in English, a sentence must begin with a capital letter and end with a period. this sentence contains a syntax error. So does this one For most readers, a few syntax errors are not a significant problem, which is why we can read the poetry of e. e. cummings without spewing error messages. Python is not so forgiving. If there is a single syntax error anywhere in your program, Python will print an error message and quit, and you will not be able to run your program. During the first few weeks of your programming career, you will probably spend a lot of time tracking down syntax errors. As you gain experience, though, you will make fewer errors and find them faster.

Runtime Errors

The second type of error is a runtime error, so called because the error does not appear until you run the program. These errors are also called exceptions because they usually indicate that something exceptional (and bad) has happened.

Semantic Errors

The third type of error is the semantic error. If there is a semantic error in your program, it will run successfully, in the sense that the computer will not generate any error messages, but it will not do the right thing. It will do something else. Specifically, it will do what you told it to do. The problem is that the program you wrote is not the program you wanted to write. The meaning of the program (its semantics) is wrong. Identifying semantic errors can be tricky because it requires you to work backward by looking at the output of the program and trying to figure out what it is doing.

Experimental Debugging

One of the most important skills you will acquire is debugging. Although it can be frustrating, debugging is one of the most intellectually rich, challenging, and interesting parts of programming. In some ways, debugging is like detective work. You are confronted with clues, and you have to infer the processes and events that led to the results you see. Debugging is also like an experimental science. Once you have an idea what is going wrong, you modify your program and try again. If your hypothesis was correct, then you can predict the result of the modification, and you take a step closer to a working program. If your hypothesis was wrong, you have to come up with a new one. As Sherlock Holmes pointed out, "When you have eliminated the impossible, whatever remains, however improbable, must be the truth." (A. Conan Doyle, *The Sign of Four*)

For some people, programming and debugging are the same thing. That is, programming is the process of gradually debugging a program until it does what you want. The idea is that you should start with a program that does *something* and make small modifications, debugging them as you go, so that you always have a working program.

Linux is an operating system that contains thousands of lines of code, but it started out as a simple program Linus Torvalds used to explore the Intel 80386 chip. According to Larry Greenfield, "One of Linus's earlier projects was a program that would switch between printing AAAA and BBBB.

NATURAL AND FORMAL LANGUAGES

Natural languages are the languages that people speak, such as English, Spanish, and French. They were not designed by people (although people try to impose some order on them); they evolved naturally.

Formal languages are languages that are designed by people for specific applications. For example, the notation that mathematicians use is a formal language that is particularly good at denoting relationships among numbers and symbols. Chemists use a formal language to represent the chemical structure of molecules. And most importantly:

Programming languages are formal languages that have been designed to express computations. Formal languages tend to have strict rules about syntax. For example, 3+3=6 is a syntactically correct mathematical statement, but 3=+6$ is not. H2O is a syntactically correct chemical name, but 2Zz is not.

Syntax rules come in two flavours, pertaining to tokens and structure. Tokens are the basic elements of the language, such as words, numbers, and chemical elements. The second type of syntax error pertains to the structure of a statement that is, the way the tokens are arranged. The statement 3=+6$ is structurally illegal because you can't place a plus sign immediately after an equal sign. Similarly, molecular formulas have to have subscripts after the element name, not before.

When you read a sentence in English or a statement in a formal language, you have to figure out what the structure of the sentence is (although in a natural language you do this subconsciously). This process is called parsing.

For example, when you hear the sentence, "The other shoe fell," you understand that "the other shoe" is the subject and "fell" is the predicate. Once you have parsed a sentence, you can figure out what it means, or the semantics of the sentence. Assuming that you know what a shoe is and what it means to fall, you will understand the general implication of this sentence.

Although formal and natural languages have many features in common tokens, structure, syntax, and semantics there are many differences:

Ambiguity

Natural languages are full of ambiguity, which people deal with by using contextual clues and other information. Formal languages are designed to be nearly or completely unambiguous, which means that any statement has exactly one meaning, regardless of context.

Redundancy

In order to make up for ambiguity and reduce misunderstandings, natural languages employ lots of redundancy. As a result, they are often verbose. Formal languages are less redundant and more concise.

Literalness

Natural languages are full of idiom and metaphor. If I say, "The other shoe fell," there is probably no shoe and nothing falling. Formal languages mean exactly what they say. People who grow up speaking a natural language everyone often have a hard time adjusting to formal languages.

Poetry

Words are used for their sounds as well as for their meaning, and the whole poem together creates an effect or emotional response. Ambiguity is not only common but often deliberate.

Prose

The literal meaning of words is more important, and the structure contributes more meaning. Prose is more amenable to analysis than poetry but still often ambiguous.

Programs

The meaning of a computer program is unambiguous and literal, and can be understood entirely by analysis of the tokens and structure. Here are some suggestions for reading programs (and other formal languages). First, remember that formal languages are much more dense than natural languages, so it takes longer to read them.

Also, the structure is very important, so it is usually not a good idea to read from top to bottom, left to right. Instead, learn to parse the program in your head, identifying the tokens and interpreting the structure. Finally, the details matter. Little things like spelling errors and bad punctuation, which you can get away with in natural languages, can make a big difference in a formal language.

The First Program

Traditionally, the first program written in a new language is called "Hello, World!" because all it does is display the words, "Hello, World!"

In Python, it looks like this:

```
print "Hello, World!"
```

This is an example of a print statement, which doesn't actually print anything on paper. It displays a value on the screen.

In this case, the result is the words:

```
Hello, World!
```

The quotation marks in the program mark the beginning and end of the value; they don't appear in the result. Some people judge the quality of a programming language by the simplicity of the "Hello, World!" program. By this standard, Python does about as well as possible.

GLOSSARY

- *Problem solving*: The process of formulating a problem, finding a solution, and expressing the solution.
- *High-level language*: A programming language like Python that is designed to be easy for humans to read and write.
- *Low-level language*: A programming language that is designed to be easy for a computer to execute; also called "machine language" or "assembly language."
- *Portability*: A property of a program that can run on more than one kind of computer.
- *Interpret*: To execute a program in a high-level language by translating it one line at a time.

- *Compile*: To translate a program written in a high-level language into a low-level language all at once, in preparation for later execution.
- *Source code*: A program in a high-level language before being compiled.
- *Object code*: The output of the compiler after it translates the program.
- *Executable*: Another name for object code that is ready to be executed.
- *Script*: A program stored in a file (usually one that will be interpreted).
- *Program*: A set of instructions that specifies a computation.
- *Algorithm*: A general process for solving a category of problems.
- *Bug*: An error in a program.
- *Debugging*: The process of finding and removing any of the three kinds of programming errors.
- *Syntax*: The structure of a program.
- *Syntax error*: An error in a program that makes it impossible to parse (and therefore impossible to interpret).
- *Runtime error*: An error that does not occur until the program has started to execute but that prevents the program from continuing.
- *Exception*: Another name for a runtime error.
- *Semantic error*: An error in a program that makes it do something other than what the programmer intended.
- *Semantics*: The meaning of a program.
- *Natural language*: Any one of the languages that people speak that evolved naturally.
- *Formal language*: Any one of the languages that people have designed for specific purposes, such as representing mathematical ideas or computer programs; all programming languages are formal languages.
- *Token*: One of the basic elements of the syntactic

structure of a program, analogous to a word in a natural language.

- *Parse*: To examine a program and analyse the syntactic structure.
- *Print statement*: An instruction that causes the Python interpreter to display a value on the screen.
- *Warning*: the HTML version of this document is generated from Latex and may contain translation errors. In particular, some mathematical expressions are not translated correctly.

VARIABLES AND EXPRESSIONS

VALUES

A value is one of the fundamental things like a letter or a number that a programme manipulates. The values we have seen so far are 2 (the result when we added 1 + 1), and 'Hello, World!'.

These values belong to different types: 2 is an integer, and 'Hello, World!' is astring, so-called because it contains a "string" of letters. You (and the interpreter) can identify strings because they are enclosed in quotation marks. The print statement also works for integers.

```
print 4
4
```

If you are not sure what type a value has, the interpreter can tell you.

```
type('Hello, World!')
type 'str'>
type(17)
type 'int'>
```

Not surprisingly, strings belong to the type str and integers belong to the type int. Less obviously, numbers with a decimal point belong to a type called float, because these numbers are represented in a format called floating-point.

```
type(3.2)
type 'float'>
```

What about values like '17' and '3.2'? They look like numbers, but they are in quotation marks like strings.

```
type('17')
type 'str'>
type('3.2')
type 'str'>
```

They're strings: When you type a large integer, you might be tempted to use commas between groups of three digits, as in 1,000,000.

This is not a legal integer in Python, but it is a legal expression:

```
print 1,000,000
1 0 0
```

VARIABLES

One of the most powerful features of a programming language is the ability to manipulate variables. A variable is a name that refers to a value.

The assignment statement creates new variables and gives them values:

```
message = "What's up, Doc?"
n = 17
pi = 3.14159
```

This example makes three assignments. The first assigns the string "What's up, Doc?" to a new variable named message. The second gives the integer 17 to n, and the third gives the floating-point number 3.14159 to pi. Notice that the first statement uses double quotes to enclose the string. In general, single and double quotes do the same thing, but if the string contains a single quote (or an apostrophe, which is the same character), you have to use double quotes to enclose it.

A common way to represent variables on paper is to write the name with an arrow pointing to the variable's value. This kind of figure is called a state diagrambecause it shows what state each of the variables is in (think of it as the variable's state of mind).

This diagram shows the result of the assignment statements:

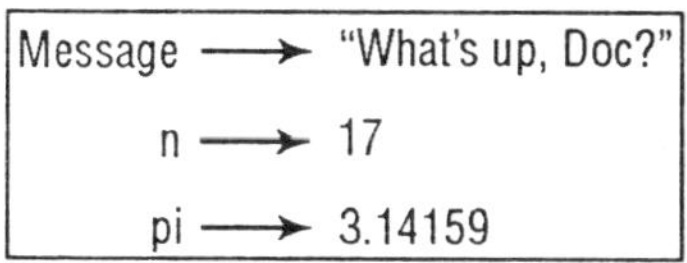

The print statement also works with variables.

```
print message
What's up, Doc?
print n
7
print pi
3.14159
```

In each case the result is the value of the variable. Variables also have types; again, we can ask the interpreter what they are.

```
type(message)
type 'str'>
type(n)
type 'int'>
type(pi)
type 'float'>
```

The type of a variable is the type of the value it refers to.

VARIABLE NAMES AND KEYWORDS

Programmers generally choose names for their variables that are meaningful they document what the variable is used for. Variable names can be arbitrarily long. They can contain both letters and numbers, but they have to begin with a letter. Although it is legal to use uppercase letters, by convention we don't. If you do, remember that case matters. Bruce and bruce are different variables.

The underscore character (_) can appear in a name. It is often used in names with multiple words, such as my_name or price_of_tea_in_china.

If you give a variable an illegal name, you get a syntax error:

```
76trombones = 'big parade'
SyntaxError: invalid syntax
more$ = 1000000
SyntaxError: invalid syntax
class = 'Computer Science 101'
SyntaxError: invalid syntax
```

76trombones is illegal because it does not begin with a letter. more$ is illegal because it contains an illegal character, the dollar sign. But what's wrong with class? It turns out that class is one of the Python keywords. Keywords define the language's rules and structure, and they cannot be used as variable names.

Python has twenty-nine keywords:

and	def	exec	if	not	return
assert	del	finally	import	or	try
break	elif	for	in	pass	while
class	else	from	is	print	yield
continue	except	global	lambda	raise	

If the interpreter complains about one of your variable names and you don't know.

STATEMENTS

A statement is an instruction that the Python interpreter can execute. We have seen two kinds of statements: print and assignment. When you type a statement on the command line, Python executes it and displays the result, if there is one. The result of a print statement is a value. Assignment statements don't produce a result.

A script usually contains a sequence of statements. If there is more than one statement, the results appear one at a time as the statements execute.

For example, the script,

```
print 1
x = 2
print x
```

produces the output,

```
1
2
```

Again, the assignment statement produces no output.

EVALUATING EXPRESSIONS

An expression is a combination of values, variables, and operators. If you type an expression on the command line, the interpreter evaluates it and displays the result:

```
1 + 1
2
```

Although expressions contain values, variables, and operators, not every expression contains all of these elements. A value all by itself is considered an expression, and so is a variable.

```
17
17
>>> x
2
```

Confusingly, evaluating an expression is not quite the same thing as printing a value.

```
message = 'Hello, World!'
message
'Hello, World!'
print message
Hello, World!
```

When the Python interpreter displays the value of an expression, it uses the same format you would use to enter a value. In the case of strings, that means that it includes the quotation marks. But if you use a print statement, Python displays the contents of the string without the quotation marks.

In a script, an expression all by itself is a legal statement, but it doesn't do anything.

```
17
3.2
'Hello, World!'
1 + 1
```

OPERATORS AND OPERANDS

Operators are special symbols that represent computations like addition and multiplication. The values the operator uses are called operands.

The following are all legal Python expressions whose meaning is more or less clear:

```
20+32 hour-1 hour*60+minute minute/60 5**2
(5+9)*(15-7)
```

The symbols +, –, and/, and the use of parenthesis for grouping, mean in Python what they mean in mathematics.

The asterisk (*) is the symbol for multiplication, and ** is the symbol for exponentiation. When a variable name appears in the place of an operand, it is replaced with its value before the operation is performed. Addition, subtraction, multiplication, and exponentiation all do what you expect, but you might be surprised by division.

The following operation has an unexpected result:

```
minute = 59
minute/60
0
```

The value of minute is 59, and in conventional arithmetic 59 divided by 60 is 0.98333, not 0. The reason for the discrepancy is that Python is performinginteger division. When both of the operands are integers, the result must also be an integer, and by convention, integer division always rounds *down*, even in cases like this where the next integer is very close.

A possible solution to this problem is to calculate a percentage rather than a fraction:

```
minute*100/60
98
```

Again the result is rounded down, but at least now the answer is approximately correct. Another alternative is to use floating-point division.

ORDER OF OPERATIONS

When more than one operator appears in an expression, the order of evaluation depends on the rules of precedence. Python follows the same precedence rules for its mathematical operators that mathematics does.

The acronym PEMDAS is a useful way to remember the order of operations:

- Parentheses have the highest precedence and can be used to force an expression to evaluate in the order you want. Since expressions in parentheses are evaluated first, 2 * (3–1) is 4, and (1+1)**(5–2) is 8. You can also use parentheses to make an expression easier to read, as in (minute * 100)/60, even though it doesn't change the result.

- Exponentiation has the next highest precedence, so 2**1+1 is 3 and not 4, and 3*1**3 is 3 and not 27.
- Multiplication and Division have the same precedence, which is higher thanAddition and Subtraction, which also have the same precedence. So 2*3-1yields 5 rather than 4, and 2/3–1 is –1, not 1 (remember that in integer division, 2/3=0).
- Operators with the same precedence are evaluated from left to right. So in the expression minute*100/60, the multiplication happens first, yielding 5900/60, which in turn yields 98. If the operations had been evaluated from right to left, the result would have been 59*1, which is 59, which is wrong.

OPERATIONS ON STRINGS

In general, you cannot perform mathematical operations on strings, even if the strings look like numbers. The following are illegal (assuming that message has typestring):

```
message-1  'Hello'/123 message*'Hello'  '15'+2
```

Interestingly, the + operator does work with strings, although it does not do exactly what you might expect. For strings, the + operator representsconcatenation, which means joining the two operands by linking them end-to-end.

For example:

```
fruit = 'banana'
bakedGood = ' nut bread'
print fruit + bakedGood
```

The output of this programme is banana nut bread. The space before the word nut is part of the string, and is necessary to produce the space between the concatenated strings.

The * operator also works on strings; it performs repetition. For example, 'Fun'*3is 'FunFunFun'. One of the operands has to be a string; the other has to be an integer.

On one hand, this interpretation of + and * makes sense by analogy with addition and multiplication. Just as 4*3 is equivalent to 4+4+4, we expect 'Fun'*3 to be the same as 'Fun'+'Fun'+'Fun', and it is. On the other hand, there is a significant way in which string concatenation and repetition are different from integer addition and multiplication. Can you think of a property that addition and multiplication have that string concatenation and repetition do not?

COMPOSITION

So far, we have looked at the elements of a programme variables, expressions, and statements in isolation, without talking about how to combine them.

One of the most useful features of programming languages is their ability to take small building blocks and compose them. For example, we know how to add numbers and we know how to print; it turns out we can do both at the same time:

```
print 17 + 3
20
```

In reality, the addition has to happen before the printing, so the actions aren't actually happening at the same time. The point is that any expression involving numbers, strings, and variables can be used inside a print statement.

You've already seen an example of this:

```
print 'Number of minutes since midnight: ',
hour*60+minute
```

You can also put arbitrary expressions on the right-hand side of an assignment statement:

```
percentage = (minute * 100)/60
```

This ability may not seem impressive now, but you will see other examples where composition makes it possible to express complex computations neatly and concisely. There are limits on where you can use certain expressions. For example, the left-hand side of an assignment statement has to be a *variable* name, not an expression. So, the following is illegal: minute+1 = hour.

COMMENTS

As programmes get bigger and more complicated, they get more difficult to read. Formal languages are dense, and it is often difficult to look at a piece of code and figure out what it is doing, or why.

For this reason, it is a good idea to add notes to your programmes to explain in natural language what the programme is doing.

These notes are called comments, and they are marked with the # symbol:

```
# compute the percentage of the hour that
has elapsed
percentage = (minute * 100)/60
```

In this case, the comment appears on a line by itself. You can also put comments at the end of a line:

```
percentage = (minute * 100)/60 # caution:
integer division
```

Everything from the # to the end of the line is ignored it has no effect on the programme. The message is intended for the programmer or for future programmers who might use this code. In this case, it reminds the reader about the ever-surprising behaviour of integer division. This sort of comment is less necessary if you use the integer division operation,//. It has the same effect as the division operator * Note, but it signals that the effect is deliberate.

```
percentage = (minute * 100)//60
```

The integer division operator is like a comment that says, "I know this is integer division, and I like it that way!"

GLOSSARY

- *Value*: A number or string (or other thing to be named later) that can be stored in a variable or computed in an expression.
- *Type*: A set of values. The type of a value determines how it can be used in expressions. So far, the types you have seen are integers (type int), floating-point numbers (type float), and strings (type string).
- *Floating-point*: A format for representing numbers with fractional parts.
- *Variable*: A name that refers to a value.
- *Statement*: A section of code that represents a command or action. So far, the statements you have seen are assignments and print statements.

- *Assignment*: A statement that assigns a value to a variable.
- *State diagram*: A graphical representation of a set of variables and the values to which they refer.
- *Keyword*: A reserved word that is used by the compiler to parse a programme; you cannot use keywords like if, def, and while as variable names.
- *Operator*: A special symbol that represents a simple computation like addition, multiplication, or string concatenation.
- *Operand*: One of the values on which an operator operates.
- *Expression*: A combination of variables, operators, and values that represents a single result value.
- *Evaluate*: To simplify an expression by performing the operations in order to yield a single value.
- *Integer division*: An operation that divides one integer by another and yields an integer. Integer division yields only the whole number of times that the numerator is divisible by the denominator and discards any remainder.
- *Rules of precedence*: The set of rules governing the order in which expressions involving multiple operators and operands are evaluated.
- *Concatenate*: To join two operands end-to-end.
- *Composition*: The ability to combine simple expressions and statements into compound statements and expressions in order to represent complex computations concisely.
- *Comment*: Information in a programme that is meant for other programmers (or anyone reading the source code) and has no effect on the execution of the programme.
- *Warning*: the HTML version of this document is generated from Latex and may contain translation errors. In particular, some mathematical expressions are not translated correctly.

FUNCTIONS

FUNCTION CALLS

You have already seen one example of a function call:

```
>>> type("32")
<type 'str'>
```

The name of the function is type, and it displays the type of a value or variable.

The value or variable, which is called the argument of the function, has to be enclosed in parentheses. It is common to say that a function "takes" an argument and "returns" a result. The result is called the return value.

Instead of printing the return value, we could assign it to a variable:

```
betty = type("32")
print betty
type 'str'>
```

As another example, the id function takes a value or a variable and returns an integer that acts as a unique identifier for the value:

```
id(3)
134882108
betty = 3
id(betty)
134882108
```

Every value has an id, which is a unique number related to where it is stored in the memory of the computer. The id of a variable is the id of the value to which it refers.

TYPE CONVERSION

Python provides a collection of built-in functions that convert values from one type to another. The int function takes any value and converts it to an integer, if possible, or complains otherwise:

```
int("32")
32
int("Hello")
ValueError: invalid literal for int(): Hello
```

int *can also convert floating-point values to integers, but remember that it truncates the fractional part*:

```
int(3.99999)
3
int(-2.3)
-2
```

The float *function converts integers and strings to floating-point numbers*:

```
float(32)
32.0
float("3.14159")
3.14159
```

Finally, the str *function converts to type string*:

```
str(32)
'32'
str(3.14149)
'3.14149'
```

It may seem odd that Python distinguishes the integer value 1 from the floating-point value 1.0. They may represent the same number, but they belong to different types. The reason is that they are represented differently inside the computer.

TYPE COERCION

Now that we can convert between types, we have another way to deal with integer division. The most obvious expression, minute/60, does integer arithmetic, so the result is always 0, even at 59 minutes past the hour.

One solution is to convert minute to floating-point and do floating-point division:

```
minute = 59
float(minute)/60
0.983333333333
```

Alternatively, we can take advantage of the rules for automatic type conversion, which is called type coercion. For the mathematical operators, if either operand is a float, the other is automatically converted to a float:

```
minute = 59
```

```
minute/60.0
0.983333333333
```

By making the denominator a float, we force Python to do floating-point division.

MATH FUNCTIONS

In mathematics, you have probably seen functions like sin and log, and you have learned to evaluate expressions like sin(pi/2) and log(1/x). First, you evaluate the expression in parentheses (the argument). For example, pi/2 is approximately 1.571, and 1/x is 0.1 (if x happens to be 10.0).

Then, you evaluate the function itself, either by looking it up in a table or by performing various computations. The sin of 1.571 is 1, and the log of 0.1 is –1 (assuming that log indicates the logarithm base 10).

This process can be applied repeatedly to evaluate more complicated expressions like log(1/sin(pi/2)). First, you evaluate the argument of the innermost function, then evaluate the function, and so on.

Python has a math module that provides most of the familiar mathematical functions. A module is a file that contains a collection of related functions grouped together.

Before we can use the functions from a module, we have to import them:

```
import math
```

To call one of the functions, we have to specify the name of the module and the name of the function, separated by a dot, also known as a period. This format is called dot notation.

```
decibel = math.log10 (17.0)
angle = 1.5
height = math.sin(angle)
```

The first statement sets decibel to the logarithm of 17, base 10. There is also a function called log that takes logarithm base e. The third statement finds the sine of the value of the variable angle.

Sin and the other trigonometric functions (cos, tan, etc.) take arguments in radians. To convert from degrees to radians, divide by 360 and multiply by 2*pi. For example, to find the sine of 45 degrees, first calculate the angle in radians and then take the sine:

```
degrees = 45
angle = degrees * 2 * math.pi/360.0
math.sin(angle)
0.707106781187
```

The constant pi is also part of the math module. If you know your geometry, you can check the previous result by comparing it to the square root of two divided by two:

```
math.sqrt(2)/2.0
0.707106781187
```

COMPOSITION

Just as with mathematical functions, Python functions can be composed, meaning that you use one expression as part of another.

For example, you can use any expression as an argument to a function:

```
x = math.cos(angle + math.pi/2)
```

This statement takes the value of pi, divides it by 2, and adds the result to the value of angle. The sum is then passed as an argument to the cos function.

You can also take the result of one function and pass it as an argument to another:

```
x = math.exp(math.log(10.0))
```

This statement finds the log base e of 10 and then raises e to that power. The result gets assigned to x.

ADDING NEW FUNCTIONS

So far, we have only been using the functions that come with Python, but it is also possible to add new functions. Creating new functions to solve your particular problems is one of the most useful things about a general-purpose programming language.

In the context of programming, a function is a named sequence of statements that performs a desired operation. This operation is specified in a function definition. The functions we have been using so far have been defined for us, and these definitions have been hidden. This is a good thing, because it allows us to use the functions without worrying about the details of their definitions.

The syntax for a function definition is:

```
def NAME(LIST OF PARAMETERS):
    STATEMENTS
```

You can make up any names you want for the functions you create, except that you can't use a name that is a Python keyword. The list of parameters specifies what information, if any, you have to provide in order to use the new function.

There can be any number of statements inside the function, but they have to be indented from the left margin. In the examples in this book, we will use an indentation of two spaces.

The first couple of functions we are going to write have no parameters, so the syntax looks like this:

```
def newLine():
print
```

This function is named newLine. The empty parentheses indicate that it has no parameters.

It contains only a single statement, which outputs a newline character.

The syntax for calling the new function is the same as the syntax for built-in functions:

```
print "First Line."
newLine()
print "Second Line."
```

The output of this programme is:

```
First line.
Second line.
```

Notice the extra space between the two lines. What if we wanted more space between the lines?

We could call the same function repeatedly:

```
print "First Line."
newLine()
newLine()
newLine()
print "Second Line."
```

Or we could write a new function named threeLines *that prints three new lines*:

```
def threeLines():
newLine()
newLine()
newLine()
print "First Line."
threeLines()
print "Second Line."
```

This function contains three statements, all of which are indented by two spaces. Since the next statement is not indented, Python knows that it is not part of the function.

You should notice a few things about this programme:

- You can call the same procedure repeatedly. In fact, it is quite common and useful to do so.
- You can have one function call another function; in this case threeLines callsnewLine.

So far, it may not be clear why it is worth the trouble to create all of these new functions.

Actually, there are a lot of reasons, but this example demonstrates two:

- Creating a new function gives you an opportunity to name a group of statements. Functions can simplify a programme by hiding a complex computation behind a single command and by using English words in place of arcane code.
- Creating a new function can make a programme smaller by eliminating repetitive code. For example, a short way to print nine consecutive new lines is to call threeLines three times.

As an exercise, write a function called nineLines that usesthreeLines to print nine blank lines. How would you print twenty-seven new lines?

DEFINITIONS AND USE

Pulling together the code fragments, the whole programme looks like this:

```
def newLine():
```

```
    print
  def threeLines():
    newLine()
    newLine()
    newLine()
  print "First Line."
  threeLines()
  print "Second Line."
```

This programme contains two function definitions: newLine and threeLines. Function definitions get executed just like other statements, but the effect is to create the new function. The statements inside the function do not get executed until the function is called, and the function definition generates no output. As you might expect, you have to create a function before you can execute it. In other words, the function definition has to be executed before the first time it is called.

FLOW OF EXECUTION

In order to ensure that a function is defined before its first use, you have to know the order in which statements are executed, which is called the flow of execution. Execution always begins at the first statement of the programme. Statements are executed one at a time, in order from top to bottom.

Function definitions do not alter the flow of execution of the programme, but remember that statements inside the function are not executed until the function is called. Although it is not common, you can define one function inside another. In this case, the inner definition isn't executed until the outer function is called.

Function calls are like a detour in the flow of execution. Instead of going to the next statement, the flow jumps to the first line of the called function, executes all the statements there, and then comes back to pick up where it left off.

That sounds simple enough, until you remember that one function can call another. While in the middle of one function, the programme might have to execute the statements in another function. But while executing that new function, the programme might have to execute yet another function! Fortunately, Python is adept at keeping track of where it is, so each time a function completes, the programme picks up where it left off in the function that called it. When it gets to the end of the programme, it terminates. What's the moral of this sordid tale? When you read a programme, don't read from top to bottom. Instead, follow the flow of execution.

PARAMETERS AND ARGUMENTS

Some of the built-in functions you have used require arguments, the values that control how the function does its job. For example, if you want to find the sine of a number, you have to indicate what the number is. Thus, sin takes a numeric value as an argument.

Some functions take more than one argument. For example, pow takes two arguments, the base and the exponent. Inside the function, the values that are passed get assigned to variables called parameters.

Here is an example of a user-defined function that has a parameter:

```
def printTwice(bruce):
print bruce, bruce
```

This function takes a single argument and assigns it to a parameter named bruce. The value of the parameter (at this point we have no idea what it will be) is printed twice, followed by a newline. The name bruce was chosen to suggest that the name you give a parameter is up to you, but in general, you want to choose something more illustrative than *bruce*.

The function printTwice *works for any type that can be printed*:

```
>>> printTwice('Spam')
Spam Spam
printTwice(5)
5 5
printTwice(3.14159)
3.14159 3.14159
```

In the first function call, the argument is a string. In the second, it's an integer. In the third, it's a float. The same rules of composition that apply to built-in functions also apply to user-defined functions, so we can use any kind of expression as an argument forprintTwice:

```
printTwice('Spam'*4)
SpamSpamSpamSpam SpamSpamSpamSpam
printTwice(math.cos(math.pi))
-1.0 -1.0
```

As usual, the expression is evaluated before the function is run, so printTwice printsSpamSpamSpamSpam SpamSpam SpamSpam instead of 'Spam'*4 'Spam'*4.

As an exercise, write a call to printTwice that does print 'Spam'*4'Spam'*4.

Hint: Strings can be enclosed in either single or double quotes, and the type of quote not used to enclose the string can be used inside it as part of the string.

We can also use a variable as an argument:

```
michael = 'Eric, the half a bee.'
printTwice(michael)
Eric, the half a bee. Eric, the half a bee.
```

Notice something very important here. The name of the variable we pass as an argument (michael) has nothing to do with the name of the parameter (bruce). It doesn't matter what the value was called back home (in the caller); here inprintTwice, we call everybody bruce.

VARIABLES AND PARAMETERS ARE LOCAL

When you create a local variable inside a function, it only exists inside the function, and you cannot use it outside.

For example:

```
def catTwice(part1, part2):
cat = part1 + part2
printTwice(cat)
```

This function takes two arguments, concatenates them, and then prints the result twice. We can call the function with two strings:

```
chant1 = "Pie Jesu domine, "
chant2 = "Dona eis requiem."
catTwice(chant1, chant2)
Pie Jesu domine, Dona eis requiem. Pie Jesu
domine, Dona eis requiem.
```

When catTwice *terminates, the variable* cat *is destroyed. If we try to print it, we get an error:*

```
print cat
NameError: cat
```

Parameters are also local. For example, outside the function printTwice, there is no such thing as bruce. If you try to use it, Python will complain.

STACK DIAGRAMS

To keep track of which variables can be used where, it is sometimes useful to draw a stack diagram. Like state diagrams, stack diagrams show the value of each variable, but they also show the function to which each variable belongs.

Each function is represented by a frame. A frame is a box with the name of a function beside it and the parameters and variables of the function inside it.

The stack diagram for the previous example looks like this:

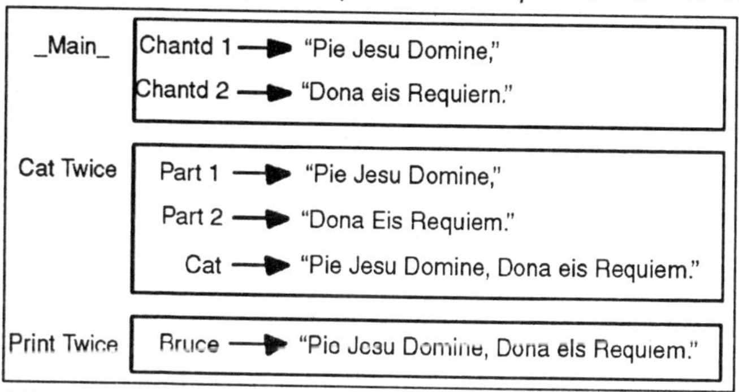

The order of the stack shows the flow of execution. printTwice was called bycatTwice, and catTwice was called by __main__, which is a special name for the topmost function. When you create a variable outside of any function, it belongs to__main__.

Each parameter refers to the same value as its corresponding argument. So, part1has the same value as chant1, part2 has the same value as chant2, and bruce has the same value as cat.

If an error occurs during a function call, Python prints the name of the function, and the name of the function that called it, and the name of the function that called*that,* all the way back to __main__.

For example, if we try to access cat from within printTwice, *we get a* NameError:

```
Traceback (innermost last):
  File "test.py", line 13, in __main__
    catTwice(chant1, chant2)
  File "test.py", line 5, in catTwice
    printTwice(cat)
  File "test.py", line 9, in printTwice
    print cat
NameError: cat
```

This list of functions is called a traceback. It tells you what programme file the error occurred in, and what line, and what functions were executing at the time. It also shows the line of code that caused the error. Notice the similarity between the traceback and the stack diagram. It's not a coincidence.

FUNCTIONS WITH RESULTS

You might have noticed by now that some of the functions we are using, such as the math functions, yield results. Other functions, like newLine, perform an action but don't return a value.

That raises some questions:

- What happens if you call a function and you don't do anything with the result (*i.e.,* you don't assign it to a variable or use it as part of a larger expression)?
- What happens if you use a function without a result as part of an expression, such as newLine() + 7?
- Can you write functions that yield results, or are you stuck with simple function like newLine and printTwice?

As an exercise, answer the other two questions by trying them out. When you have a question about what is legal or illegal in Python, a good way to find out is to ask the interpreter.

GLOSSARY

- *Function call*: A statement that executes a function. It

consists of the name of the function followed by a list of arguments enclosed in parentheses.

- *Argument*: A value provided to a function when the function is called. This value is assigned to the corresponding parameter in the function.
- *Return value*: The result of a function. If a function call is used as an expression, the return value is the value of the expression.
- *Type conversion*: An explicit statement that takes a value of one type and computes a corresponding value of another type.
- *Type coercion*: A type conversion that happens automatically according to Python's coercion rules.
- *Module*: A file that contains a collection of related functions and classes.
- *Dot notation*: The syntax for calling a function in another module, specifying the module name followed by a dot (period) and the function name.
- *Function*: A named sequence of statements that performs some useful operation. Functions may or may not take arguments and may or may not produce a result.
- *Function definition*: A statement that creates a new function, specifying its name, parameters, and the statements it executes.
- *Flow of execution*: The order in which statements are executed during a programme run.
- *Parameter*: A name used inside a function to refer to the value passed as an argument.
- *Local variable*: A variable defined inside a function. A local variable can only be used inside its function.
- *Stack diagram*: A graphical representation of a stack of functions, their variables, and the values to which they refer.
- *Frame*: A box in a stack diagram that represents a function call. It contains the local variables and parameters of the function.
- *Traceback*: A list of the functions that are executing, printed when a runtime error occurs.

CONDITIONALS AND RECURSION

THE MODULUS OPERATOR

The modulus operator works on integers (and integer expressions) and yields the remainder when the first operand is divided by the second. In Python, the modulus operator is a percent sign (%).

The syntax is the same as for other operators:

```
quotient = 7/3
print quotient
2
remainder = 7 % 3
>>> print remainder
1
```

So 7 divided by 3 is 2 with 1 left over. The modulus operator turns out to be surprisingly useful. For example, you can check whether one number is divisible by another if × % y is zero, then x is divisible by y.

Also, you can extract the right-most digit or digits from a number. For example, × % 10 yields the right-most digit of × (in base 10). Similarly × % 100 yields the last two digits.

BOOLEAN EXPRESSIONS

A boolean expression is an expression that is either true or false. One way to write a boolean expression is to use the operator ==, which compares two values and produces a boolean value:

```
5 == 5
True
5 == 6
False
```

In the first statement, the two operands are equal, so the value of the expression isTrue; in the second statement, 5 is not equal to 6, so we get False. True and Falseare special values that are built into Python.

The == operator is one of the comparison operators; the others are:

```
x != y    #  x is not equal to y
```

```
x > y      #  x is greater than y
x < y      #  x is less than y
x ⇒ y      #  x is greater than or equal to y
x ⇐ y      #  x is less than or equal to y
```

Although these operations are probably familiar to you, the Python symbols are different from the mathematical symbols. A common error is to use a single equal sign (=) instead of a double equal sign (==). Remember that = is an assignment operator and == is a comparison operator. Also, there is no such thing as ⇒ or ⇐.

LOGICAL OPERATORS

There are three logical operators: and, or, and not. The semantics (meaning) of these operators is similar to their meaning in English. For example, x > 0 and x < 10 is true only if x is greater than 0 *and* less than 10.

n%2 == 0 or n%3 == 0 is true if *either* of the conditions is true, that is, if the number is divisible by 2 *or* 3. Finally, the not operator negates a boolean expression, so not(x > y) is true if (x > y) is false, that is, if x is less than or equal to y. Strictly speaking, the operands of the logical operators should be boolean expressions, but Python is not very strict. Any nonzero number is interpreted as "true."

```
x = 5
x and 1
1
y = 0
y and 1
0
```

In general, this sort of thing is not considered good style. If you want to compare a value to zero, you should do it explicitly.

CONDITIONAL EXECUTION

In order to write useful programmes, we almost always need the ability to check conditions and change the behaviour of the programme accordingly. Conditional statements give us this ability.

The simplest form is the if statement:

```
if x > 0:
   print "x is positive"
```

The boolean expression after the if statement is called the condition. If it is true, then the indented statement gets executed. If not, nothing happens.

Like other compound statements, the if *statement is made up of a header and a block of statements:*

```
HEADER:
   FIRST STATEMENT
   ...
   LAST STATEMENT
```

The header begins on a new line and ends with a colon (:). The indented statements that follow are called a block. The first unindented statement marks the end of the block. A statement block inside a compound statement is called thebody of the statement.

There is no limit on the number of statements that can appear in the body of an if statement, but there has to be at least one. Occasionally, it is useful to have a body with no statements (usually as a place keeper for code you haven't written yet). In that case, you can use the pass statement, which does nothing.

SECOND FORM OF EXECUTION

A second form of the if statement is alternative execution, in which there are two possibilities and the condition determines which one gets executed.

The syntax looks like this:

```
if x%2 == 0:
    print x, "is even"
else:
   print x, "is odd"
```

If the remainder when x is divided by 2 is 0, then we know that x is even, and the programme displays a message to that effect. If the condition is false, the second set of statements is executed. Since the condition must be true or false, exactly one of the alternatives will be executed. The alternatives are called branches, because they are branches in the flow of execution.

As an aside, if you need to check the parity (evenness or oddness) of numbers often, you might "wrap" this code in a function:

```
def printParity(x):
  if x%2 == 0:
    print x, "is even"
else:
    print x, "is odd"
```

For any value of x, printParity displays an appropriate message. When you call it, you can provide any integer expression as an argument.

```
>>> printParity(17)
17 is odd
>>> y = 17
>>> printParity(y+1)
18 is even
```

CHAINED CONDITIONALS

Sometimes there are more than two possibilities and we need more than two branches.

One way to express a computation like that is a chained conditional:

```
if x < y:
  print x, "is less than", y
elif x > y:
  print x, "is greater than", y
else:
  print x, "and", y, "are equal"
```

elif is an abbreviation of "else if." Again, exactly one branch will be executed. There is no limit of the number of elif statements, but the last branch has to be anelse statement:

```
if choice == 'A':
  functionA()
elif choice == 'B':
  functionB()
elif choice == 'C':
  functionC()
```

```
else:
  print "Invalid choice."
```

Each condition is checked in order. If the first is false, the next is checked, and so on. If one of them is true, the corresponding branch executes, and the statement ends. Even if more than one condition is true, only the first true branch executes. As an exercise, wrap these examples in functions called compare(x, y) and dispatch(choice).

NESTED CONDITIONALS

One conditional can also be nested within another. We could have written the trichotomy example as follows:

```
if x == y:
  print x, "and", y, "are equal"
else:
  if x < y:
print x, "is less than", y
  else:
    print x, "is greater than", y
```

The outer conditional contains two branches. The first branch contains a simple output statement. The second branch contains another if statement, which has two branches of its own. Those two branches are both output statements, although they could have been conditional statements as well.

Although the indentation of the statements makes the structure apparent, nested conditionals become difficult to read very quickly. In general, it is a good idea to avoid them when you can. Logical operators often provide a way to simplify nested conditional statements.

For example, we can rewrite the following code using a single conditional:

```
if 0 < x:
  if x < 10:
    print "x is a positive single digit."
```

The print statement is executed only if we make it past both the conditionals, so we can use the and operator:

```
if 0 < x and x < 10:
    print "x is a positive single digit."
```

These kinds of conditions are common, so Python provides an alternative syntax that is similar to mathematical notation:

```
if 0 < x < 10:
  print "x is a positive single digit."
```

This condition is semantically the same as the compound boolean expression and the nested conditional.

THE RETURN STATEMENT

The return statement allows you to terminate the execution of a function before you reach the end.

One reason to use it is if you detect an error condition:

```
import math
def printLogarithm(x):
    if x ⇐ 0:
        print "Positive numbers only, please."
        return
  result = math.log(x)
  print "The log of x is", result
```

The function printLogarithm has a parameter named x. The first thing it does is check whether x is less than or equal to 0, in which case it displays an error message and then uses return to exit the function. The flow of execution immediately returns to the caller, and the remaining lines of the function are not executed. Remember that to use a function from the math module, you have to import it.

RECURSION

We mentioned that it is legal for one function to call another, and you have seen several examples of that. We neglected to mention that it is also legal for a function to call itself. It may not be obvious why that is a good thing, but it turns out to be one of the most magical and interesting things a programme can do.

For example, look at the following function:

```
def countdown(n):
  if n == 0:
print "Blastoff!"
  else:
```

```
    print n
    countdown(n-1)
```

countdown expects the parameter, n, to be a positive integer. If n is 0, it outputs the word, "Blastoff!" Otherwise, it outputs n and then calls a function named countdown-itself passing n-1 as an argument.

What happens if we call this function like this:

```
>>> countdown(3)
```

The execution of countdown begins with n=3, and since n is not 0, it outputs the value 3, and then calls itself...

The execution of countdown begins with n=2, and since n is not 0, it outputs the value 2, and then calls itself...

The execution of countdown begins with n=1, and since nis not 0, it outputs the value 1, and then calls itself...

The execution of countdown begins withn=0, and since n is 0, it outputs the word, "Blastoff!" and then returns.

The countdown that got n=1 returns.

The countdown that got n=2 returns.

The countdown that got n=3 returns.

And then you're back in __main__ (what a trip). So, the total output looks like this:

```
3
2
1
Blastoff!
```

As a second example, look again at the functions newLine and threeLines:

```
def newline():
  print
def threeLines():
  newLine()
  newLine()
  newLine()
```

Although these work, they would not be much help if we wanted to output 2 newlines, or 106.

A better alternative would be this:

```
def nLines(n):
  if n > 0:
```

```
print
nLines(n-1)
```

This programme is similar to countdown; as long as n is greater than 0, it outputs one newline and then calls itself to output n-1 additional newlines. Thus, the total number of newlines is 1 + (n – 1) which, if you do your algebra right, comes out ton. The process of a function calling itself is recursion, and such functions are said to be recursive.

STACK DIAGRAMS FOR RECURSIVE FUNCTIONS

Every time a function gets called, Python creates a new function frame, which contains the function's local variables and parameters. For a recursive function, there might be more than one frame on the stack at the same time.

This figure shows a stack diagram for countdown *called with* n = 3:

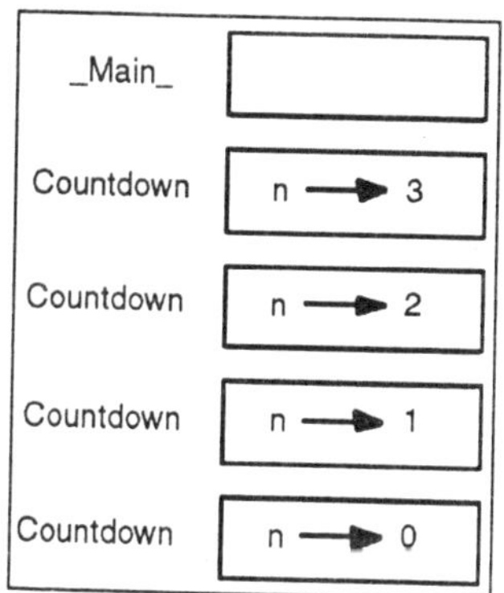

As usual, the top of the stack is the frame for __main__. It is empty because we did not create any variables in __main__ or pass any arguments to it. The four countdown frames have different values for the parameter n. The bottom of the stack, where n=0, is called the base case. It does not make a recursive call, so there are no more frames.

As an exercise, draw a stack diagram for nLines called with n=4.

INFINITE RECURSION

If a recursion never reaches a base case, it goes on making

recursive calls forever, and the programme never terminates. This is known as infinite recursion, and it is generally not considered a good idea.

Here is a minimal programme with an infinite recursion:

```
def recurse():
    recurse()
```

In most programming environments, a programme with infinite recursion does not really run forever.

Python reports an error message when the maximum recursion depth is reached:

```
File "<stdin>", line 2, in recurse
(98 repetitions omitted)
File "<stdin>", line 2, in recurse
RuntimeError: Maximum recursion depth exceeded
```

This traceback is a little bigger. When the error occurs, there are 100 recurse frames on the stack!

As an exercise, write a function with infinite recursion and run it in the Python interpreter.

KEYBOARD INPUT

The programmes we have written so far are a bit rude in the sense that they accept no input from the user. They just do the same thing every time.

Python provides built-in functions that get input from the keyboard. The simplest is called raw_input. When this function is called, the programme stops and waits for the user to type something. When the user presses Return or the Enter key, the programme resumes and raw_input returns what the user typed as a string:

```
input = raw_input ()
What are you waiting for?
print input
What are you waiting for?
```

Before calling raw_input, it is a good idea to print a message telling the user what to input. This message is called a prompt.

We can supply a prompt as an argument to raw_input:

```
name = raw_input ("What...is your name?")
```

```
What...is your name? Arthur, King of the
Britons!
>>> print name
Arthur, King of the Britons!
```

If we expect the response to be an integer, we can use the input function:

```
prompt = "What...is the airspeed velocity of
an unladen
swallow?\n"
speed = input(prompt)
```

The sequence \n at the end of the string represents a newline, so the user's input appears below the prompt. If the user types a string of digits, it is converted to an integer and assigned tospeed.

Unfortunately, if the user types a character that is not a digit, the programme crashes:

```
speed = input (prompt)
What...is the airspeed velocity of an unladen
  swallow?
What do you mean, an African or a European
  swallow?
SyntaxError: invalid syntax
```

To avoid this kind of error, it is generally a good idea to use raw_input to get a string and then use conversion functions to convert to other types.

GLOSSARY

- *Modulus operator*: An operator, denoted with a per cent sign (%), that works on integers and yields the remainder when one number is divided by another.
- *Boolean expression*: An expression that is either true or false.
- *Comparison operator*: One of the operators that compares two values: ==, !=, >, <, ⇒, and ⇐.
- *Logical operator*: One of the operators that combines boolean expressions: and, or, and not.
- *Conditional statement*: A statement that controls the flow of execution depending on some condition.

- *Condition*: The boolean expression in a conditional statement that determines which branch is executed.
- *Compound statement*: A statement that consists of a header and a body. The header ends with a colon (:). The body is indented relative to the header.
- *Block*: A group of consecutive statements with the same indentation.
- *Body*: The block in a compound statement that follows the header.
- *Nesting*: One programme structure within another, such as a conditional statement inside a branch of another conditional statement.
- *Recursion*: The process of calling the function that is currently executing.
- *Base case*: A branch of the conditional statement in a recursive function that does not result in a recursive call.
- *Infinite recursion*: A function that calls itself recursively without ever reaching the base case. Eventually, an infinite recursion causes a runtime error.
- *Prompt*: A visual cue that tells the user to input data.
- *Warning*: The HTML version of this document is generated from Latex and may contain translation errors. In particular, some mathematical expressions are not translated correctly.

FRUITFUL FUNCTIONS

RETURN VALUES

Some of the built-in functions we have used, such as the math functions, have produced results. Calling the function generates a new value, which we usually assign to a variable or use as part of an expression.

```
e = math.exp(1.0)
height = radius * math.sin(angle)
```

But so far, none of the functions we have written has returned a value. In this, we are going to write functions that return values, which we will call fruitful functions, for want of a better name.

The first example is area, which returns the area of a circle with the given radius:

```
import math
def area(radius):
  temp = math.pi * radius**2
  return temp
```

We have seen the return statement before, but in a fruitful function the returnstatement includes a return value. This statement means: "Return immediately from this function and use the following expression as a return value."

The expression provided can be arbitrarily complicated, so we could have written this function more concisely:

```
def area(radius):
    return math.pi * radius**2
```

On the other hand, temporary variables like temp often make debugging easier.

Sometimes it is useful to have multiple return statements, one in each branch of a conditional:

```
def absoluteValue(x):
    if x < 0:
        return -x
else:
  return x
```

Since these return statements are in an alternative conditional, only one will be executed. As soon as one is executed, the function terminates without executing any subsequent statements. Code that appears after a return statement, or any other place the flow of execution can never reach, is called dead code.

In a fruitful function, it is a good idea to ensure that every possible path through the programme hits a return statement.

For example:

```
def absoluteValue(x):
  if x < 0:
      return -x
  elif x > 0:
    return x
```

This programme is not correct because if x happens to be 0, neither condition is true, and the function ends without hitting a return statement. In this case, the return value is a special value called None:

```
print absoluteValue(0)
None
```

As an exercise, write a compare function that returns1 if $x > y$, 0 if $x == y$, and -1 if $x < y$.

PROGRAMME DEVELOPMENT

At this point, you should be able to look at complete functions and tell what they do. Also, if you have been doing the exercises, you have written some small functions. As you write larger functions, you might start to have more difficulty, especially with runtime and semantic errors.

To deal with increasingly complex programmes, we are going to suggest a technique called incremental development. The goal of incremental development is to avoid long debugging sessions by adding and testing only a small amount of code at a time.

As an example, suppose you want to find the distance between two points, given by the coordinates (x1, y1) and (x2, y2).

By the Pythagorean theorem, the distance is:

$$\text{Distance} = \sqrt{(x_2 - x_1)^2 + (y_2 - y_1)^2}$$

The first step is to consider what a distance function should look like in Python. In other words, what are the inputs (parameters) and what is the output (return value)?

In this case, the two points are the inputs, which we can represent using four parameters. The return value is the distance, which is a floating-point value.

Already we can write an outline of the function:

```
def distance(x1, y1, x2, y2):
  return 0.0
```

Obviously, this version of the function doesn't compute distances; it always returns zero. But it is syntactically correct, and it will run, which means that we can test it before we make it more complicated.

To test the new function, we call it with sample values:

```
distance(1, 2, 4, 6)
0.0
```

We chose these values so that the horizontal distance equals 3 and the vertical distance equals 4; that way, the result is 5 (the hypotenuse of a 3–4–5 triangle). When testing a function, it is useful to know the right answer.

At this point we have confirmed that the function is syntactically correct, and we can start adding lines of code. After each incremental change, we test the function again. If an error occurs at any point, we know where it must be in the last line we added.

A logical first step in the computation is to find the differences x2 – x1 and y2 – y1. We will store those values in temporary variables named dx and dy and print them.

```
def distance(x1, y1, x2, y2):
  dx = x2 - x1
  dy = y2 - y1
  print "dx is", dx
  print "dy is", dy
  return 0.0
```

If the function is working, the outputs should be 3 and 4. If so, we know that the function is getting the right arguments and performing the first computation correctly. If not, there are only a few lines to check.

Next we compute the sum of squares of dx *and* dy:

```
def distance(x1, y1, x2, y2):
  dx = x2 - x1
  dy = y2 - y1
  dsquared = dx**2 + dy**2
  print "dsquared is: ", dsquared
  return 0.0
```

Notice that we removed the print statements we wrote in the previous step. Code like that is called scaffolding because it is helpful for building the programme but is not part of the final product.

Again, we would run the programme at this stage and check the output (which should be 25).

Finally, if we have imported the math module, we can use the sqrt *function to compute and return the result:*

```
def distance(x1, y1, x2, y2):
  dx = x2 - x1
  dy = y2 - y1
  dsquared = dx**2 + dy**2
  result = math.sqrt(dsquared)
  return result
```

If that works correctly, you are done. Otherwise, you might want to print the value of result before the return statement.

When you start out, you should add only a line or two of code at a time. As you gain more experience, you might find yourself writing and debugging bigger chunks. Either way, the incremental development process can save you a lot of debugging time.

The key aspects of the process are:

- Start with a working programme and make small incremental changes. At any point, if there is an error, you will know exactly where it is.
- Use temporary variables to hold intermediate values so you can output and check them.
- Once the programme is working, you might want to remove some of the scaffolding or consolidate multiple statements into compound expressions, but only if it does not make the programme difficult to read.

As an exercise, use incremental development to write a function called hypotenuse that returns the length of the hypotenuse of a right triangle given the lengths of the two legs as arguments. Record each stage of the incremental development process as you go.

COMPOSITION

As you should expect by now, you can call one function from within another. This ability is called composition.

As an example, we'll write a function that takes two points, the centre of the circle and a point on the perimeter, and computes the area of the circle. Assume that the centre point is stored in the variables xc and yc, and the perimeter point is in xp and yp. The first step is to find the radius of the circle, which is the distance between the two points.

Fortunately, there is a function, distance, *that does that:*

```
radius = distance(xc, yc, xp, yp)
```

The second step is to find the area of a circle with that radius and return it:

```
result = area(radius)
return result
```

Wrapping that up in a function, we get:

```
def area2(xc, yc, xp, yp):
  radius = distance(xc, yc, xp, yp)
  result = area(radius)
  return result
```

We called this function area2 to distinguish it from the area function defined earlier. There can only be one function with a given name within a given module. The temporary variables radius and result are useful for development and debugging, but once the programme is working, we can make it more concise by composing the function calls:

```
def area2(xc, yc, xp, yp):
return area(distance(xc, yc, xp, yp))
```

As an exercise, write a function slope(x1, y1, x2, y2) that returns the slope of the line through the points (x1, y1) and (x2, y2). Then use this function in a function called intercept(x1, y1, x2, y2) that returns the y-intercept of the line through the points(x1, y1) and (x2, y2).

BOOLEAN FUNCTIONS

Functions can return boolean values, which is often convenient for hiding complicated tests inside functions.

For example:

```
def isDivisible(x, y):
  if x % y == 0:
    return True
else:
  return False
```

The name of this function is isDivisible. It is common to give boolean functions names that sound like yes/no questions. isDivisible returns either True or False to indicate whether the x is or is not divisible by y.

We can make the function more concise by taking advantage of the fact that the condition of the if statement is itself a boolean expression.

We can return it directly, avoiding the if statement altogether:

```
def isDivisible(x, y):
    return x % y == 0
```

This session shows the new function in action:

```
is Divisible(6, 4)
False
is Divisible(6, 3)
True
```

Boolean functions are often used in conditional statements:

```
if isDivisible(x, y):
    print "x is divisible by y"
else:
    print "x is not divisible by y"
```

It might be tempting to write something like:

```
if isDivisible(x, y) == True:
```

But the extra comparison is unnecessary.

As an exercise, write a function isBetween(x, y, z) that returnsTrue if y le x le z or False otherwise.

MORE RECURSION

So far, you have only learned a small subset of Python, but you might be interested to know that this subset is a *complete* programming language, which means that anything that can be computed can be expressed in this language. Any programme ever written could be rewritten using only the language features you have learned so far (actually, you would need a few commands to control devices like the keyboard, mouse, disks, etc., but that's all).

Proving that claim is a nontrivial exercise first accomplished by Alan Turing, one of the first computer scientists (some would argue that he was a mathematician, but a lot of early computer scientists started as mathematicians). Accordingly, it is known as the Turing Thesis. If you take a course on the Theory of Computation, you will have a chance to see the proof.

To give you an idea of what you can do with the tools you have learned so far, we'll evaluate a few recursively defined mathematical functions. A recursive definition is similar to a circular definition, in the sense that the definition contains a reference to the thing being defined. A truly circular definition is not very useful:

Frabjuous: An adjective used to describe something that is frabjuous.

If you saw that definition in the dictionary, you might be annoyed. On the other hand, if you looked up the definition of the mathematical function factorial, you might get something like this:

```
0! = 1
n! = n (n-1)!
```

This definition says that the factorial of 0 is 1, and the factorial of any other value,n, is n multiplied by the factorial of n-1. So 3! is 3 times 2!, which is 2 times 1!, which is 1 times 0!. Putting it all together, 3! equals 3 times 2 times 1 times 1, which is 6.

If you can write a recursive definition of something, you can usually write a Python programme to evaluate it. The first step is to decide what the parameters are for this function. *With little effort, you should conclude that* factorial *has a single parameter*:

```
def factorial(n):
```

If the argument happens to be 0, all we have to do is return 1:

```
def factorial(n):
  if n == 0:
    return 1
```

Otherwise, and this is the interesting part, we have to make a recursive call to find the factorial of n-1 and then multiply it by n:

```
def factorial(n):
  if n == 0:
    return 1
```

```
  else:
    recurse = factorial(n-1)
    result = n * recurse
    return result
```

The flow of execution for this programme is similar to the flow of countdown. If we call factorial with the value 3:

Since 3 is not 0, we take the second branch and calculate the factorial of n-1...

Since 2 is not 0, we take the second branch and calculate the factorial of n-1...

Since 1 is not 0, we take the second branch and calculate the factorial of n-1...

Since 0 *is* 0, we take the first branch and return 1 without making any more recursive calls.

The return value (1) is multiplied by n, which is 1, and the result is returned.

The return value (1) is multiplied by n, which is 2, and the result is returned.

The return value (2) is multiplied by n, which is 3, and the result, 6, becomes the return value of the function call that started the whole process.

LEAP OF FAITH

Following the flow of execution is one way to read programmes, but it can quickly become labyrinthine. An alternative is what we call the "leap of faith." When you come to a function call, instead of following the flow of execution, you *assume*that the function works correctly and returns the appropriate value. In fact, you are already practicing this leap of faith when you use built-in functions. When you call math.cos or math.exp, you don't examine the implementations of those functions. You just assume that they work because the people who wrote the built-in functions were good programmers. The same is true when you call one of your own functions. For example, inSection 5.4, we wrote a function called isDivisible that determines whether one number is divisible by another. Once we have convinced ourselves that this function is correct by testing and examining the code we can use the function without looking at the code again. The same is true of recursive programmes. When you get to the recursive call, instead of following the flow of execution, you should assume that the recursive call works (yields the correct result) and then ask yourself, "Assuming that I can find the factorial of n-1, can I compute the factorial of n?" In this case, it is clear that you can, by multiplying by n.

MORE EXAMPLE

In the example, we used temporary variables to spell out the steps and to make the code easier to debug, but we could have saved a few lines:

```
def factorial(n):
    if n == 0:
      return 1
else:
    return n * factorial(n-1)
```

From now on, we will tend to use the more concise form, but we recommend that you use the more explicit version while you are developing code. When you have it working, you can tighten it up if you are feeling inspired.

After factorial, *the most common example of a recursively defined mathematical function is* fibonacci, *which has the following definition*:

```
fibonacci(0) = 1
fibonacci(1) = 1
fibonacci(n) = fibonacci(n 1) + fibonacci(n-
2);
```

Translated into Python, it looks like this:

```
def fibonacci (n):
  if n == 0 or n == 1:
      return 1
  else:
    return fibonacci(n-1) + fibonacci(n 2)
```

If you try to follow the flow of execution here, even for fairly small values of n, your head explodes. But according to the leap of faith, if you assume that the two recursive calls work correctly, then it is clear that you get the right result by adding them together.

CHECKING TYPES

What happens if we call factorial and give it 1.5 as an argument?

```
factorial (1.5)
RuntimeError: Maximum recursion depth
exceeded
```

It looks like an infinite recursion. But how can that be? There is a base case when n == 0. The problem is that the values of n *miss* the base case. In the first recursive call, the value of n is 0.5. In the next, it is –0.5. From there, it gets smaller and smaller, but it will never be 0.

We have two choices. We can try to generalize the factorial function to work with floating-point numbers, or we can make factorial check the type of its argument. The first option is called the gamma function and it's a little beyond the scope of this book. So we'll go for the second. We can use the built-in function isinstance to verify the type of the argument.

While we're at it, we also make sure the argument is positive:

```
def factorial (n):
  if not isinstance(n, int):
      print "Factorial is only defined for
      integers."
      return -1
elif n < 0:
    print "Factorial is only defined for
    positive integers."
      return -1
    elif n == 0:
      return 1
    else:
      return n * factorial(n-1)
```

Now we have three base cases. The first catches nonintegers. The second catches negative integers. In both cases, the programme prints an error message and returns a special value, –1, to indicate that something went wrong:

```
factorial ("fred")
Factorial is only defined for integers.
-1
```

```
factorial (-2)
Factorial is only defined for positive
integers.
-1
```

If we get past both checks, then we know that n is a positive integer, and we can prove that the recursion terminates. This programme demonstrates a pattern sometimes called a guardian. The first two conditionals act as guardians, protecting the code that follows from values that might cause an error. The guardians make it possible to prove the correctness of the code.

ITERATION

MULTIPLE ASSIGNMENT

A new assignment makes an existing variable refer to a new value (and stop referring to the old value).

```
bruce = 5
print bruce,
bruce = 7
print bruce
```

The output of this programme is 5 7, because the first time bruce is printed, his value is 5, and the second time, his value is 7. The comma at the end of the first printstatement suppresses the newline after the output, which is why both outputs appear on the same line. With multiple assignment it is especially important to distinguish between an assignment operation and a statement of equality. Because Python uses the equal sign (=) for assignment, it is tempting to interpret a statement like a = b as a statement of equality.

First, equality is commutative and assignment is not. For example, in mathematics, if a = 7 then 7 = a. But in Python, the statement a = 7 is legal and 7 = a is not.

Furthermore, in mathematics, a statement of equality is always true. If a = b now, then a will always equal b.

In Python, an assignment statement can make two variables equal, but they don't have to stay that way:

```
a = 5
```

```
b = a   # a and b are now equal
a = 3   # a and b are no longer equal
```

The third line changes the value of a but does not change the value of b, so they are no longer equal. (In some programming languages, a different symbol is used for assignment, such as ← or:=, to avoid confusion.)

Although multiple assignment is frequently helpful, you should use it with caution. If the values of variables change frequently, it can make the code difficult to read and debug.

THE WHILE STATEMENT

Computers are often used to automate repetitive tasks. Repeating identical or similar tasks without making errors is something that computers do well and people do poorly.

We have seen two programmes, nLines and countdown, that use recursion to perform repetition, which is also called iteration. Because iteration is so common, Python provides several language features to make it easier. The first feature we are going to look at is the while statement.

Here is what countdown looks like with a while statement:

```
def countdown(n):
  while n > 0:
    print n
    n = n-1
print "Blastoff!"
```

Since we removed the recursive call, this function is not recursive. You can almost read the while statement as if it were English. It means, "While n is greater than 0, continue displaying the value of n and then reducing the value of nby 1. When you get to 0, display the word Blastoff!"

More formally, here is the flow of execution for a while *statement*:

- Evaluate the condition, yielding **0** or **1**.
- If the condition is false (0), exit the **while** statement and continue execution at the next statement.
- If the condition is true (1), execute each of the statements in the body and then go back to step 1.

The body consists of all of the statements below the header with the same indentation. This type of flow is called a loop because the third step loops back around to the top. Notice that if the condition is false the first time through the loop, the statements inside the loop are never executed.

The body of the loop should change the value of one or more variables so that eventually the condition becomes false and the loop terminates. Otherwise the loop will repeat forever, which is called an infinite loop. An endless source of amusement for computer scientists is the observation that the directions on shampoo, "Lather, rinse, repeat," are an infinite loop. In the case of countdown, we can prove that the loop terminates because we know that the value of n is finite, and we can see that the value of n gets smaller each time through the loop, so eventually we have to get to 0.

In other cases, it is not so easy to tell:

```
def sequence(n):
  while n != 1:
    print n,
    if n%2 == 0:          # n is even
      n = n/2
    else:                 # n is odd
      n = n*3+1
```

The condition for this loop is n != 1, so the loop will continue until n is 1, which will make the condition false. Each time through the loop, the programme outputs the value of n and then checks whether it is even or odd. If it is even, the value of n is divided by 2. If it is odd, the value is replaced by n*3+1. For example, if the starting value (the argument passed to sequence) is 3, the resulting sequence is 3, 10, 5, 16, 8, 4, 2, 1. Since n sometimes increases and sometimes decreases, there is no obvious proof that n will ever reach 1, or that the programme terminates. For some particular values of n, we can prove termination. For example, if the starting value is a power of two, then the value of n will be even each time through the loop until it reaches 1. The previous example ends with such a sequence, starting with 16. Particular values aside, the interesting question is whether we can prove that this programme terminates for *all positive values* of n. So far, no one has been able to prove it *or* disprove it!

As an exercise, rewrite the function nLines from Section 4.9using iteration instead of recursion.

TABLES

One of the things loops are good for is generating tabular data. Before computers were readily available, people had to calculate logarithms, sines and cosines, and other mathematical functions by hand. To make that easier, mathematics books contained long tables listing the values of these functions. Creating the tables was slow and boring, and they tended to be full of errors. When computers appeared on the scene, one of the initial reactions was, "This is great! We can use the computers to generate the tables, so there will be no errors." That turned out to be true (mostly) but shortsighted. Soon thereafter, computers and calculators were so pervasive that the tables became obsolete. Well, almost. For some operations, computers use tables of values to get an approximate answer and then perform computations to improve the approximation. In some cases, there have been errors in the underlying tables, most famously in the table the Intel Pentium used to perform floating-point division.

Although a log table is not as useful as it once was, it still makes a good example of iteration. The following programme outputs a sequence of values in the left column and their logarithms in the right column:

```
x = 1.0
while x < 10.0:
  print x, '\t', math.log(x)
  x = x + 1.0
```

The string '\t' represents a tab character. As characters and strings are displayed on the screen, an invisible marker called the cursor keeps track of where the next character will go. After a printstatement, the cursor normally goes to the beginning of the next line. The tab character shifts the cursor to the right until it reaches one of the tab stops.

Tabs are useful for making columns of text line up, as in the output of the previous programme:

```
1.0     0.0
```

```
2.0    0.69314718056
3.0    1.09861228867
4.0    1.38629436112
5.0    1.60943791243
6.0    1.79175946923
7.0    1.94591014906
8.0    2.07944154168
9.0    2.19722457734
```

If these values seem odd, remember that the log function uses base e. Since powers of two are so important in computer science, we often want to find logarithms with respect to base 2. To do that, we can use the following formula:

$$\log_2 x = \frac{\log_e x}{\log_e 2}$$

Changing the output statement to:

```
print x, '\t', math.log(x)/math.log(2.0)
```

yields:

```
1.0    0.0
2.0    1.0
3.0    1.58496250072
4.0    2.0
5.0    2.32192809489
6.0    2.58496250072
7.0    2.80735492206
8.0    3.0 9.0 3.16992500144
```

We can see that 1, 2, 4, and 8 are powers of two because their logarithms base 2 are round numbers. If we wanted to find the logarithms of other powers of two, we could modify the programme like this:

```
x = 1.0
while x < 100.0:
    print x, '\t', math.log(x)/math.log(2.0)
    x = x * 2.0
```

Now instead of adding something to x each time through the loop, which yields an arithmetic sequence, we multiply x by something, yielding a geometric sequence.

The result is:

```
1.0      0.0
```

```
2.0       1.0
4.0       2.0
8.0       3.0
16.0      4.0
32.0      5.0
64.0      6.0
```

Because of the tab characters between the columns, the position of the second column does not depend on the number of digits in the first column. Logarithm tables may not be useful any more, but for computer scientists, knowing the powers of two is! *As an exercise, modify this programme so that it outputs the powers of two up to 65,536 (that's 2^{16}). Print it out and memorize it.* The backslash character in '\t' indicates the beginning of an escape sequence.

Escape sequences are used to represent invisible characters like tabs and newlines. The sequence \n represents a newline. An escape sequence can appear anywhere in a string; in the example, the tab escape sequence is the only thing in the string. How do you think you represent a backslash in a string?

As an exercise, write a single string that,

```
produces
           this
                 output.
```

TWO-DIMENSIONAL TABLES

A two-dimensional table is a table where you read the value at the intersection of a row and a column. A multiplication table is a good example. Let's say you want to print a multiplication table for the values from 1 to 6.

A good way to start is to write a loop that prints the multiples of 2, all on one line:

```
i = 1
while i <= 6:
  print 2*i, ' ',
  i = i + 1
print
```

The first line initializes a variable named i, which acts as a counter or loop variable. As the loop executes, the value of i increases from 1 to 6. When i is 7, the loop terminates. Each time through the loop, it displays the value of 2*i, followed by three spaces. Again, the comma in the print statement suppresses the newline. After the loop completes, the second print statement starts a new line.

The output of the programme is:

```
2    4    6    8    10    12
```

So far, so good. The next step is to encapsulate and generalize.

ENCAPSULATION AND GENERALIZATION

Encapsulation is the process of wrapping a piece of code in a function, allowing you to take advantage of all the things functions are good. Generalization means taking something specific, such as printing the multiples of 2, and making it more general, such as printing the multiples of any integer.

This function encapsulates the previous loop and generalizes it to print multiples ofn:

```
def printMultiples(n):
  i = 1
  while i <= 6:
    print n*i, '\t',
    i = i + 1
  print
```

To encapsulate, all we had to do was add the first line, which declares the name of the function and the parameter list. To generalize, all we had to do was replace the value 2 with the parameter n.

If we call this function with the argument 2, we get the same output as before. With the argument 3, the output is:

```
3    6    9    12    15    18
```

With the argument 4, the output is:

```
4    8    12    16    20    24
```

By now you can probably guess how to print a multiplication table by callingprintMultiples repeatedly with different arguments.

In fact, we can use another loop:

```
i = 1
```

```
while i <= 6:
  printMultiples(i)
  i = i + 1
```

Notice how similar this loop is to the one inside printMultiples. All we did was replace the print statement with a function call.

Table. The Output of This Programme is a Multiplication Table.

1	2	3	4	5	6
2	4	6	8	10	12
3	6	9	12	15	18
4	8	12	16	20	24
5	10	15	20	25	30
6	12	18	24	30	36

MORE ENCAPSULATION

To demonstrate encapsulation again, let's take the code from the end of Section 6.5 and wrap it up in a function:

```
def printMultTable():
i = 1
  while i Ü 6:
    printMultiples(i)
    i = i + 1
```

This process is a common development plan. We develop code by writing lines of code outside any function, or typing them in to the interpreter. When we get the code working, we extract it and wrap it up in a function.

This development plan is particularly useful if you don't know, when you start writing, how to divide the programme into functions. This approach lets you design as you go along.

LOCAL VARIABLES

Variables created inside a function definition are local; you can't access a local variable from outside its "home" function. That means you are free to have multiple variables with the same name as long as they are not in the same function. Inside print Multiples, the value of i goes from 1 to

6. In the diagram, it happens to be 2. Changing this variable has no effect on the value of i in print MultTable.

It is common and perfectly legal to have different local variables with the same name. In particular, names like i and j are used frequently as loop variables. If you avoid using them in one function just because you used them somewhere else, you will probably make the programme harder to read.

MORE GENERALIZATION

As another example of generalization, imagine you wanted a programme that would print a multiplication table of any size, not just the six-by-six table.

You could add a parameter to printMultTable:

```
def printMultTable(high):
  i = 1
  while i Ü high:
    printMultiples(i)
    i = i + 1
```

We replaced the value 6 with the parameter high. *If we call* printMultTable *with the argument 7, it displays:*

1	2	3	4	5	6
2	4	6	8	10	12
3	6	9	12	15	18
4	8	12	16	20	24
5	10	15	20	25	30
6	12	18	24	30	36
7	14	21	28	35	42

This is fine, except that we probably want the table to be square with the same number of rows and columns. To do that, we add another parameter toprintMultiples to specify how many columns the table should have.

Just to be annoying, we call this parameter high, demonstrating that different functions can have parameters with the same name (just like local variables).

Here's the whole programme:

```
def printMultiples(n, high):
  i = 1
  while i Ü high:
```

```
      print n*i, '\t',
      i = i + 1
    print
  def printMultTable(high):
    i = 1
    while i <= high:
      printMultiples(i, high)
      i = i + 1
```

Notice that when we added a new parameter, we had to change the first line of the function (the function heading), and we also had to change the place where the function is called in printMultTable.

Table: As Expected, this Programme Generates a Square Seven-by-seven.

1	2	3	4	5	6	7
2	4	6	8	10	12	14
3	6	9	12	15	18	21
4	8	12	16	20	24	28
5	10	15	20	25	30	35
6	12	18	24	30	36	42
7	14	21	28	35	42	49

When you generalize a function appropriately, you often get a programme with capabilities you didn't plan. For example, you might notice that, because ab = ba, all the entries in the table appear twice. You could save ink by printing only half the table.

```
printMultiples(i, high)
  to
printMultiples(i, i)
  and you get
```

1						
2	4					
3	6	9				
4	8	12	16			
5	10	15	20	25		
6	12	18	24	30	36	
7	14	21	28	35	42	49

As an exercise, trace the execution of this version ofprintMultTable and figure out how it works.

6.9 Functions

A few times now, we have mentioned "all the things functions are good for." By now, you might be wondering what exactly those things are.

Here are some of them:

- Giving a name to a sequence of statements makes your programme easier to read and debug.
- Dividing a long programme into functions allows you to separate parts of the program, debug them in isolation, and then compose them into a whole.
- Functions facilitate both recursion and iteration.
- Well-designed functions are often useful for many programmes. Once you write and debug one, you can reuse it.

4

Object Oriented Programming

REAL TOOL

A type of programming in which programmers define not only the data type of a data structure, but also the types of operations (functions) that can be applied to the data structure. In this way, the data structure becomes an object that includes both data and functions. In addition, programmers can create relationships between one object and another. For example, objects can inherit characteristics from other objects. One of the principal advantages of object-oriented programming techniques over procedural programming techniques is that they enable programmers to create modules that do not need to be changed when a new type of object is added.

A programmer can simply create a new object that inherits many of its features from existing objects. This makes object-oriented programs easier to modify. To perform object-oriented programming, one needs an object-oriented programming language (OOPL). Java, C++ and Smalltalk are three of the more popular languages, and there are also object-oriented versions of Pascal.

OBJECTS

An object is a software bundle of related state and behaviour. Software objects are often used to model the real-world objects that you find in everyday life. This lesson explains how state and behaviour are represented within an object, introduces the concept of data encapsulation, and explains the benefits of designing your software in this manner.

CLASS

A class is a blueprint or prototype from which objects are created. This section defines a class that models the state and behaviour of a real-world object. It intentionally focuses on the basics, showing how even a simple class can cleanly model state and behaviour.

INHERITANCE

Inheritance provides a powerful and natural mechanism for organizing and structuring your software. This section explains how classes inherit state and behaviour from their superclasses, and explains how to derive one class from another using the simple syntax provided by the Java programming language.

INTERFACE

An interface is a contract between a class and the outside world. When a class implements an interface, it promises to provide the behaviour published by that interface. This section defines a simple interface and explains the necessary changes for any class that implements it.

PACKAGE

A package is a namespace for organizing classes and interfaces in a logical manner. Placing your code into packages makes large software projects easier to manage. This section explains why this is useful, and introduces you to the Application Programming Interface (API) provided by the Java platform. Object-oriented programming (OOP) is a programming language model organized around "objects" rather than "actions" and data rather than logic. Historically, a program has been viewed as a logical procedure that takes input data, processes it, and produces output data. The programming challenge was seen as how to write the logic, not how to define the data. Object-oriented programming takes the view that what we really care about are the objects we want to manipulate rather than the logic required to manipulate them. Examples of objects range from human beings to buildings and floors (whose properties can be described and managed) down to the little widgets on your computer desktop (such as buttons and scroll bars).

The first step in OOP is to identify all the objects you want to manipulate and how they relate to each other, an exercise often known as data modeling. Once you've identified an object, you generalize it as a class of objects (think of Plato's concept of the "ideal" chair that stands for all chairs) and define the kind of data it contains and any logic sequences that can manipulate it. Each distinct logic sequence is known as a method.

A real instance of a class is called (no surprise here) an "object" or, in some environments, an "instance of a class." The object or class instance is what you run in the computer. Its methods provide computer instructions and the class object characteristics provide relevant data. You communicate with objects - and they communicate with each other - with well-defined interfaces called messages.

The concepts and rules used in object-oriented programming provide these important benefits: The concept of a data class makes it possible to define subclasses of data objects that share some or all of the main class characteristics. Called inheritance, this property of OOP forces a more thorough data analysis, reduces development time, and ensures more accurate coding. Since a class defines only the data it needs to be concerned with, when an instance of that class (an object) is run, the code will not be able to accidentally access other program data. This characteristic of data hiding provides greater system security

ROLE

The demand for businesses to deploy solutions across multiple servers is bound to increase. With the growth and acceptance of the Internet, businesses have come to think of their applications and information be connected and distributed across multiple servers from remote locations. Also data can be processed and accessed through the use of Web browsers and by user interfaces. But a number of problems stands on the way towards developing and deploying mission-critical business applications on several server systems. These applications are named as distributed software applications. They are communication issues among different programming languages and platforms and security. There are a few promising technologies for promoting these critical applications.. Microsoft has come out with a new technology called as Component Object Model (COM) that addresses these problems towards the goal of design of distributed software components.

COMPONENT OBJECT MODEL

COM is an outgrowth of the OO technology. It is a specification that is based on a binary standard for reuse through interfaces. That is, components, which are pre-compiled blocks of code, written for COM can be reused without any dependencies on the language in which they are coded.

The programming language may be Visual Basic, C++ etc. COM uses system-level code that is implemented in the form of dynamic link libraries, which are collectively called COM library. The COM library consists of several application programming interface (API) functions that are necessary for COM components to do various tasks. COM library is responsible for locating and activating server applications. With client applications, COM APIs contains the necessary functions for instantiating objects that the client want to use. Also the COM library provides locator services using the System Control Manager (SCM), which also provides transparent remote procedure calls when an object is executing out-of-process in a local or remote server.

COMPONENT-BASED DEVELOPMENT

CBD camc from OO software development methodology towards facilitating software reusability in larger scale.

Suppose there is an object and we want to use that in an application. For that, we have to cut and paste the code in the application. If there is any changes made in the object, we have to search for all the object copies in the application to insert the relevant changes. This becomes cumbersome when there are more applications with more copies of the same object.

Here comes the idea of designing components as a robust solution. A component can be technically defined as a coarse-grained object. It is also defined as a reusable software module, which displays its services through interfaces for use by client software. On using a component, which is stored in a single place, applications can use the object directly from the component and get the same functionality. Thus both classes, where objects get derived from and components provide same type of services.

Classes pro! vide services to single applications because they can not communicate with other applications due to the differences in language and platform, while components provide services to numerous applications irrespective of the languages used. There came a number of architecture for developing both client-side and server-side components. They are OMG's CORBA, Sun's JaveBeans and Enterprise JavaBeans and Microsoft's COM.

Thus the world is full of software components, which in turn can be of greater use for hundreds of different applications. As both CORBA and COM supports language independence, a different software vendor can create components using different programming languages without any integration problems.

ADVANTAGES

- COM promotes component-based software development - before component-based development came, software programs have been coded using procedural programming paradigm, which supports linear form of program execution. But component-based program development comes with a number of advantages, such as the ability to use pre-packaged components and tools from third party vendors into an application and support for code reusability in other parts of the same application.

- COM promotes code reusability - standard classes are normally reused in the same application but not to be used easily in other applications. But COM components are designed to separate themselves from single applications and hence can be accessed and used by several different applications without any hassle.
- COM promotes Object-oriented programming (OOP) - The primary characteristics of OOP are encapsulation, which allows the implementation details of an object to be hidden, polymorphism, which is the ability to exhibit multiple behaviours, and inheritance, which allows for the reuse of existing classes in order to design new and more specialized classes. Among these, encapsulation is one of COM's most important characteristics. Encapsulation helps to hide how an object has implemented a method internally. This ultimately helps to incorporate more vigourously implemented or advanced implementation into an object at later time without affecting the client which uses it.
- COM comprises the necessary mechanisms for COM components to communicate with each other - In the normal case, two components coded using two different programming languages can not communicate with each other. But COM can make it possible for different language components, which adhere to the COM specification, to interact with each other and hence COM is language-independent.
- COM helps to access components loaded in different machines on the network - COM component can reside anywhere on our computer or even on another computer connected to a network. That is, applications using COM can access and share COM

components regardless of their locations. Thus COM abstracts away the nitty-gritty of clients to locate COM components anywhere in the network. Thus COM provides location transparency and COM components are location independent.

COM INTERFACES

Components, especially server-side ones, are bound to have their own interfaces. An interface is simply a list of methods a COM component implements and makes them available to consumers. COM interface are immutable. That is, once a COM component has been released with an interface, this interface must never be manipulated. COM interfaces are the mechanisms by which a client contacts, connects and use components. If the client component is using a different language from the one a server component is coded, there will be language problem for interactions. In order to remove this barrier, COM interfaces provide an universal way so that components coded in different languages can communicate with each other.

Thus every interface constitutes a binding contract between a COM object (no interface is attached with this) and a COM component with an interface. COM specification makes life easier by allowing a component to publish more than one interface at a time. New interfaces can! be incorporated to support new features of the components while keeping the original interface intact. We have to increment a version number for the new interface. A class module then would need to be implemented for both old and new interfaces in order to support both old clients that rely on the old interface and new clients that can take advantage of the new interface. Thus the immutability factor of COM interfaces can be overcome.

INTERFACE DEFINITION LANGUAGE (IDL)

To successfully make COM language-independent, the COM interfaces have to coded using IDL. IDL is just a declaration language, not a programming language. The syntax for IDL is almost similar to C++ language. But IDL goes beyond what C++ can offer by being able to define functions that extend process boundaries.

IDL provides many vital extensions that allow attributes such as type libraries, co-classes, interfaces, and method parameters to be specified quite elegantly. But if there is no language problem, it is not mandatory to use IDL for defining COM interfaces.

Here comes an model interface definition for a COM component coded using Microsoft IDL.

```
[object,
  uuid (122323FAGAd098776)
]
  interface IFindSum: IUnknown
{
  import "unknown.idl"
  HRESULT SumOfNumbers ([in] long lnum1, [in]
  long lnum2, [out, retval] long* sum);
}
```

The interface definition begins with an object attribute. The object attribute is used to identify a COM interface. Then a UUID (universally unique identifier), which provides an unique identifying number (a string of hexadecimal digits) for each interface and this number is being generated by an algorithm, which takes into account the unique value from the network card on the programmer's PC and the current system date and time, follows that. The interface keyword is followed by the name of the interface (IFindSum).

The QueryInterface method is the mechanism that a client uses to discover and navigate the interfaces of a component dynamically. It is the most significant method of all COM interfaces available for a component since this method allows run-time checking of all of these interfaces. When the QueryInterface method provides an interface pointer to a client, the QueryInterface calls the method AddRef. The only way to access a COM object is through a pointer to an interface.

An interface pointer is actually a pointer to a pointer in a virtual table that is implemented in memory. That is, for every class that contains public methods, a virtual table will be created and placed in memory at run time. Virtual tables are generated for each class and not for objects of that class. Each virtual table contains an array of function pointers whose elements contain the address of each specific function that an object can implement. At the top of every virtual table array will be three fundamental methods that make up this IUnknown interface. The methods AddRef and Release manage reference counting. This reference count is an internal count of the number of clients using a particular COM object. It is possible for several clients to invoke the services available with a COM object at the same time. When a client begins a session with an object, it calls the AddRef method, which increments one to the existing count. Once the session is over, the corresponding Release method gets invoked to decrement one from the existing count.

An HRESULT is used with COM to indicate whether a method call is successfully accomplished or not. Almost all COM interfaces return a special 32-bit code, called as HRESULT, from their methods to return status information. It is actually the method COM utilizes to return errors to the caller of the method. The reason for this mechanism is due to the inability of COM to transmit error messages back to the client if there is anything wrong on the server side or on the way to the server. As components are being written using different programming languages and each language follows its own exception mechanisms, COM can not correctly pass on the error messages and hence HRESULT.

Following the HRESULT are three parameters for the interface method SumOfNumbers. The [in] in the first two parameters specifies that these parameters are input values to be passed to the interface method and the [out, retval] in the last parameter indicates that this parameter returns a value that will be ultimately passed to back to the client.

WINDOWS REGISTRY AND COMPONENTS

COM components may be loaded in different address spaces in the same machine or machine connected with the network. Before an object can be created, the COM runtime must first locate the COM components. The COM runtime is able to locate COM components through the use of Windows registry. COM components may be out-of-process or in-process. An out-of-process component can effectively be a separate program containing objects. This type runs in its own process space and will thus be largely independent from any client programs. These components are often large applications themselves, and provide access to their objects to make it easy for other programs to create macros or otherwise make use of existing functionality. This can be very beneficial, because the component developer can choose his own threading models. The drawback here is that the developer has to write the code for threading. This work can be handled by automatically COM+ , the latest one from the COM family.

There is also a performance issue. Because the client application is communicating with objects which are in an entirely different process there is quite a bit of overhead. COM steps in between the client and the server and handles all the communication between them. Mainly out-of-process components are useful if we are trying to make use of the objects in a pre-existing application. An in-process component is one where the objects run inside the client's process. Each client gets its own private copy of the component and hence a copy of all the objects in that component. An in-process component is often called COM DLLs or ActiveX DLLs.

In-process component does not have a process of its own and it always runs within the context of another process. Often this other process is the client application itself but may be run within the context of a different process entirely. In this case, we can get performance boost as the component is loaded in the client application itself. There is almost no overhead when client interacts with an object that is running in the same process.

COM OBJECT

There is a lot of communication that must occur behind the scenes in order for a COM object to be created. First of all, a client looking for an object has to make a call to an API function called CoCreate Instance with the CLSID for the class, which comprises the particular object. The prefix Co in this function is a typical naming convention for COM runtime API functions. Co Create Instance in turn as a second step calls another API function called Co Get Class Object. Basically the function Co Create Instance asks the SCM to search the Windows registry location, which is HKEY_CLASSES _ROOT\ CLSID. The function of SCM is to locate the requested class object by using the specified CLSID. The first place the SCM looks to locate the class object is within its own internal database.

If the class is not located inside its database, the SCM turns to the system registry as a third step. As soon as the class object is found, the SCM immediately returns to COM an interface pointer referred to as IClass Factory. Every COM class must have a factory object associated with it. The main purpose of these class objects is to implement the IClass Factory interface. Once the client gets the IClass Factory pointer, two things happen. One, by obtaining a pointer to the IClass Factory, Co Create Instance can call IClass Factory:: Create Instance in order to create the requested COM object. Once the object is created, a second step occurs: the interface pointer to the IClass Factory gets released.

The interface called IClass Factory's job is to talk to other class objects. Further, Co Get Class Object is a COM class object whose sole purpose is to create a new instance of a different class. Because this COM class creates class objects by implementing the IClass Factory interface, CoGet Class Object is referred to as a class factory.

LOCKSERVER

When an object is created it resides in memory. It is the client's job to notify the object when it is no longer needed. The Release method told above can decrement the reference count for the interface. If there are several interfaces for an object, it is possible that the object is still being accessed somewhere else. The idea is that the reference count has to reach zero before the object is to be released from the memory. Releasing objects from memory usually improves performance. Some special clients constantly create and destroy objects, which normally affects the application's performance.

The Lock Server method allows components to remain in memory by incrementing the reference count by one. Because LockServer keeps a count of one in the reference counter, the object will stay in memory even if it is not being accessed currently. Having the component reside in memory has the advantage of allowing the object to be called without having to go through the process of recre! ating it. But on the other hand, if objects are not destroyed when they are not in use, there will be reduction of system memory resources.

5

High Level Language

INTRODUCTION

C is sometimes referred to as a "high-level assembly language." Some people think that's an insult, but it's actually a deliberate and significant aspect of the language. If you have programmed in assembly language, you'll probably find C very natural and comfortable (although if you continue to focus too heavily on machine-level details, you'll probably end up with unnecessarily nonportable programs). If you haven't programmed in assembly language, you may be frustrated by C's lack of certain higher-level features. In either case, you should understand why C was designed this way: so that seemingly-simple constructions expressed in C would not expand to arbitrarily expensive (in time or space) machine language constructions when compiled.

If you write a C program simply and succinctly, it is likely to result in a succinct, efficient machine language executable. If you find that the executable program resulting from a C program is not efficient, it's probably because of something silly you did, not because of something the compiler did behind your back which you have no control over. In any case, there's no point in complaining about C's low-level flavour: C is what it is.

A programming language is a tool, and no tool can perform every task unaided. If you're building a house, and I'm teaching you how to use a hammer, and you ask how to assemble rafters and trusses into gables, that's a legitimate question, but the answer has fallen out of the realm of "How do I use a hammer?" and into "How do I build a house?". In the same way, we'll see that C does not have built-in features to perform every function that we might ever need to do while programming.

As mentioned above, C imposes relatively few built-in ways of doing things on the programmer. Some common tasks, such as manipulating strings, allocating memory, and doing input/output (I/O), are performed by calling on library functions. Other tasks which you might want to do, such as creating or listing directories, or interacting with a mouse, or displaying windows or other user-interface elements, or doing colour graphics, are not defined by the C language at all. You can do these things from a C program, of course, but you will be calling on services which are peculiar to your programming environment (compiler, processor, and operating system) and which are not defined by the C standard. Since this course is about portable C programming, it will also be steering clear of facilities not provided in all C environments.

Another aspect of C that's worth mentioning here is that it is, to put it bluntly, a bit dangerous. C does not, in general, try hard to protect a programmer from mistakes. If you write a piece of code which will (through some oversight of yours) do something wildly different from what you intended it to do, up to and including deleting your data or trashing your disk, and if it is possible for the compiler to compile it, it generally will. You won't get warnings of the form "Do you really mean to...?" or "Are you sure you really want to...?". C is often compared to a sharp knife: it can do a surgically precise job on some exacting task you have in mind, but it can also do a surgically precise job of cutting off your finger. It's up to you to use it carefully.

This aspect of C is very widely criticized; it is also used (justifiably) to argue that C is not a good teaching language. C aficionados love this aspect of C because it means that C does not try to protect them from themselves: when they know what they're doing, even if it's risky or obscure, they can do it. Students of C hate this aspect of C because it often seems as if the language is some kind of a conspiracy specifically designed to lead them into booby traps. This is another aspect of the language which it's fairly pointless to complain about. If you take care and pay attention, you can avoid many of the pitfalls. These notes will point out many of the obvious (and not so obvious) trouble spots. If you have a C compiler, the first thing to do is figure out how to type this program in and compile it and run it and see where its output went.The first line is practically boilerplate; it will appear in almost all programs we write. It asks that some definitions having to do with the "Standard I/O Library" be included in our program; these definitions are needed if we are to call the library function printf correctly.

The second line says that we are defining a function named main. Most of the time, we can name our functions anything we want, but the function name main is special: it is the function that will be "called" first when our program starts running. The empty pair of parentheses indicates that our main function accepts no*arguments,* that is, there isn't any information which needs to be passed in when the function is called.

The braces { and } surround a list of statements in C. Here, they surround the list of statements making up the function main.

The line,

```
printf("Hello, world!\n");
```

is the first statement in the program. It asks that the function printf be called; printf is a library function which prints formatted output. The parentheses surroundprintf's argument list: the information which is handed to it which it should act on. The semicolon at the end of the line terminates the statement. (printf's name reflects the fact that C was first developed when Teletypes and other printing terminals were still in widespread use. Today, of course, video displays are far more common. printf's "prints" to the *standard output,* that is, to the default location for program output to go. Nowadays, that's almost always a video screen or a window on that screen. printf's first (and, in this case, only) argument is the string which it should print. The string, enclosed in double quotes "", consists of the words "Hello, world!" followed by a special sequence: \n. In strings, any two-character sequence beginning with the backslash \ represents a single special character. The sequence \nrepresents the "new line" character, which prints a carriage return or line feed or whatever it takes to end one line of output and move down to the next. (This program only prints one line of output, but it's still important to terminate it.)

The second line in the main function is,

```
return 0;
```

In general, a function may return a value to its caller, and main is no exception. When main returns (that is, reaches its end and stops functioning), the program is at its end, and the return value from main tells the operating system (or whatever invoked the program that main is the main function of) whether it succeeded or not. By convention, a return value of 0 indicates success.

This program may look so absolutely trivial that it seems as if it's not even worth typing it in and trying to run it, but doing so may be a big (and is certainly a vital) first hurdle. On an unfamiliar computer, it can be arbitrarily difficult to figure out how to enter a text file containing program source, or how to compile and link it, or how to invoke it, or what happened after it ran. The most experienced C programmers immediately go back to this one, simple program whenever they're trying out a new system or a new way of entering or building programs or a new way of printing output from within programs. As Kernighan and Ritchie say, everything else is comparatively easy.

How *you* compile and run this (or any) program is a function of the compiler and operating system you're using. The first step is to type it in, exactly as shown; this may involve using a text editor to create a file containing the program text. You'll have to give the file a name, and all C compilers require that files containing C source end with the extension .c. So you might place the program text in a file called hello.c. The second step is to compile the program. (Strictly speaking, compilation consists of two steps, compilation proper followed by linking, but we can overlook this distinction at first, especially because the compiler often takes care of initiating the linking step automatically.) On many Unix systems, the command to compile a C program from a source file hello.c is,

```
cc -o hello hello.c
```

You would type this command at the Unix shell prompt, and it requests that the cc (C compiler) program be run, placing its output (*i.e.* the new executable program it creates) in the file hello, and taking its input (*i.e.* the source code to be compiled) from the file hello.c. The third step is to run (execute, invoke) the newly-built hello program. Again on a Unix system, this is done simply by typing the program's name:

```
hello
```

Depending on how your system is set up (in particular, on whether the current directory is searched for executables, based on the PATH variable), you may have to type,

```
./hello
```

to indicate that the hello program is in the current directory (as opposed to some "bin" directory full of executable programs, elsewhere).

You may also have your choice of C compilers. On many Unix machines, the cc command is an older compiler which does not recognize modern, ANSI Standard C syntax. An old compiler will accept the simple programs we'll be starting with, but it will not accept most of our later programs.

If you find yourself getting baffling compilation errors on programs which you've typed in exactly as they're shown, it probably indicates that you're using an older compiler. On many machines, another compiler called acc or gcc is available, and you'll want to use it, instead. (Both acc and gcc are typically invoked the same as cc; that is, the above cc command would instead be typed, say, gcc -o hello hello.c .)

In an integrated or "visual" progamming environment, such as those on the Macintosh or under various versions of Microsoft Windows, the steps you take to enter, compile, and run a program are somewhat different (and, theoretically, simpler). Typically, there is a way to open a new source window, type source code into it, give it a file name, and add it to the program (or "project") you're building. If necessary, there will be a way to specify what other source files (or "modules") make up the program. Then, there's a button or menu selection which compiles and runs the program, all from within the programming environment. (There will also be a way to create a standalone executable file which you can run from outside the environment.) In a PC-compatible environment, you may have to choose between creating DOS programs or Windows programs. (If you have troubles pertaining to the printf function, try specifying a target environment of MS-DOS.

Supposedly, some compilers which are targeted at Windows environments won't let you call printf, because until you call some fancier functions to request that a window be created, there's no window for printf to print to.) Again, check the introductory or tutorial manual that came with the programming package; it should walk you through the steps necessary to get your first program running.

Our second example is of little more practical use than the first, but it introduces a few more programming language elements:

```
#include <stdio.h>
/* print a few numbers, to illustrate a
simple loop */
main()
{
int i;
for(i = 0; i < 10; i = i + 1)
 printf("i is %d\n", i);
return 0;
}
```

As before, the line #include <stdio.h> is boilerplate which is necessary since we're calling the printf function, and main() and the pair of braces {} indicate and delineate the function named main we're (again) writing.

The first new line is the line,

```
/* print a few numbers, to illustrate a
```

```
        simple loop */
```

which is a *comment*. Anything between the characters /* and */ is ignored by the compiler, but may be useful to a person trying to read and understand the program. You can add comments anywhere you want to in the program, to document what the program is, what it does, who wrote it, how it works, what the various functions are for and how *they* work, what the various variables are for, etc.

The second new line, down within the function main, is,

```
int i;
```

which *declares* that our function will use a variable named i. The variable's type is int, which is a plain integer.

Next, we set up a loop:

```
for(i = 0; i < 10; i = i + 1)
```

The keyword for indicates that we are setting up a "for loop." A for loop is controlled by three expressions, enclosed in parentheses and separated by semicolons. These expressions say that, in this case, the loop starts by setting i to 0, that it continues as long as i is less than 10, and that after each iteration of the loop, i should be incremented by 1 (that is, have 1 added to its value).

Finally, we have a call to the printf function, as before, but with several differences. First, the call to printf is within the *body* of the for loop. This means that control flow does not pass once through the printf call, but instead that the call is performed as many times as are dictated by the for loop. In this case, printfwill be called several times: once when i is 0, once when i is 1, once when i is 2, and so on until i is 9, for a total of 10 times.

A second difference in the printf call is that the string to be printed, "i is %d", contains a per cent sign. Whenever printf sees a per cent sign, it indicates thatprintf is not supposed to print the exact text of the string, but is instead supposed to read another one of its arguments to decide what to print. The letter after the per cent sign tells it what type of argument to expect and how to print it. In this case, the letter d indicates that printf is to expect an int, and to print it in decimal. Finally, we see that printf is in fact being called with another argument, for a total of two, separated by commas. The second argument is the variable i, which is in fact an int, as required by %d. The effect of all of this is that each time it is called, printf will print a line containing the current value of the variable i:

```
i is 0
i is 1
i is 2
...
```

After several trips through the loop, i will eventually equal 9. After that trip through the loop, the third control expression i = i + 1 will increment its value to 10. The condition i < 10 is no longer true, so no more trips through the loop are taken. Instead, control flow jumps down to the statement following the for loop, which is the return statement. The main function returns, and the program is finished.

STRUCTURE OF THE PROGRAM

A program consists of one or more functions; it may also contain global variables. (Our two example programs so far have contained one function apiece, and no global variables.) At the top of a source file are typically a few boilerplate lines such as #include <stdio.h>, followed by the definitions (*i.e.* code) for the functions. (It's also possible to split up the several functions making up a larger program into several source files.)

Each function is further composed of *declarations* and *statements*, in that order. When a sequence of statements should act as one (for example, when they should all serve together as the body of a loop) they can be enclosed in braces (just as for the outer body of the entire function). The simplest kind of statement is an *expression statement*, which is an expression (presumably performing some useful operation) followed by a semicolon. Expressions are further composed of *operators*, *objects*(variables), and *constants*.

C source code consists of several *lexical elements*. Some are words, such as for, return, main, and i, which are either *keywords* of the language (for, return) or *identifiers* (names) we've chosen for our own functions and variables (main, i). There are *constants* such as 1 and 10 which introduce new values into the program. There are *operators* such as =, +, and >, which manipulate variables and values. There are other punctuation characters (often called *delimiters*), such as parentheses and squiggly braces {}, which indicate how the other elements of the program are grouped. Finally, all of the preceding elements can be separated by*whitespace*: spaces, tabs, and the "carriage returns" between lines.

The source code for a C program is, for the most part, "free form." This means that the compiler does not care how the code is arranged: how it is broken into lines, how the lines are indented, or whether whitespace is used between things like variable names and other punctuation. (Lines like #include <stdio.h> are an exception; they must appear alone on their own lines, generally unbroken. Only lines beginning with # are affected by this rule; we'll see other examples later.)

You can use whitespace, indentation, and appropriate line breaks to make your programs more readable for yourself and other people (even though the compiler doesn't care). You can place explanatory *comments* anywhere in your program—any text between the characters /* and */ is ignored by the compiler. (In fact, the compiler pretends that all it saw was whitespace.) Though comments are ignored by the compiler, well-chosen comments can make a program *much* easier to read.

The usage of whitespace is our first *style* issue. It's typical to leave a blank line between different parts of the program, to leave a space on either side of operators such as + and =, and to *indent* the bodies of loops and other control flow constructs. Typically, we arrange the indentation so that the subsidiary statements controlled by a loop statement (the "loop body," such as the printf call in our second example program) are all aligned with each other and placed one tab stop (or some consistent number of spaces) to the right of the controlling statement.

This indentation (like all whitespace) is not required by the compiler, but it makes programs*much* easier to read. (However, it can also be misleading, if used incorrectly or in the face of inadvertent mistakes. The compiler will decide what "the body of the loop" is based on its own rules, not the indentation, so if the indentation does not match the compiler's interpretation, confusion is inevitable.)

To drive home the point that the compiler doesn't care about indentation, line breaks, or other whitespace, here are a few (extreme) examples:

The fragments,

```
for(i = 0; i < 10; i = i + 1)
printf("%d\n", i);
```

and

```
for(i = 0; i < 10; i = i + 1) printf("%d\n",
i);
```

and

```
for(i=0;i<10;i=i+1)printf("%d\n",i);
```

and

```
for(i = 0; i < 10; i = i + 1)
printf("%d\n", i);
```

and

```
for     (       i
=       0       ;
i       <       10
;       i       =
i       +       1
)       printf          (
"%d\n"  ,       i
)       ;
```

and

```
for
(i=0;
i<10;i=
i+1)printf
("%d\n", i);
```

are all treated exactly the same way by the compiler. Some programmers argue forever over the best set of "rules" for indentation and other aspects of programming style, calling to mind the old philosopher's debates about the number of angels that could dance on the head of a pin. Style issues (such as how a program is laid out) *are* important, but they're not something to be too dogmatic about, and there are also other, deeper style issues besides mere layout and typography: Although C compilers do not care about how a program looks, proper indentation and spacing are critical in making programs easy for people to read.

We recommend writing only one statement per line, and using blanks around operators to clarify grouping. The position of braces is less important, although people hold passionate beliefs. We have chosen one of several popular styles. Pick a style that suits you, then use it consistently.

DATA TYPES

There are only a few basic data types in C.

The first ones we'll be encountering and using are:

- Char a character
- Int an integer, in the range -32,767 to 32,767
- Long int a larger integer (up to +-2,147,483,647)
- Float a floating-point number
- Double a floating-point number, with more precision and perhaps greater range than float

If you can look at this list of basic types and say to yourself, "Oh, how simple, there are only a few types, I won't have to worry much about choosing among them," you'll have an easy time with declarations. (Some masochists wish that the type system were more complicated so that they could specify more things about each variable, but those of us who would rather not have to specify these extra things each time are glad that we don't have to.)

The ranges listed above for types int and long int are the guaranteed minimum ranges. On some systems, either of these types (or, indeed, any C type) may be able to hold larger values, but a program that depends on extended ranges will not be as portable. Some programmers become obsessed with knowing exactly what the sizes of data objects will be in various situations, and go on to write programs which depend on these exact sizes. Determining or controlling the size of an object is occasionally important, but most of the time we can sidestep size issues and let the compiler do most of the worrying. (From the ranges listed above, we can determine that type int must be at least 16 bits, and that type long int must be at least 32 bits. But neither of these sizes is exact; many systens have 32-bit ints, and some systems have 64-bit long ints.)

Most machines today use the ASCII character set, in which the letter A is represented by the code 65, the ampersand and is represented by the code 38, the digit 1 is represented by the code 49, the space character is represented by the code 32, etc. (Most of the time, of course, you have *no* need to know or even worry about these particular code values; they're automatically translated into the right shapes on the screen or printer when characters are printed out, and they're automatically generated when you type characters on the keyboard.

Eventually, though, we'll appreciate, and even take some control over, exactly when these translations—from characters to their numeric codes—are performed.) Character codes are usually small—the largest code value in ASCII is 126, which is the ~ (tilde or circumflex) character. Characters usually fit in a byte, which is usually 8 bits. In C, type char is defined as occupying one byte, so it is usually 8 bits.

CONSTANTS

A *constant* is just an immediate, absolute value found in an expression. The simplest constants are decimal integers, *e.g.* 0,1, 2, 123 . Occasionally it is useful to specify constants in base 8 or base 16 (octal or hexadecimal); this is done by prefixing an extra 0 (zero) for octal, or 0x for hexadecimal: the constants 100, 0144, and 0x64 all represent the same number. (If you're not using these non-decimal constants, just remember not to use any leading zeroes. If you accidentally write 0123 intending to get one hundred and twenty three, you'll get 83 instead, which is 123 base 8.)

We write constants in decimal, octal, or hexadecimal for our convenience, not the compiler's. The compiler doesn't care; it always converts everything into binary internally, anyway. (There is, however, no good way to specify constants in source code in binary.) A constant can be forced to be of type long int by suffixing it with the letter L (in upper or lower case, although upper case is strongly recommended, because a lower case l looks too much like the digit 1).

A constant that contains a decimal point or the letter e (or both) is a floating-point constant: 3.14, 10..01, 123e4, 123.456e7 . The e indicates multiplication by a power of 10; 123.456e7 is 123.456 times 10 to the 7th, or 1,234,560,000. (Floating-point constants are of type double by default.)

We also have constants for specifying characters and strings. (Make sure you understand the difference between a character and a string: a character is exactly one character; a string is a set of zero or more characters; a string containing one character is distinct from a lone character.) A character constant is simply a single character between single quotes:'A', '.', '%'. The numeric value of a character constant is, naturally enough, that character's value in the machine's character set. (In ASCII, for example, 'A' has the value 65.)

A *string* is represented in C as a sequence or array of characters. (We'll have more to say about arrays in general, and strings in particular, later.)

A string constant is a sequence of zero or more characters enclosed in double quotes: "apple","hello, world", "this is a test". Within character and string constants, the backslash character \ is special, and is used to represent characters not easily typed on the keyboard or for various reasons not easily typed in constants.

The most common of these "character escapes" are:

\n	a "newline" character
\b	a backspace
\r	a carriage return (without a line feed)
\'	a single quote (*e.g.* in a character constant)
\"	a double quote (*e.g.* in a string constant)
\\	a single backslash

DECLARATIONS

Informally, a *variable* (also called an *object*) is a place you can store a value. So that you can refer to it unambiguously, a variable needs a name. You can think of the variables in your program as a set of boxes or cubbyholes, each with a label giving its name; you might imagine that storing a value "in" a variable consists of writing the value on a slip of paper and placing it in the cubbyhole.

A *declaration* tells the compiler the name and type of a variable you'll be using in your program. In its simplest form, a declaration consists of the type, the name of the variable, and a terminating semicolon:

```
char c;
int i;
float f;
```

You can also declare several variables of the same type in one declaration, separating them with commas:

```
int i1, i2;
```

Later we'll see that declarations may also contain *initializers*, *qualifiers* and *storage classes*, and that we can declare *arrays,functions*, *pointers*, and other kinds of data structures.

The placement of declarations is significant. You can't place them just anywhere (*i.e.* they cannot be interspersed with the other statements in your program). They must either be placed at the beginning of a function, or at the beginning of a brace-enclosed block of statements or outside of any function. Furthermore, the placement of a declaration, as well as its storage class, controls several things about its *visibility* and *lifetime*,

You may wonder *why* variables must be declared before use.

There are two reasons:

- It makes things somewhat easier on the compiler; it knows right away what kind of storage to allocate and what code to emit to store and manipulate each variable; it doesn't have to try to intuit the programmer's intentions.

- It forces a bit of useful discipline on the programmer: you cannot introduce variables willy-nilly; you must think about them enough to pick appropriate types for them. (The compiler's error messages to you, telling you that you apparently forgot to declare a variable, are as often helpful as they are a nuisance: they're helpful when they tell you that you misspelled a variable, or forgot to think about exactly how you were going to use it.)

Although there are a few places where declarations can be omitted making use of these removes the advantages of reason 2 above, so I recommend always declaring everything explicitly. Most of the time, I recommend writing one declaration per line.

For the most part, the compiler doesn't care what order declarations are in. You can order the declarations alphabetically, or in the order that they're used, or to put related declarations next to each other. Collecting all variables of the same type together on one line essentially orders declarations by type, which isn't a very useful order (it's only slightly more useful than random order).

A declaration for a variable can also contain an initial value. This *initializer* consists of an equals sign and an expression, which is usually a single constant:

```
int i = 1;
int i1 = 10, i2 = 20;
```

VARIABLE NAMES

Within limits, you can give your variables and functions any names you want. These names (the formal term is "identifiers") consist of letters, numbers, and underscores. For our purposes, names must begin with a letter.

Theoretically, names can be as long as you want, but extremely long ones get tedious to type after a while, and the compiler is not required to keep track of extremely long ones perfectly. (What this means is that if you were to name a variable, say,supercalafragalisticespialidocious, the compiler might get lazy and pretend that you'd named it super calafragalisticespialidocio, such that if you later misspelled itsupercalafragalisticespialidociouz, the compiler wouldn't catch your mistake.

Nor would the compiler necessarily be able to tell the difference if for some perverse reason you *deliberately* declared a second variable namedsupercalafragalisticespialidociouz.) The capitalization of names in C is significant: the variable names variable, Variable, and VARIABLE (as well as silly combinations like variAble) are all distinct. A final restriction on names is that you may not use *keywords* (the words such as int and for which are part of the syntax of the language) as the names of variables or functions (or as identifiers of any kind).

ARITHMETIC OPERATORS

The basic operators for performing arithmetic are the same in many computer languages:

```
+        addition
-        subtraction
*        multiplication
/        division
%        modulus (remainder)
```

The - operator can be used in two ways: to subtract two numbers (as in a - b), or to negate one number (as in -a + bor a + -b). When applied to integers, the division operator / discards any remainder, so 1/2 is 0 and 7/4 is 1. But when either operand is a floating-point quantity (type float or double), the division operator yields a floating-point result, with a potentially nonzero fractional part. So 1/2.0 is 0.5, and 7.0/4.0 is 1.75.

The *modulus* operator % gives you the remainder when two integers are divided: 1 % 2 is 1; 7 % 4 is 3. (The modulus operator can only be applied to integers.) An additional arithmetic operation you might be wondering about is exponentiation. Some languages have an exponentiation operator (typically ^ or **), but C doesn't. (To square or cube a number, just multiply it by itself.)

Multiplication, division, and modulus all have

higher *precedence* than addition and subtraction. The term "precedence" refers to how "tightly" operators bind to their operands (that is, to the things they operate on). In mathematics, multiplication has higher precedence than addition, so 1 + 2 * 3 is 7, not 9. In other words, 1 + 2 * 3 is equivalent to1 + (2 * 3). C is the same way. All of these operators "group" from left to right, which means that when two or more of them have the same precedence and participate next to each other in an expression, the evaluation conceptually proceeds from left to right. For example, 1 - 2 - 3 is equivalent to (1 - 2) - 3 and gives -4, not +2. ("Grouping" is sometimes called *associativity*, although the term is used somewhat differently in programming than it is in mathematics. Not all C operators group from left to right; a few group from right to left.)

Whenever the default precedence or associativity doesn't give you the grouping you want, you can always use explicit parentheses. For example, if you wanted to add 1 to 2 and then multiply the result by 3, you could write (1 + 2) * 3. By the way, the word "arithmetic" as used in the title of this section is an adjective, not a noun, and it's pronounced differently than the noun: the accent is on the third syllable.

ASSIGNMENT OPERATORS

The assignment operator = assigns a value to a variable. For example,

```
x = 1
```

sets x to 1, and

```
a = b
```

sets a to whatever b's value is. The expression

```
i = i + 1
```

is, as we've mentioned elsewhere, the standard programming idiom for increasing a variable's value by 1: this expression takes i's old value, adds 1 to it, and stores it back into i. (C provides several "shortcut" operators for modifying variables in this and similar ways, which we'll meet later.)

We've called the = sign the "assignment operator" and referred to "assignment expressions" because, in fact, = *is* an operator just like + or -. C does not have "assignment statements"; instead, an assignment like a = b is an expression and can be used wherever any expression can appear. Since it's an expression, the assignment a = b has a value, namely, the same value that's assigned to a.

This value can then be used in a larger expression; for example, we might write,

```
c = a = b
```

which is equivalent to,

```
c = (a = b)
```

and assigns b's value to both a and c. (The assignment operator, therefore, groups from right to left.). It's usually a matter of style whether you initialize a variable with an initializer in its declaration or with an assignment expression near where you first use it.

That is, there's no particular difference between,

```
int a = 10;
and
int a;
/* later... */
a = 10;
```

FUNCTION CALLS

We'll have much more to say about functions, but for now let's just look at how they're called.You call a function by mentioning its name followed by a pair of parentheses. If the function takes any arguments, you place the arguments between the parentheses, separated by commas.

These are all function calls:

```
printf("Hello, world!\n")
printf("%d\n", i)
sqrt(144.)
getchar()
```

The arguments to a function can be arbitrary expressions. Therefore, you don't have to say things like,

```
int sum = a + b + c;
printf("sum = %d\n", sum);
```

if you don't want to; you can instead collapse it to

```
printf("sum = %d\n", a + b + c);
```

Many functions return values, and when they do, you can embed calls to these functions within larger expressions:

```
c = sqrt(a * a + b * b)
x = r * cos(theta)
i = f1(f2(j))
```

The first expression squares a and b, computes the square root of the sum of the squares, and assigns the result to c. (In other words, it computes a * a + b * b, passes that number to the sqrt function, and assigns sqrt's return value toc.) The second expression passes the value of the variable theta to the cos (cosine) function, multiplies the result by r, and assigns the result to x. The third expression passes the value of the variable j to the function f2, passes the return value of f2 immediately to the function f1, and finally assigns f1's return value to the variable i.

EXPRESSION STATEMENTS

Most of the statements in a C program are *expression statements*. An expression statement is simply an expression followed by a semicolon.

The lines,

```
i = 0;
i = i + 1;
```

and

```
printf("Hello, world!\n");
```

are all expression statements. (In some languages, such as Pascal, the semicolon separates statements, such that the last statement is not followed by a semicolon. In C, however, the semicolon is a statement terminator; all simple statements are followed by semicolons. The semicolon is also used for a few other things in C; we've already seen that it terminates declarations, too.)

Expression statements do all of the real work in a C program. Whenever you need to compute new values for variables, you'll typically use expression statements (and they'll typically contain assignment operators). Whenever you want your program to do something visible, in the real world, you'll typically call a function (as part of an expression statement). We've already seen the most basic example: calling the function printf to print text to the screen. But anything else you might do—read or write a disk file, talk to a modem or printer, draw pictures on the screen—will also involve function calls. (Furthermore, the functions you call to do these things are usually different depending on which operating system you're using. The C language does not define them, so we won't be talking about or using them much.) Expressions and expression statements can be arbitrarily complicated.

They don't have to consist of exactly one simple function call, or of one simple assignment to a variable. For one thing, many functions return values, and the values they return can then be used by other parts of the expression.

For example, C provides a sqrt (square root) function, which we might use to compute the hypotenuse of a right triangle like this:

```
c = sqrt(a*a + b*b);
```

To be useful, an expression statement must do something; it must have some lasting effect on the state of the program. (Formally, a useful statement must have at least one *side effect*.) The first two sample expression statements in this section (above) assign new values to the variable i, and the third one calls printf to print something out, and these are good examples of statements that do something useful. (To make the distinction clear, we may note that degenerate constructions such as,

```
0;
i;
  or
i + 1;
```

are syntactically valid statements—they consist of an expression followed by a semicolon—but in each case, they compute a value without doing anything with it, so the computed value is discarded, and the statement is useless. But if the "degenerate" statements in this paragraph don't make much sense to you, don't worry; it's because they, frankly, don't make much sense.)

It's also possible for a single expression to have multiple side effects, but it's easy for such an expression to be:

- Confusing or
- Undefined.

For now, we'll only be looking at expressions (and, therefore, statements) which do one well-defined thing at a time.

IF STATEMENTS

The simplest way to modify the control flow of a program is with an if statement, which in its simplest form looks like this:

```
if(x > max)
max = x;
```

Even if you didn't know any C, it would probably be pretty obvious that what happens here is that if x is greater than max,x gets assigned to max. (We'd use code like this to keep track of the maximum value of x we'd seen—for each new x, we'd compare it to the old maximum value max, and if the new value was greater, we'd update max.)

More generally, we can say that the syntax of an if statement is:

```
if(expression)
statement
```

where *expression* is any expression and *statement* is any statement.

What if you have a series of statements, all of which should be executed together or not at all depending on whether some condition is true?

The answer is that you enclose them in braces:

```
if(expression)
{
statement<sub>1</sub>
statement<sub>2</sub>
statement<sub>3</sub>
}
```

As a general rule, anywhere the syntax of C calls for a statement, you may write a series of statements enclosed by braces. (You do not need to, and should not, put a semicolon after the closing brace, because the series of statements enclosed by braces is not itself a simple expression statement.)

An if statement may also optionally contain a second statement, the "else clause," which is to be executed if the condition is not met.

Here is an example:

```
if(n > 0)
average = sum/n;
else {
printf("can't compute average\n");
average = 0;
}
```

The first statement or block of statements is executed if the condition *is* true, and the second statement or block of statements (following the keyword else) is executed if the condition is *not* true. In this example, we can compute a meaningful average only if n is greater than 0; otherwise, we print a message saying that we cannot compute the average.

The general syntax of an if statement is therefore,

```
if(expression)
statement<sub>1</sub>
else
statement<sub>2</sub>
```

(where both *statement₁* and *statement₂* may be lists of statements enclosed in braces).

It's also possible to nest one if statement inside another. (For that matter, it's in general possible to nest any kind of statement or control flow construct within another.) For example, here is a little piece of code which decides roughly which quadrant of the compass you're walking into, based on an x value which is positive if you're walking east, and a y value which is positive if you're walking north:

```
if(x > 0)
{
if(y > 0)
printf("Northeast.\n");
else printf("Southeast.\n");
}
```

```
else {
if(y > 0)
printf("Northwest.\n");
else printf("Southwest.\n");
}
```

When you have one if statement (or loop) nested inside another, it's a very good idea to use explicit braces {}, as shown, to make it clear (both to you and to the compiler) how they're nested and which else goes with which if. It's also a good idea to indent the various levels, also as shown, to make the code more readable to humans. Why do both? You use indentation to make the code visually more readable to yourself and other humans, but the compiler doesn't pay attention to the indentation (since all whitespace is essentially equivalent and is essentially ignored). Therefore, you also have to make sure that the punctuation is right.

Here is an example of another common arrangement of if and else. Suppose we have a variable grade containing a student's numeric grade, and we want to print out the corresponding letter grade.

Here is code that would do the job:

```
if(grade >= 90)
  printf("A");
else if(grade >= 80)
  printf("B");
else if(grade >= 70)
  printf("C");
else if(grade >= 60)
  printf("D");
else printf("F");
```

What happens here is that exactly one of the five printf calls is executed, depending on which of the conditions is true. Each condition is tested in turn, and if one is true, the corresponding statement is executed, and the rest are skipped. If none of the conditions is true, we fall through to the last one, printing "F".

In the cascaded if/else/if/else/... chain, each else clause is another if statement. This may be more obvious at first if we reformat the example, including every set of braces and indenting each if statement relative to the previous one:

```
if(grade >= 90)
{
printf("A");
}
else {
if(grade >= 80)
{
printf("B");
}
else {
if(grade >= 70)
{
printf("C");
}
else {
if(grade >= 60)
{
printf("D");
}
else {
printf("F");
}
}
}
}
```

By examining the code this way, it should be obvious that exactly one of the printf calls is executed, and that whenever one of the conditions is found true, the remaining conditions do not need tó be checked and none of the later statements within the chain will be executed. But once you've convinced yourself of this and learned to recognize the idiom, it's generally preferable to arrange the statements as in the first example, without trying to indent each successive if statement one tabstop further out. (Obviously, you'd run into the right margin very quickly if the chain had just a few more cases!)

BOOLEAN EXPRESSIONS

An if statement like,

```
if(x > max)
max = x;
```

is perhaps deceptively simple. Conceptually, we say that it checks whether the condition x > max is "true" or "false". The mechanics underlying C's conception of "true" and "false," however, deserve some explanation. We need to understand how true and false values are represented, and how they are interpreted by statements like if. As far as C is concerned, a true/false condition can be represented as an integer. (An integer can represent many values; here we care about only two values: "true" and "false." The study of mathematics involving only two values is called Boolean algebra, after George Boole, a mathematician who refined this study.) In C, "false" is represented by a value of 0 (zero), and "true" is represented by any value that is nonzero. Since there are many nonzero values (at least 65,534, for values of type int), when we have to pick a specific value for "true," we'll pick 1.

The *relational operators* such as <, <=, >, and >= are in fact operators, just like +, -, *, and /. The relational operators take two values, look at them, and "return" a value of 1 or 0 depending on whether the tested relation was true or false.

The complete set of relational operators in C is:

```
<  less than
<= less than or equal
>  greater than
>= greater than or equal
== equal
!= not equal
```

For example, 1 < 2 is 1, 3 > 4 is 0, 5 == 5 is 1, and 6 != 6 is 0. We've now encountered perhaps the most easy-to-stumble-on "gotcha!" in C: the equality-testing operator is ==, not a single =, which is assignment. If you accidentally write,

```
if(a = 0)
```

(and you probably will at some point; everybody makes this mistake), it will *not* test whether a is zero, as you probably intended. Instead, it will *assign* 0 to a, and then perform the "true" branch of the if statement if a is *non*zero. But a will have just been assigned the value 0, so the "true" branch will never be taken! (This could drive you crazy while debugging—you wanted to do something if a was 0, and after the test, a *is* 0, whether it was supposed to be or not, but the "true" branch is nevertheless not taken.)

The relational operators work with arbitrary numbers and generate true/false values. You can also combine true/false values by using the *Boolean operators*, which take true/false values as operands and compute new true/false values.

The three Boolean operators are:

```
&&  and
||  or
!  not  (takes  one  operand;  "unary")
```

The && ("and") operator takes two true/false values and produces a true (1) result if both operands are true (that is, if the left-hand side is true and the right-hand side is true). The || ("or") operator takes two true/false values and produces a true (1) result if either operand is true. The ! ("not") operator takes a single true/false value and negates it, turning false to true and true to false (0 to 1 and nonzero to 0).

For example, to test whether the variable i lies between 1 and 10, you might use,

```
if(1 < i && i < 10)
...
```

Here we're expressing the relation "i is between 1 and 10" as "1 is less than i and i is less than 10." It's important to understand why the more obvious expression,

```
if(1 < i < 10) /* WRONG */
```

would not work. The expression 1 < i < 10 is parsed by the compiler analogously to 1 + i + 10. The expression 1 + i + 10 is parsed as (1 + i) + 10 and means "add 1 to i, and then add the result to 10." Similarly, the expression 1 < i < 10 is parsed as (1 < i) < 10 and means "see if 1 is less than i, and then see if the result is less than 10." But in this case, "the result" is 1 or 0, depending on whether i is greater than 1. Since both 0 and 1 are less than 10, the expression 1 < i < 10 would *always* be true in C, regardless of the value of i!

Relational and Boolean expressions are usually used in contexts such as an if statement, where something is to be done or not done depending on some condition. In these cases what's actually checked is whether the expression representing the condition has a zero or nonzero value. As long as the expression is a relational or Boolean expression, the interpretation is just what we want. For example, when we wrote,

```
if(x > max)
```

the > operator produced a 1 if x was greater than max, and a 0 otherwise. The if statement interprets 0 as false and 1 (or any nonzero value) as true. But what if the expression is not a relational or Boolean expression? As far as C is concerned, the controlling expression (of conditional statements like if) can in fact be *any* expression: it doesn't have to "look like" a Boolean expression; it doesn't have to contain relational or logical operators. All C looks at (when it's evaluating an if statement, or anywhere else where it needs a true/false value) is whether the expression evaluates to 0 or nonzero. For example, if you have a variable x, and you want to do something if x is nonzero, it's possible to write,

```
if(x)
statement
```

and the statement will be executed if x is nonzero (since nonzero means "true").

This possibility (that the controlling expression of an if statement doesn't have to "look like" a Boolean expression) is both useful and potentially confusing. It's useful when you have a variable or a function that is "conceptually Boolean," that is, one that you consider to hold a true or false (actually nonzero or zero) value. For example, if you have a variableverbose which contains a nonzero value when your program should run in verbose mode and zero when it should be quiet, you can write things like,

```
if(verbose)
printf("Starting first pass\n");
```

and this code is both legal and readable, besides which it does what you want. The standard library contains a functionisupper() which tests whether a character is an upper-case letter, so if c is a character, you might write

```
if(isupper(c))
...
```

Both of these examples (verbose and isupper()) are useful and readable. However, you will eventually come across code like,

```
if(n)
average = sum/n;
```

where n is just a number. Here, the programmer wants to compute the average only if n is nonzero (otherwise, of course, the code would divide by 0), and the code works, because, in the context of the if statement, the trivial expression n is (as always) interpreted as "true" if it is nonzero, and "false" if it is zero.

"Coding shortcuts" like these can seem cryptic, but they're also quite common, so you'll need to be able to recognize them even if you don't choose to write them in your own code. Whenever you see code like

```
if(x)
```

or

```
if(f())
```

where x or f() do not have obvious "Boolean" names, you can read them as "if x is nonzero" or "if f() returns nonzero."

WHILE LOOPS

Loops generally consist of two parts: one or more *control expressions* which (not surprisingly) control the execution of the loop, and the *body*, which is the statement or set of statements which is executed over and over.

The most basic *loop* in C is the while loop. A while loop has one control expression, and executes as long as that expression is true. This example repeatedly doubles the number 2 (2, 4, 8, 16...) and prints the resulting numbers as long as they are less than 1000:

```
int x = 2;
while(x < 1000)
{
```

```
printf("%d\n", x);
x = x * 2;
}
```

(Once again, we've used braces {} to enclose the group of statements which are to be executed together as the body of the loop.)

The general syntax of a while loop is,

```
while(expression)
statement
```

A while loop starts out like an if statement: if the condition expressed by the *expression* is true, the *statement* is executed. However, after executing the statement, the condition is tested again, and if it's still true, the statement is executed again. (Presumably, the condition depends on some value which is changed in the body of the loop.) As long as the condition remains true, the body of the loop is executed over and over again. (If the condition is false right at the start, the body of the loop is not executed at all.)

As another example, if you wanted to print a number of blank lines, with the variable n holding the number of blank lines to be printed, you might use code like this:

```
while(n > 0)
{
printf("\n");
n = n - 1;
}
```

After the loop finishes (when control "falls out" of it, due to the condition being false), n will have the value 0.

You use a while loop when you have a statement or group of statements which may have to be executed a number of times to complete their task. The controlling expression represents the condition "the loop is not done" or "there's more work to do." As long as the expression is true, the body of the loop is executed; presumably, it makes at least some progress at its task.

When the expression becomes false, the task is done, and the rest of the program (beyond the loop) can proceed. When we think about a loop in this way, we can seen an additional important property: if the expression evaluates to "false" before the very first trip through the loop, we make *zero* trips through the loop. In other words, if the task is already done (if there's no work to do) the body of the loop is not executed at all. (It's always a good idea to think about the "boundary conditions" in a piece of code, and to make sure that the code will work correctly when there is no work to do, or when there is a trivial task to do, such as sorting an array of one number. Experience has shown that bugs at boundary conditions are quite common.)

FOR LOOPS

Our second loop, which we've seen at least one example of already, is the for loop.

The first one we saw was:

```
for (i = 0; i < 10; i = i + 1)
printf("i is %d\n", i);
```

More generally, the syntax of a for loop is for,

```
(expr<sub>1</sub>; expr<sub>2</sub>; expr<sub>
 3</sub>)
statement
```

(Here we see that the for loop has three control expressions. As always, the *statement* can be a brace-enclosed block.)

Many loops are set up to cause some variable to step through a range of values, or, more generally, to set up an initial condition and then modify some value to perform each succeeding loop as long as some condition is true.

The three expressions in a for loop encapsulate these conditions: *expr₁* sets up the initial condition,*expr<sub>2</ sub>* tests whether another trip through the loop should be taken, and *expr₃* increments or updates things after each trip through the loop and prior to the next one.

In our first example, we had i = 0 as*expr₁*, i < 10 as *expr₂*, i = i + 1 as *expr₃*, and the call to printf as*statement*, the body of the loop. So the loop began by setting i to 0, proceeded as long as i was less than 10, printed outi's value during each trip through the loop, and added 1 to i between each trip through the loop.

When the compiler sees a for loop, first, *expr₁* is evaluated. Then, *expr₂* is evaluated, and if it is true, the body of the loop (*statement*) is executed. Then, *expr₃* is evaluated to go to the next step, and*expr₂* is evaluated again, to see if there *is* a next step. During the execution of a for loop, the sequence is:

```
expr<sub>1</sub>
expr<sub>2</sub>
statement
expr<sub>3</sub>
expr<sub>2</sub>
statement
expr<sub>3</sub>
...
expr<sub>2</sub>
statement
expr<sub>3</sub>
expr<sub>2</sub>
```

The first thing executed is *expr₁*. *expr₃* is evaluated after *every* trip through the loop. The last thing executed is always *expr₂*, because when *expr₂* evaluates false, the loop exits.

All three expressions of a for loop are optional. If you leave out *expr₁*, there simply is no initialization step, and the variable(s) used with the loop had better have been initialized already.

If you leave out *expr₂*, there is no test, and the default for the for loop is that another trip through the loop should be taken (such that unless you break out of it some other way, the loop runs forever). If you leave out *expr₃*, there is no increment step.

The semicolons separate the three controlling expressions of a for loop. (These semicolons, by the way, have nothing to do with statement terminators.) If you leave out one or more of the expressions, the semicolons remain. Therefore, one way of writing a deliberately infinite loop in C is,

```
for(;;)
...
```

It's useful to compare C's for loop to the equivalent loops in other computer languages you might know.

The C loop,

```
for(i = x; i <= y; i = i + z)
```

is roughly equivalent to:

```
for I = X to Y step Z  (BASIC)
do 10 i=x,y,z (FORTRAN)
for i:= x to y (Pascal)
```

In C (unlike FORTRAN), if the test condition is false before the first trip through the loop, the loop won't be traversed at all. In C (unlike Pascal), a loop control variable (in this case, i) is guaranteed to retain its final value after the loop completes, and it is also legal to modify the control variable within the loop, if you really want to. (When the loop terminates due to the test condition turning false, the value of the control variable after the loop will be the first value for which the condition failed, not the last value for which it succeeded.) It's also worth noting that a for loop can be used in more general ways than the simple, iterative examples we've seen so far. The "control variable" of a for loop does not have to be an integer, and it does not have to be incremented by an additive increment. It could be "incremented" by a multiplicative factor (1, 2, 4, 8...) if that was what you needed, or it could be a floating-point variable, or it could be another type of variable which we haven't met yet which would step, not over numeric values, but over the elements of an array or other data structure. Strictly speaking, a for loop doesn't have to have a "control variable" at all; the three expressions can be anything, although the loop will make the most sense if they are related and together form the expected initialize, test, increment sequence.

The powers-of-two example of the previous section does fit this pattern, so we could rewrite it like this:

```
int x;
for(x = 2; x < 1000; x = x * 2)
printf("%d\n", x);
```

There is no earth-shaking or fundamental difference between the while and for loops.

In fact, given the general for loop, for,

```
(expr<sub>1</sub>; expr<sub>2</sub>; expr<sub>
 3</sub>)
statement
```

you could usually rewrite it as a while loop, moving the initialize and increment expressions to statements before and within the loop:

```
expr<sub>1</sub>;
while(expr<sub>2</sub>)
{
statement
expr<sub>3</sub>;
}
```

Similarly, given the general while loop:

```
while(expr)
statement
```

you could rewrite it as a for loop:

```
for(; expr;)
statement
```

Another contrast between the for and while loops is that although the test expression (*expr₂*) is optional in a for loop, it is required in a while loop. If you leave out the controlling expression of a while loop, the compiler will complain about a syntax error. (To write a deliberately infinite while loop, you have to supply an expression which is always nonzero. The most obvious one would simply be while(1) .) If it's possible to rewrite a for loop as a while loop and vice versa, why do they both exist? Which one should you choose? In general, when you choose a for loop, its three expressions should all manipulate the same variable or data structure, using the initialize, test, increment pattern. If they don't manipulate the same variable or don't follow that pattern, wedging them into a for loop buys nothing and a while loop would probably be clearer. (The reason that one loop or the other can be clearer is simply that, when you see a for loop, you *expect* to see an idiomatic initialize/test/increment of a single variable, and if the for loop you're looking at doesn't end up matching that pattern, you've been momentarily misled.)

BREAK AND CONTINUE

Sometimes, due to an exceptional condition, you need to jump out of a loop early, that is, before the main controlling expression of the loop causes it to terminate normally. Other times, in an elaborate loop, you may want to jump back to the top of the loop (to test the controlling expression again, and perhaps begin a new trip through the loop) without playing out all the steps of the current loop.

The break and continue statements allow you to do these two things. (They are, in fact, essentially restricted forms of goto.).

To put everything together, as well as demonstrate the use of the break statement, here is a program for printing prime numbers between 1 and 100:

```
#include <stdio.h>
#include <math.h>
main()
{
int i, j;
printf("%d\n", 2);
for(i = 3; i <= 100; i = i + 1)
{
for(j = 2; j < i; j = j + 1)
{
if(i % j == 0)
break;
if(j > sqrt(i))
{
printf("%d\n", i);
break;
}
}
}
return 0;
}
```

The outer loop steps the variabie i through the numbers from 3 to 100; the code tests to see if each number has any divisors other than 1 and itself. The trial divisor j loops from

2 up to i. j is a divisor of i if the remainder of i divided by jis 0, so the code uses C's "remainder" or "modulus" operator % to make this test.

Remember that i % j gives the remainder when i is divided by j. If the program finds a divisor, it uses break to break out of the inner loop, without printing anything. But if it notices that jhas risen higher than the square root of i, without its having found any divisors, then i must not have any divisors, so i is prime, and its value is printed.

Once we've determined that i is prime by noticing that j > sqrt(i), there's no need to try the other trial divisors, so we use a second break statement to break out of the loop in that case, too.

The simple algorithm and implementation we used here (like many simple prime number algorithms) does not work for 2, the only even prime number, so the program "cheats" and prints out 2 no matter what, before going on to test the numbers from 3 to 100.

Many improvements to this simple program are of course possible; you might experiment with it. (Did you notice that the "test" expression of the inner loop for(j = 2; j < i; j = j + 1) is in a sense unnecessary, because the loop always terminates early due to one of the two break statements?)

ARRAYS

So far, we've been declaring simple variables: the declaration,

```
int i;
```

declares a single variable, named i, of type int. It is also possible to declare an *array* of several elements.

The declaration,

```
int a[10];
```

declares an array, named a, consisting of ten elements, each of type int. Simply speaking, an array is a variable that can hold more than one value. You specify which of the several values you're referring to at any given time by using a numeric*subscript*. (Arrays in programming are similar to vectors or matrices in mathematics.)

We can represent the array a above with a picture like this:

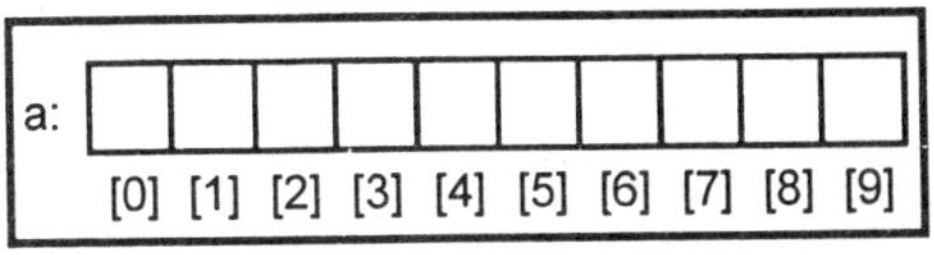

a:										
	[0]	[1]	[2]	[3]	[4]	[5]	[6]	[7]	[8]	[9]

In C, arrays are *zero-based*: the ten elements of a 10-element array are numbered from 0 to 9. The subscript which specifies a single element of an array is simply an integer expression in square brackets. The first element of the array isa[0], the second element is a[1], etc.

You can use these "array subscript expressions" anywhere you can use the name of a simple variable, for example:

```
a[0] = 10;
a[1] = 20;
a[2] = a[0] + a[1];
```

Notice that the subscripted array references (*i.e.* expressions such as a[0] and a[1]) can appear on either side of the assignment operator. The subscript does not have to be a constant like 0 or 1; it can be any integral expression. For example, it's common to loop over all elements of an array:

```
int i;
for(i = 0; i < 10; i = i + 1)
a[i] = 0;
```

This loop sets all ten elements of the array a to 0. Arrays are a real convenience for many problems, but there is not a lot that C will do with them for you automatically.

In particular, you can neither set all elements of an array at once nor assign one array to another; both of the assignments,

```
a = 0; /* WRONG */
and
int b[10];
b = a; /* WRONG */
are illegal.
```

To set all of the elements of an array to some value, you must do so one by one, as in the loop example above. To copy the contents of one array to another, you must again do so one by one:

```
int b[10];
for(i = 0; i < 10; i = i + 1)
b[i] = a[i];
```

Remember that for an array declared:

```
int a[10];
```

there is no element a[10]; the topmost element is a[9]. This is one reason that zero-based loops are also common in C.

Note that the for loop,

```
for(i = 0; i < 10; i = i + 1)
...
```

does just what you want in this case: it starts at 0, the number 10 suggests (correctly) that it goes through 10 iterations, but the less-than comparison means that the last trip through the loop has i set to 9. (The comparison i <= 9 would also work, but it would be less clear and therefore poorer style.) In the little examples so far, we've always looped over all 10 elements of the sample array a. It's common, however, to use an array that's bigger than necessarily needed, and to use a second variable to keep track of how many elements of the array are currently in use. For example, we might have an integer variable,

```
int na;  /* number of elements of a[] in use */
```

Then, when we wanted to do something with a (such as print it out), the loop would run from 0 to na, not 10 (or whatevera's size was):

```
for(i = 0; i < na; i = i + 1)
printf("%d\n", a[i]);
```

Naturally, we would have to ensure ensure that na's value was always less than or equal to the number of elements actually declared in a.

Arrays are not limited to type int; you can have arrays of char or double or any other type. Here is a slightly larger example of the use of arrays. Suppose we want to investigate the behaviour of rolling a pair of dice. The total roll can be anywhere from 2 to 12, and we want to count how often each roll comes up. We will use an array to keep track of the counts: a[2] will count how many times we've rolled 2, etc.

We'll simulate the roll of a die by calling C's random number generation function, rand(). Each time you call rand(), it returns a different, pseudo-random integer. The values that rand() returns typically span a large range, so we'll use C's*modulus* (or "remainder") operator % to produce random numbers in the range we want. The expression rand() % 6produces random numbers in the range 0 to 5, and rand() % 6 + 1 produces random numbers in the range 1 to 6.

Here is the program:

```
#include <stdio.h>
#include <stdlib.h>
main()
{
int i;
int d1, d2;
int a[13];/* uses [2..12] */
for(i = 2; i <= 12; i = i + 1)
a[i] = 0;
for(i = 0; i < 100; i = i + 1)
{
d1 = rand() % 6 + 1;
d2 = rand() % 6 + 1;
a[d1 + d2] = a[d1 + d2] + 1;
}
for(i = 2; i <= 12; i = i + 1)
printf("%d: %d\n", i, a[i]);
return 0;
}
```

We include the header <stdlib.h> because it contains the necessary declarations for the rand() function. We declare the array of size 13 so that its highest element will be a[12]. (We're wasting a[0] and a[1]; this is no great loss.) The variables d1 and d2 contain the rolls of the two individual dice; we add them together to decide which cell of the array to increment, in the line,

```
a[d1 + d2] = a[d1 + d2] + 1;
```

After 100 rolls, we print the array out. Typically (as craps players well know), we'll see mostly 7's, and relatively few 2's and 12's. (By the way, it turns out that using the % operator to reduce the range of the rand function is *not* always a good idea. We'll say more about this problem in an exercise.)

ARRAY INITIALIZATION

Although it is not possible to assign to all elements of an array at once using an assignment expression, it is possible to initialize some or all elements of an array when the array is defined.

The syntax looks like this:

```
int a[10] = {0, 1, 2, 3, 4, 5, 6, 7, 8, 9};
```

The list of values, enclosed in braces {}, separated by commas, provides the initial values for successive elements of the array. (Under older, pre-ANSI C compilers, you could not always supply initializers for "local" arrays inside functions; you could only initialize "global" arrays, those outside of any function. Those compilers are now rare, so you shouldn't have to worry about this distinction any more. We'll talk more about local and global variables.)

If there are fewer initializers than elements in the array, the remaining elements are automatically initialized to 0.

For example,

```
int a[10] = {0, 1, 2, 3, 4, 5, 6};
```

would initialize a[7], a[8], and a[9] to 0. When an array definition includes an initializer, the array dimension may be omitted, and the compiler will infer the dimension from the number of initializers.

For example,

```
int b[] = {10, 11, 12, 13, 14};
```

would declare, define, and initialize an array b of 5 elements (*i.e.* just as if you'd typed int b[5]). Only the dimension is omitted; the brackets [] remain to indicate that b is in fact an array.

In the case of arrays of char, the initializer may be a string constant:

```
char s1[7] = "Hello,";
char s2[10] = "there,";
char s3[] = "world!";
```

As before, if the dimension is omitted, it is inferred from the size of the string initializer. (We haven't covered strings in detail yet—but it turns out that all strings in C are terminated by a special character with the value 0. Therefore, the array s3 will be of size 7, and the explicitly-sized s1 does need to be of size at least 7. For s2, the last 4 characters in the array will all end up being this zero-value character.)

MULTIDIMENSIONAL ARRAYS

When we said that "Arrays are not limited to type int; you can have arrays of... any other type," we meant that more literally than you might have guessed. If you have an "array of int," it means that you have an array each of whose elements is of type int. But you can have an array each of whose elements is of type *x*, where *x* is any type you choose. In particular, you can have an array each of whose elements is another array! We can use these arrays of arrays for the same sorts of tasks as we'd use multidimensional arrays in other computer languages (or matrices in mathematics). Naturally, we are not limited to arrays of arrays, either; we could have an array of arrays of arrays, which would act like a 3-dimensional array, etc.

The declaration of an array of arrays looks like this:

```
int a2[5][7];
```

You have to read complicated declarations like these "inside out." What this one says is that a2 is an array of 5 somethings, and that each of the somethings is an array of 7 ints. More briefly, "a2 is an array of 5 arrays of 7 ints," or, "a2 is an array of array of int." In the declaration of a2, the brackets closest to the identifier a2 tell you what a2 first and foremost is. That's how you know it's an array of 5 arrays of size 7, not the other way around. You can think of a2 as having 5 "rows" and 7 "columns," although this interpretation is not mandatory. (You could also treat the "first" or inner subscript as "x" and the second as "y." Unless you're doing something fancy, all you have to worry about is that the subscripts when you access the array match those that you used when you declared it, as in the examples below.) To illustrate the use of multidimensional arrays, we might fill in the elements of the above array a2 using this piece of code:

```
int i, j;
for(i = 0; i < 5; i = i + 1)
{
```

```
for(j = 0; j < 7; j = j + 1)
a2[i][j] = 10 * i + j;
}
```

This pair of nested loops sets a[1][2] to 12, a[4][1] to 41, etc. Since the first dimension of a2 is 5, the first subscripting index variable, i, runs from 0 to 4. Similarly, the second subscript varies from 0 to 6.

We could print a2 out (in a two-dimensional way, suggesting its structure) with a similar pair of nested loops:

```
for(i = 0; i < 5; i = i + 1)
{
for(j = 0; j < 7; j = j + 1)
printf("%d\t", a2[i][j]);
printf("\n");
}
```

(The character \t in the printf string is the tab character.) Just to see more clearly what's going on, we could make the "row" and "column" subscripts explicit by printing them, too:

```
for(j = 0; j < 7; j = j + 1)
printf("\t%d:", j);
printf("\n");
for(i = 0; i < 5; i = i + 1)
{
printf("%d:", i);
for(j = 0; j < 7; j = j + 1)
printf("\t%d", a2[i][j]);
printf("\n");
}
```

This last fragment would print:

0: 1: 2: 3: 4: 5: 6:
0: 0 1 2 3 4 5 6
1: 10 11 12 13 14 15 16
2: 20 21 22 23 24 25 26
3: 30 31 32 33 34 35 36
4: 40 41 42 43 44 45 46

Finally, there's no reason we have to loop over the "rows" first and the "columns" second; depending on what we wanted to do, we could interchange the two loops, like this:

```
for(j = 0; j < 7; j = j + 1)
{
for(i = 0; i < 5; i = i + 1)
printf("%d\t", a2[i][j]);
printf("\n");
}
```

Notice that i is still the first subscript and it still runs from 0 to 4, and j is still the second subscript and it still runs from 0 to 6.

VISIBILITY

We haven't said so explicitly, but variables are channels of communication within a program. You set a variable to a value at one point in a program, and at another point (or points) you read the value out again. The two points may be in adjoining statements, or they may be in widely separated parts of the program. How long does a variable last? How widely separated can the setting and fetching parts of the program be, and how long after a variable is set does it persist? Depending on the variable and how you're using it, you might want different answers to these questions.

The *visibility* of a variable determines how much of the rest of the program can access that variable. You can arrange that a variable is visible only within one part of one function, or in one function, or in one source file, or anywhere in the program. (We haven't really talked about source files yet; we'll be exploring them soon.) Why would you want to limit the visibility of a variable? For maximum flexibility, wouldn't it be handy if all variables were potentially visible everywhere? As it happens, that arrangement would be *too* flexible: everywhere in the program, you would have to keep track of the names of all the variables declared anywhere else in the program, so that you didn't accidentally re-use one. Whenever a variable had the wrong value by mistake, you'd have to search the entire program for the bug, because any statement in the entire program could potentially have modified that variable. You would constantly be stepping all over yourself by using a common variable name like i in two parts of your program, and having one snippet of code accidentally overwrite the values being used by another part of the code. The communication would be sort of like an old party line—you'd always be accidentally interrupting other conversations, or having your conversations interrupted.

To avoid this confusion, we generally give variables the narrowest or smallest visibility they need. A variable declared within the braces {} of a function is visible only within that function; variables declared within functions are called *local variables*. If another function somewhere else declares a local variable with the same name, it's a different variable entirely, and the two don't clash with each other.

On the other hand, a variable declared outside of any function is a *global variable*, and it is potentially visible anywhere within the program. You use global variables when you *do* want the communications path to be able to travel to any part of the program. When you declare a global variable, you will usually give it a longer, more descriptive name (not something generic like i) so that whenever you use it you will remember that it's the same variable everywhere. Another word for the visibility of variables is *scope*.

How long do variables last? By default, local variables (those declared within a function) have *automatic duration*: they spring into existence when the function is called, and they (and their values) disappear when the function returns. Global variables, on the other hand, have *static duration*: they last, and the values stored in them persist, for as long as the program does. (Of course, the values can in general still be overwritten, so they don't necessarily persist forever.)

Finally, it is possible to split a function up into several source files, for easier maintenance. When several source files are combined into one program the compiler must have a way of correlating the global variables which might be used to communicate between the several source files. Furthermore, if a global variable is going to be useful for communication, there must be exactly one of it: you wouldn't want one function in one source file to store a value in one global variable named globalvar, and then have another function in another source file read from a*different* global variable named globalvar. Therefore, a global variable should have exactly one *defining instance,* in one place in one source file. If the same variable is to be used anywhere else (*i.e.* in some other source file or files), the variable is declared in those other file(s) with an *external declaration,* which is not a defining instance. The external declaration says, "hey, compiler, here's the name and type of a global variable I'm going to use, but don't define it here, don't allocate space for it; it's one that's defined somewhere else, and I'm just referring to it here." If you accidentally have two distinct defining instances for a variable of the same name, the compiler (or the linker) will complain that it is "multiply defined." It is also possible to have a variable which is global in the sense that it is declared outside of any function, but private to the one source file it's defined in. Such a variable is visible to the functions in that source file but not to any functions in any other source files, even if they try to issue a matching declaration.

You get any extra control you might need over visibility and lifetime, and you distinguish between defining instances and external declarations, by using *storage classes.* A storage class is an extra keyword at the beginning of a declaration which modifies the declaration in some way. Generally, the storage class (if any) is the first word in the declaration, preceding the type name. (Strictly speaking, this ordering has not traditionally been necessary, and you may see some code with the storage class, type name, and other parts of a declaration in an unusual order.)

We said that, by default, local variables had automatic duration. To give them static duration (so that, instead of coming and going as the function is called, they persist for as long as the function does), you precede their declaration with thestatic keyword:

```
static int i;
```

By default, a declaration of a global variable (especially if it specifies an initial value) is the defining instance. To make it an external declaration, of a variable which is defined somewhere else, you precede it with the keyword extern:

```
extern int j;
```

Finally, to arrange that a global variable is visible only within its containing source file, you precede it with the statickeyword:

```
static int k;
```

Notice that the static keyword can do two different things: it adjusts the duration of a local variable from automatic to static, or it adjusts the visibility of a global variable from truly global to private-to-the-file.

DEFAULT INITIALIZATION

The duration of a variable (whether static or automatic) also affects its default initialization. If you do not explicitly initialize them, automatic-duration variables (that is, local, non-static ones) are not guaranteed to have any particular initial value; they will typically contain garbage. It is therefore a fairly serious error to attempt to use the value of an automatic variable which has never been initialized or assigned to: the program will either work incorrectly, or the garbage value may just happen to be "correct" such that the program appears to work correctly! However, the particular value that the garbage takes on can vary depending literally on *anything*: other parts of the program, which compiler was used, which hardware or operating system the program is running on, the time of day, the phase of the moon.So you hardly want to say that a program which uses an uninitialized variable "works"; it may seem to work, but it works for the wrong reason, and it may stop working tomorrow.

Static-duration variables (global and static local), on the other hand, are guaranteed to be initialized to 0 if you do not use an explicit initializer in the definition. (Once upon a time, there was another distinction between the initialization of automatic vs. static variables: you could initialize *aggregate* objects, such as arrays, only if they had static duration. If your compiler complains when you try to initialize a local array, it's probably an old, pre-ANSI compiler. Modern, ANSI-compatible compilers remove this limitation, so it's no longer much of a concern.)

EXAMPLES

Here is an example demonstrating almost everything we've seen so far:

```
int globalvar = 1;
extern int anotherglobalvar;
static int privatevar;
f()
{
int localvar;
int localvar2 = 2;
static int persistentvar;
}
```

Here we have six variables, three declared outside and three declared inside of the function f(). Globalvar is a global variable. The declaration we see is its defining instance (it happens also to include an initial value).globalvar can be used anywhere in this source file, and it could be used in other source files, too (as long as corresponding external declarations are issued in those other source files). Anotherglobalvar is a second global variable. It is *not* defined here; the defining instance for it (and its initialization) is somewhere else.

Privatevar is a "private" global variable. It can be used anywhere within this source file, but functions in other source files cannot access it, even if they try to issue external declarations for it. (If other source files try to declare a global variable called "privatevar", they'll get their own; they won't be sharing this one.) Since it has static duration and receives no explicit initialization, privatevar will be initialized to 0.

Localvar is a local variable within the function f(). It can be accessed only within the function f(). (If any other part of the program declares a variable named "localvar", that variable will be distinct from the one we're looking at here.)localvar is conceptually "created" each time f() is called, and disappears when f() returns. Any value which was stored in localvar last time f() was running will be lost and will not be available next time f() is called. Furthermore, since it has no explicit initializer, the value of localvar will in general be garbage each time f() is called. Localvar2 is also local, and everything that we said about localvar applies to it, except that since its declaration includes an explicit initializer, it will be initialized to 2 each time f() is called.

Finally, persistentvar is again local to f(), but it *does* maintain its value between calls to f(). It has static duration but no explicit initializer, so its initial value will be 0. The defining instances and external declarations we've been looking at so far have all been of simple variables.

The term *declaration* is a general one which encompasses defining instances and external declarations; defining instances and external declarations are two different kinds of declarations. Furthermore, either kind of declaration suffices to inform the compiler of the name and type of a particular variable (or function). If you have the defining instance of a global variable in a source file, the rest of that source file can use that variable without having to issue any external declarations. It's only in source files where the defining instance hasn't been seen that you need external declarations.

You will sometimes hear a defining instance referred to simply as a "definition," and you will sometimes hear an external declaration referred to simply as a "declaration." These usages are mildly ambiguous, in that you can't tell out of context whether a "declaration" is a generic declaration (that might be a defining instance or an external declaration) or whether it's an external declaration that specifically is not a defining instance. (Similarly, there are other constructions that can be called "definitions" in C, namely the definitions of preprocessor macros, structures, and typedefs, none of which we've met.) In these notes, we'll try to make things clear by using the unambiguous terms *defining instance* and *external declaration*. Elsewhere, you may have to look at the context to determine how the terms "definition" and "declaration" are being used.

6

Program Structure

FUNCTIONS

It has a *name* that you call it by, and a list of zero or more *arguments* or *parameters* that you hand to it for it to act on or to direct its work; it has a *body* containing the actual instructions (statements) for carrying out the task the function is supposed to perform; and it may give you back a *return value*, of a particular type.

Here is a very simple function, which accepts one argument, multiplies it by 2, and hands that value back:

```
int multbytwo(int x)
{
int retval;
retval = x * 2;
return retval;
}
```

On the first line we see the return type of the function (int), the name of the function (multbytwo), and a list of the function's arguments, enclosed in parentheses. Each argument has both a name and a type; multbytwo accepts one argument, of type int, named x. The name x is arbitrary, and is used only within the definition of multbytwo.

The caller of this function only needs to know that a single argument of type int is expected; the caller does not need to know what name the function will use internally to refer to that argument. (In particular, the caller does not have to pass the value of a variable named x.) Next we see, surrounded by the familiar braces, the body of the function itself. This function consists of one declaration (of a local variable retval) and two statements. The first statement is a conventional expression statement, which computes and assigns a value to retval, and the second statement is a return statement, which causes the function to return to its caller, and also specifies the value which the function returns to its caller.

The return statement can return the value of any expression, so we don't really need the local retval variable; the function could be collapsed to,

```
int multbytwo(int x)
{
return x * 2;
}
```

How do we call a function? We've been doing so informally since day one, but now we have a chance to call one that we've written, in full detail.

Here is a tiny skeletal program to call multby2:

```
#include <stdio.h>
extern int multbytwo(int);
int main()
{
int i, j;
i = 3;
j = multbytwo(i);
printf("%d\n", j);
return 0;
}
```

This looks much like our other test programs, with the exception of the new line

```
extern int multbytwo(int);
```

This is an *external function prototype declaration.* It is an external declaration, in that it declares something which is defined somewhere else. (We've already seen the defining instance of the function multbytwo, but maybe the compiler hasn't seen it yet.) The function prototype declaration contains the three pieces of information about the function that a caller needs to know: the function's name, return type, and argument type(s). Since we don't care what name the multbytwo function will use to refer to its first argument, we don't need to mention it. (On the other hand, if a function takes several arguments, giving them names in the prototype may make it easier to remember which is which, so names may optionally be used in function prototype declarations.) Finally, to remind us that this is an external declaration and not a defining instance, the prototype is preceded by the keyword extern.

The presence of the function prototype declaration lets the compiler know that we intend to call this function, multbytwo. The information in the prototype lets the compiler generate the correct code for calling the function, and also enables the compiler to check up on our code (by making sure, for example, that we pass the correct number of arguments to each function we call).

Down in the body of main, the action of the function call should be obvious: the line

```
j = multbytwo(i);
```

calls multbytwo, passing it the value of i as its argument. When multbytwo returns, the return value is assigned to the variable j. (Notice that the value of main's local variable i will become the value of multbytwo's parameter x; this is absolutely not a problem, and is a normal sort of affair.)

This example is written out in "longhand," to make each step equivalent. The variable i isn't really needed, since we could just as well call

```
j = multbytwo(3);
```

And the variable j isn't really needed, either, since we could just as well call

```
printf("%d\n", multbytwo(3));
```

Here, the call to multbytwo is a subexpression which serves as the second argument to printf. The value returned bymultbytwo is passed immediately to printf. (Here, as in general, we see the flexibility and generality of expressions in C. An argument passed to a function may be an arbitrarily complex subexpression, and a function call is itself an expression which may be embedded as a subexpression within arbitrarily complicated surrounding expressions.) We should say a little more about the mechanism by which an argument is passed down from a caller into a function. Formally, C is *call by value*, which means that a function receives *copies* of the values of its arguments. We can illustrate this with an example. Suppose, in our implementation of multbytwo, we had gotten rid of the unnecessary retvalvariable like this:

```
int multbytwo(int x)
{
x = x * 2;
return x;
}
```

We might wonder, if we wrote it this way, what would happen to the value of the variable i when we called

```
j = multbytwo(i);
```

When our implementation of multbytwo changes the value of x, does that change the value of i up in the caller? The answer is no. x receives a copy of i's value, so when we change x we don't change i. However, there is an exception to this rule. When the argument you pass to a function is not a single variable, but is rather an array, the function does *not* receive a copy of the array, and it therefore *can* modify the array in the caller. The reason is that it might be too expensive to copy the entire array, and furthermore, it can be useful for the function to write into the caller's array, as a way of handing back more data than would fit in the function's single return value.

FUNCTION PROTOTYPES

In modern C programming, it is considered good practice to use prototype declarations for all functions that you call. As we mentioned, these prototypes help to ensure that the compiler can generate correct code for calling the functions, as well as allowing the compiler to catch certain mistakes you might make.

Strictly speaking, however, prototypes are optional. If you call a function for which the compiler has not seen a prototype, the compiler will do the best it can, assuming that you're calling the function correctly. If prototypes are a good idea, and if we're going to get in the habit of writing function prototype declarations for functions we call that we've written (such as multbytwo), what happens for library functions such as printf? Where are their prototypes? The answer is in that boilerplate line

```
#include <stdio.h>
```

we've been including at the top of all of our programs. stdio.h is conceptually a file full of external declarations and other information pertaining to the "Standard I/O" library functions, including printf. The #include directive arranges that all of the declarations within stdio.h are considered by the compiler, rather as if we'd typed them all in ourselves. Somewhere within these declarations is an external function prototype declaration forprintf, which satisfies the rule that there should be a prototype for each function we call. (For other standard library functions we call, there will be other "header files" to include.)

Finally, one more thing about external function prototype declarations. We've said that the distinction between external declarations and defining instances of normal variables hinges on the presence or absence of the keyword extern.

The situation is a little bit different for functions. The "defining instance" of a function is the function, including its body (that is, the brace-enclosed list of declarations and statements implementing the function). An external declaration of a function, even without the keyword extern, looks nothing like a function declaration. Therefore, the keyword extern is optional in function prototype declarations. If you wish, you can write

```
int multbytwo(int);
```

and this is just as good an external function prototype declaration as,

```
extern int multbytwo(int);
```

(In the first form, without the extern, as soon as the compiler sees the semicolon, it knows it's not going to see a function body, so the declaration can't be a definition.) You may want to stay in the habit of using extern in all external declarations, including function declarations, since "extern = external declaration" is an easier rule to remember.

FUNCTION PHILOSOPHY

What makes a good function? The most important aspect of a good "building block" is that have a single, well-defined task to perform. When you find that a program is hard to manage, it's often because it has not been designed and broken up into functions cleanly. Two obvious reasons for moving code down into a function are because:

- It appeared in the main program several times, such that by making it a function, it can be written just once, and the several places where it used to appear can be replaced with calls to the new function.
- The main program was getting too big, so it could be made (presumably) smaller and more manageable by lopping part of it off and making it a function.

These two reasons are important, and they represent significant benefits of well-chosen functions, but they are not sufficient to automatically identify a good function. As we've been suggesting, a good function has at least these two additional attributes:

- It does just one well-defined task, and does it well.
- Its interface to the rest of the program is clean and narrow.

Attribute 3 is just a restatement of two things we said above. Attribute 4 says that you shouldn't have to keep track of too many things when calling a function. If you know what a function is supposed to do, and if its task is simple and well-defined, there should be just a few pieces of information you have to give it to act upon, and one or just a few pieces of information which it returns to you when it's done. If you find yourself having to pass lots and lots of information to a function, or remember details of its internal implementation to make sure that it will work properly this time, it's often a sign that the function is not sufficiently well-defined. (A poorly defined function may be an arbitrary chunk of code that was ripped out of a main program that was getting too big, such that it essentially has to have access to all of that main function's local variables.)

The whole point of breaking a program up into functions is so that you don't have to think about the entire program at once; ideally, you can think about just one function at a time. We say that a good function is a "black box," which is supposed to suggest that the "container" it's in is opaque—callers can't see inside it (and the function inside can't see out). When you call a function, you only have to know what it does, not how it does it. When you're *writing* a function, you only have to know what it's supposed to do, and you don't have to know why or under what circumstances its caller will be calling it. (When designing a function, we should perhaps think about the callers just enough to ensure that the function we're designing will be easy to call, and that we aren't accidentally setting things up so that callers will have to think about any internal details.)

Some functions may be hard to write (if they have a hard job to do, or if it's hard to make them do it truly well), but that difficulty should be compartmentalized along with the function itself. Once you've written a "hard" function, you should be able to sit back and relax and watch it do that hard work on call from the rest of your program. It should be pleasant to notice (in the ideal case) how much easier the rest of the program is to write, now that the hard work can be deferred to this workhorse function. (In fact, if a difficult-to-write function's interface is well-defined, you may be able to get away with writing a quick-and-dirty version of the function first, so that you can begin testing the rest of the program, and then go back later and rewrite the function to do the hard parts. As long as the function's original interface anticipated the hard parts, you won't have to rewrite the rest of the program when you fix the function.)

What I've been trying to say in the preceding few paragraphs is that functions are important for far more important reasons than just saving typing. Sometimes, we'll write a function which we only call once, just because breaking it out into a function makes things clearer and easier.

If you find that difficulties pervade a program, that the hard parts can't be buried inside black-box functions and then forgotten about; if you find that there are hard parts which involve complicated interactions among multiple functions, then the program probably needs redesigning.

For the purposes of explanation, we've been seeming to talk so far only about "main programs" and the functions they call and the rationale behind moving some piece of code down out of a "main program" into a function. But in reality, there's obviously no need to restrict ourselves to a two-tier scheme. Any function we find ourself writing will often be appropriately written in terms of sub-functions, sub-sub-functions, etc.

SEPARATE COMPILATION LOGISTICS

When a program consists of many functions, it can be convenient to split them up into several source files. Among other things, this means that when a change is made, only the source file containing the change has to be recompiled, not the whole program.

The job of putting the pieces of a program together and producing the final executable falls to a tool called the *linker*. (We may or may not need to invoke the linker explicitly; a compiler often invokes it automatically, as needed.) The linker looks through all of the pieces making up the program, sorting out the external declarations and defining instances. The compiler has noted the definitions made by each source file, as well as the declarations of things used by each source file but (presumably) defined elsewhere. For each thing (global variable or function) used but not defined by one piece of the program, the linker looks for another piece which does define that thing.

The logistics of writing a program in several source files, and then compiling and linking all of the source files together, depend on the programming environment you're using. We'll cover two possibilities, depending on whether you're using a traditional command-line compiler or a newer integrated development environment (IDE) or other graphical user interface (GUI) compiler. When using a command-line compiler, there are usually two main steps involved in building an executable program from one or more source files.

First, each source file is compiled, resulting in an *object file* containing the machine instructions (generated by the compiler) corresponding to just the code in that source file.

Second, the various object files are *linked*together, with each other and with *libraries* containing code for functions which you did not write (such as printf), to produce a final, executable program.

Under Unix, the cc command can perform one or both steps. So far, we've been using extremely simple invocations of ccsuch as,

```
cc -o hello hello.c
```

This invocation compiles a single source file, hello.c, links it, and places the executable in a file named hello. Suppose we have a program which we're trying to build from three separate source files, x.c, y.c, and z.c. We could compile all three of them, and link them together, all at once, with the command

```
cc -o myprog x.c y.c z.c
```

Alternatively, we could compile them separately: the -c option to cc tells it to compile only, but not to link. Instead of building an executable, it merely creates an object file, with a name ending in .o, for each source file compiled.

So the three commands,

```
cc -c x.c
cc -c y.c
cc -c y.c
```

would compile x.c, y.c, and z.c and create object files x.o, y.o, and z.o. Then, the three object files could be linked together using

```
cc -o myprog x.o y.o z.o
```

When the cc command is given an .o file, it knows that it does not have to compile it (it's an object file, already compiled); it just sends it through to the link process.

Above we mentioned that the second, linking step also involves pulling in library functions. Normally, the functions from the Standard C library are linked in automatically. Occasionally, you must request a library manually; one common situation under Unix is that the math functions tend to be in a separate math library, which is requested by using -lm on the command line. Since the libraries must typically be searched *after* your program's own object files are linked (so that the linker knows which library functions your program uses), any -l option must appear *after* the names of your files on the command line. For example, to link the object file mymath.o (previously compiled with cc -c mymath.c) together with the math library, you might use,

```
cc -o mymathprog mymath.o -lm
```

Everything we've said about cc also applies to most other Unix C compilers. (Many of you will be using gcc, the FSF's GNU C Compiler.) There are command-line compilers for MS-DOS systems which work similarly. For example, the Microsoft C compiler comes with a CL ("compile and link") command, which works almost the same as Unix cc. You can compile and link in one step:

```
cl hello.c
or you can compile only:
cl/c hello.c
creating an object file named hello.obj.
```

The preceding has all been about command-line compilers. If you're using some kind of integrated development environment, such as Borland's Turbo C or the Microsoft Programmer's Workbench or Visual C or Think C or Codewarrior, most of the mechanical details are taken care of for you. Typically you define a "project," and there's a way to specify the list of files which make up your project.

7

Modelling of Program

MODEL

The I/O model does not distinguish between the types of physical devices supporting the I/O. Each source or sink of data is treated in the same way, and is viewed as a *stream* of bytes. Since the smallest object that can be represented in C is the character, access to a file is permitted at any character boundary. Any number of characters can be read or written from a movable point, known as the *file position indicator*. The characters will be read, or written, in sequence from this point, and the position indicator moved accordingly.

The position indicator is initially set to the beginning of a file when it is opened, but can also be moved by means of positioning requests. Opening a file in append mode has an implementation defined effect on the stream's file position indicator. The overall effect is to provide sequential reads or writes unless the stream was opened in append mode, or the file position indicator is explicitly moved. There are two types of file, *text files* and *binary files*, which, within a program, are manipulated as *text streams* and *binary* streams once they have been opened for I/O. The stdio package does not permit operations on the contents of files 'directly', but only by viewing them as streams.

TEXT STREAMS

The Standard specifies what is meant by the term *text stream*, which essentially considers a file to contain lines of text. A line is a sequence of zero or more characters terminated by a newline character. It is quite possible that the actual representation of lines in the external environment is different from this and there may be transformations of the data stream on the way in and out of the program; a common requirement is to translate the '\n' line-terminator into the sequence '\r\n' on output, and do the reverse on input. Other translations may also be necessary.

Data read in from a text stream is guaranteed to compare equal to the data that was earlier written out to the file if the data consists only of complete lines of printable characters and the control characters horizontal-tab and newline, no newline character is immediately preceded by space characters and the last character is a newline.

It is guaranteed that, if the last character written to a text file is a newline, it will read back as the same. It is implementation defined whether the last line written to a text file must terminate with a newline character; this is because on some implementations text files and binary files are the same. Some implementations may strip the leading space from lines consisting only of a space followed by a newline, or strip trailing spaces at the end of a line!

An implementation must support text files with lines containing at least 254 characters, including the terminating newline.

Opening a text stream in update mode may result in a binary stream in some implementations. Writing on a text stream may cause some implementations to truncate the file at that point—any data beyond the last byte of the current write being discarded.

BINARY STREAMS

A binary stream is a sequence of characters that can be used to record a program's internal data, such as the contents of structures or arrays in binary form. Data read in from a binary stream will always compare equal to data written out earlier to the same stream, under the same implementation. In some circumstances, an implementation-defined number of NUL characters may be appended to a binary stream.

STDIO.H HEADER FILE

To provide support for streams of the various kinds, a number of functions and macros exist. The <stdio.h> header file contains the various declarations necessary for the functions, together with the following macro and type declarations:

`FILE`

The type of an object used to contain stream control information. Users of stdio never need to know the contents of these objects, but simply manipulate pointers to them. It is not safe to copy these objects within the program; sometimes their addresses may be 'magic'.

`fpos_t`

A type of object that can be used to record unique values of a stream's file position indicator.

`_IOFBF _IOLBF _IONBF`

Values used to control the buffering of a stream in conjunction with thesetvbuf function.

`BUFSIZ`

The size of the buffer used by the setbuf function. An integral constant expression whose value is at least 256.

`EOF`

A negative integral constant expression, indicating the end-of-file condition on a stream i.e. that there is no more input.

`FILENAME_MAX`

The maximum length which a filename can have, if there is a limit, or otherwise the recommended size of an array intended to hold a file name.

`FOPEN_MAX`

The minimum number of files that the implementation guarantees may be held open concurrently; at least eight are guaranteed. Note that three predefined streams exist and may need to be closed if a program needs to open more than five files explicitly.

`L_tmpnam`

The maximum length of the string generated by tmpnam; an integral constant expression.

SEEK_CUR SEEK_END SEEK_SET

Integral constant expressions used to control the actions of fseek.

TMP_MAX

The minimum number of unique filenames generated by tmpnam; an integral constant expression with a value of at least 25.

stdin stdout stderr

Predefined objects of type (FILE *) referring to the standard input, output and error streams respectively. These streams are automatically open when a program starts execution.

OPENING AND BUFFERING OF STREAMS

OPENING

A stream is connected to a file by means of the fopen, freopen or tmpfilefunctions. These functions will, if successful, return a pointer to a FILE object.

Three streams are available without any special action; they are normally all connected to the physical device associated with the executing program: usually your terminal. They are referred to by the names stdin, the *standard input*, stdout, the *standard output*, and stderr, the *standard error* streams. Normal keyboard input is from stdin, normal terminal output is to stdout, and error messages are directed to stderr. The separation of error messages from normal output messages allows the stdout stream to be connected to something other than the terminal device, and still to have error messages appear on the screen in front of you, rather than to be redirected to this file. These files are only fully buffered if they do not refer to interactive devices.

As mentioned earlier, the file position indicator may or may not be movable, depending on the underlying device. It is not possible, for example, to move the file position indicator on stdin if that is connected to a terminal, as it usually is.

All non-temporary files must have a *filename*, which is a string. The rules for what constitutes valid filenames are implementation defined. Whether a file can be simultaneously open multiple times is also implementation defined. Opening a new file may involve creating the file. Creating an existing file causes its previous contents to be discarded.

CLOSING

Files are closed by explicitly calling fclose, exit or by returning from main. Any buffered data is flushed. If a program stops for some other reason, the status of files which it had open is undefined.

BUFFERING

There are three types of buffering:

`Unbuffered`

Minimum internal storage is used by stdio in an attempt to send or receive data as soon as possible.

`Line buffered`

Characters are processed on a line-by-line basis. This is commonly used in interactive environments, and internal buffers are flushed only when full or when a newline is processed.

`Fully buffered`

Internal buffers are only flushed when full. The buffering associated with a stream can always be flushed by using fflushexplicitly. Support for the various types of buffering is implementation defined, and can be controlled within these limits using setbuf and setvbuf.

DIRECT FILE MANIPULATION

A number of functions exist to operate on files directly.

```
#include <stdio.h>
int remove(const char *filename);
int rename(const char *old, const char *new);
char *tmpnam(char *s);
FILE *tmpfile(void);
```

`remove`

Causes a file to be removed. Subsequent attempts to open the file will fail, unless it is first created again. If the file is already open, the operation ofremove is implementation defined. The return value is zero for success, any other value for failure.

`rename`

Changes the name of the file identified by old to new. Subsequent attempts to open the original name will fail, unless another file is created with the old name. As with remove, rename returns zero for a successful operation, any other value indicating a failure.

If a file with the new name exists prior to calling rename, the behaviour is implementation defined. If rename fails for any reason, the original file is unaffected.

`tmpnam`

Generates a string that may be used as a filename and is guaranteed to be different from any existing filename. It may be called repeatedly, each time generating a new name. The constant TMP_MAX is used to specify how many times tmpnam may be called before it can no longer find a unique name.TMP_MAX will be at least 25. If tmpnam is called more than this number of times, its behaviour is undefined by the Standard, but many implementations offer no practical limit.

If the argument s is set to NULL, then tmpnam uses an internal buffer to build the name, and returns a pointer to that. Subsequent calls may alter the same internal buffer. The argument may instead point to an array of at leastL_tmpnam characters, in which case the name will be filled into the supplied buffer. Such a filename may then be created, and used as a temporary file. Since the name is generated by the function, it is unlikely to be very useful in any other context. Temporary files of this nature are not removed, except by direct calls to the remove function. They are most often used to pass temporary data between two separate programs.

`tmpfile`

Creates a temporary binary file, opened for update, and returns a pointer to the stream of that file. The file will be removed when the stream is closed. If no file could be opened, tmpfile returns a null pointer.

OPENING NAMED FILES

Named files are opened by a call to the fopen function, whose declaration is this:

```
#include &lt;stdio.h&gt;
```

FILE *fopen(const char *pathname, const char *mode); The pathname argument is the name of the file to open, such as that returned fromtmpnam, or some program-specific filename.

Files can be opened in a variety of *modes*, such as *read* mode for reading data,*write* mode for writing data, and so on. Note that if you only want to write data to a file, fopen will *create* the file if it does not already exist, or truncate it to zero length if it did exist.

If a file is opened in append mode, all writes will occur at the end of the file, regardless of attempts to move the file position indicator with fseek. The initial position fo the file position indicator will be implementation defined.

Attempts to open a file in read mode, indicated by an 'r' as the first character in the mode string, will fail if the file does not already exist or can't be read.

Files opened for update ('+' as the second or third character of mode) may be both read and written, but a read may not immediately follow a write, or a write follow a read, without an intervening call to one (or more) of fflush, fseek, fsetpos or rewind. The only exception is that a write may immediately follow a read if EOF was read.

It may also be possible in some implementations to omit the b in the binary modes, using the same modes for text and binary files. Streams opened by fopen are fully buffered only if they are not connected to an interactive device; this ensures that prompts and responses are handled properly.

If fopen fails to open a file, it returns a null pointer; otherwise, it returns a pointer to the object controlling the stream.

The stdin, stdout and stderr objects are not necessarily modifiable and it may not be possible to use the value returned fromfopen for assignment to one of them. For this reason, freopen is provided.

FREOPEN

The freopen function is used to take an existing stream pointer and associate it with another named file:

```
#include <stdio.h>
FILE *freopen(const char *pathname,
const char *mode, FILE *stream);
```

The mode argument is the same as for fopen. The stream is closed first, and any errors from the close are ignored. On error, NULL is returned, otherwise the new value for stream is returned.

CLOSING FILES

An open file is closed using fclose.

```
#include <stdio.h>
int fclose(FILE *stream);
```

Any unwritten data buffered for stream is flushed out and any unread data is thrown away. If a buffer had been automatically allocated for the stream, it is freed. The file is then closed. Zero is returned on success, EOF if any error occurs.

FFLUSH

```
#include <stdio.h>
int fflush(FILE *stream);
```

If stream refers to a file opened for output or update, any unwritten data is 'written' out. Exactly what that means is a function of the host environment, and C cannot guarantee, for example, that data immediately reaches the surface of a disk which might be supporting the file. If the stream is associated with a file opened for input or update, any preceding ungetc operation is forgotten.

The most recent operation on the stream must have been an output operation; if not, the behaviour is undefined. A call of fflush with an argument of zero flushes every output or update stream. Care is taken to avoid those streams that have not had an output as their last operation, thus avoiding the undefined behaviour mentioned above. EOF is returned if an error occurs, otherwise zero.

PRINTF

printf's name comes from print formatted. It generates output under the control of a *format string* (its first argument) which consists of literal characters to be printed and also special character sequences—*format specifiers*—which request that other arguments be fetched, formatted, and inserted into the string.

Our very first program was nothing more than a call to printf, printing a constant string:

```
printf("Hello, world!\n");
```

Our second program also featured a call to printf:

```
printf("i is %d\n", i);
```

In that case, whenever printf "printed" the string "i is %d", it did not print it verbatim; it replaced the two characters%d with the value of the variable i. There are quite a number of format specifiers for printf.

Here are the basic ones:

%d	print an int argument in decimal
%ld	print a long int argument in decimal
%c	print a character
%s	print a string
%f	print a float or double argument
%e	same as %f, but use exponential notation
%g	use %e or %f, whichever is better
%–	print an int argument in octal (base 8)
%x	print an int argument in hexadecimal (base 16)
%%	print a single %

It is also possible to specify the width and precision of numbers and strings as they are inserted (somewhat like FORTRAN format statements). (Very briefly, for those who are curious: a notation like %3d means to print an int in a field at least 3 spaces wide; a notation like %5.2f means to print a float ordouble in a field at least 5 spaces wide, with two places to the right of the decimal.)

To illustrate with a few more examples: The call printf

```
("%c %d %f %e %s %d%%\n", '1', 2, 3.14,
  56000000., "eight", 9); would print
1 2 3.140000 5.600000e+07 eight 9%
```

The call,

```
printf("%d %o %x\n", 100, 100, 100);
would print
100 144 64
```

Successive calls to printf just build up the output a piece at a time, so the calls,

```
printf("Hello, ");
printf("world!\n");
```

would also print Hello, world! (on one line of output). Earlier we learned that C represents characters internally as small integers corresponding to the characters' values in the machine's character set (typically ASCII). This means that there isn't really much difference between a character and an integer in C; most of the difference is in whether we choose to interpret an integer as an integer or a character. printf is one place where we get to make that choice: %d prints an integer value as a string of digits representing its decimal value, while %c prints the character corresponding to a character set value.

So the lines,

```
char c = 'A';
int i = 97;
printf("c = %c, i = %d\n", c, i);
```

would print c as the character A and i as the number 97. But if, on the other hand, we called

```
printf("c = %d, i = %c\n", c, i);
```

we'd see the decimal value (printed by %d) of the character 'A', followed by the character (whatever it is) which happens to have the decimal value 97.

You have to be careful when calling printf. It has no way of knowing how many arguments you've passed it or what their types are other than by looking for the format specifiers in the format string. If there are more format specifiers (that is, more % signs) than there are arguments, or if the arguments have the wrong types for the format specifiers, printf can misbehave badly, often printing nonsense numbers or (even worse) numbers which mislead you into thinking that some other part of your program is broken.

Because of some automatic conversion rules which we haven't covered yet, you have a small amount of latitude in the types of the expressions you pass as arguments to printf. The argument for %c may be of type char or int, and the argument for %d may be of type char or int. The string argument for %s may be a string constant, an array of characters, or a pointer to some characters (though we haven't really covered strings or pointers yet). Finally, the arguments corresponding to %e, %f, and %g may be of types float or double. But other combinations do *not* work reliably: %d will not print a long int or a float or a double; %ld will not print an int; %e, %f, and %g will not print an int.

CHARACTER INPUT AND OUTPUT

Unless a program can read some input, it's hard to keep it from doing exactly the same thing every time it's run, and thus being rather boring after a while.

The most basic way of reading input is by calling the function getchar. getchar reads one character from the "standard input," which is usually the user's keyboard, but which can sometimes be redirected by the operating system. getcharreturns the character it reads, or, if there are no more characters available, the special value EOF.

A companion function is putchar, which writes one character to the "standard output." (The standard output is, again not surprisingly, usually the user's screen, although it, too, can be redirected. printf, like putchar, prints to the standard output; in fact, you can imagine that printf calls putchar to actually print each of the characters it formats.)

Using these two functions, we can write a very basic program to copy the input, a character at a time, to the output:

```
#include <stdio.h>
/* copy input to output */
main()
{
int c;
c = getchar();
while(c != EOF)
```

```
{
putchar(c);
c = getchar();
}
return 0;
}
```

This code is straightforward, and I encourage you to type it in and try it out. It reads one character, and if it is not the EOFcode, enters a while loop, printing one character and reading another, as long as the character read is not EOF. This is a straightforward loop, although there's one mystery surrounding the declaration of the variable c: if it holds characters, why is it an int?

We said that a char variable could hold integers corresponding to character set values, and that an int could hold integers of more arbitrary values. Since most character sets contain a few hundred characters, an int variable can in general comfortably hold all char values, and then some. Therefore, there's nothing wrong with declaring c as an int.

But in fact, it's important to do so, because getchar can return every character value,*plus* that special, non-character value EOF, indicating that there are no more characters. Type char is only guaranteed to be able to hold all the character values; it is *not* guaranteed to be able to hold this "no more characters" value without possibly mixing it up with some actual character value. Therefore, you should always remember to use an int for anything you assigngetchar's return value to.

When you run the character copying program, and it begins copying its input (your typing) to its output (your screen), you may find yourself wondering how to stop it. It stops when it receives end-of-file (EOF), but how do you send EOF? The answer depends on what kind of computer you're using. On Unix and Unix-related systems, it's almost always control-D. On MS-DOS machines, it's control-Z followed by the RETURN key. Under Think C on the Macintosh, it's control-D, just like Unix. On other systems, you may have to do some research to learn how to send EOF.

Another excellent thing to know when doing any kind of programming is how to terminate a runaway program. If a program is running forever waiting for input, you can usually stop it by sending it an end-of-file, as above, but if it's running forever *not* waiting for something, you'll have to take more drastic measures. Under Unix, control-C (or, occasionally, the DELETE key) will terminate the current program, almost no matter what. Under MS-DOS, control-C or control-BREAK will sometimes terminate the current program, but by default MS-DOS only checks for control-C when it's looking for input, so an infinite loop can be unkillable.

There's a DOS command,

```
break on
```

which tells DOS to look for control-C more often, and I recommend using this command if you're doing any programming. (If a program is in a really tight infinite loop under MS-DOS, there can be no way of killing it short of rebooting.) On the Mac, try command-period or command-option-ESCAPE.

You'll type a character, and see it on the screen right away, and assume it's your program working, but it's only your computer echoing every key you type, as it always does. When you hit RETURN, a full line of characters is made available to your program. It then zips several times through its loop, reading and printing all the characters in the line in quick succession. In other words, when you run this program, it will probably seem to copy the input a line at a time, rather than a character at a time. You may wonder how a program could instead read a character right away, without waiting for the user to hit RETURN. That's an excellent question, but unfortunately the answer is rather complicated, and beyond the scope of our discussion here. (Among other things, how to read a character right away is one of the things that's not defined by the C language, and it's not defined by any of the standard library functions, either.

Stylistically, the character-copying program above can be said to have one minor flaw: it contains two calls to getchar, one which reads the first character and one which reads (by virtue of the fact that it's in the body of the loop) all the other characters.

This seems inelegant and perhaps unnecessary, and it can also be risky: if there were more things going on within the loop, and if we ever changed the way we read characters, it would be easy to change one of the getchar calls but forget to change the other one.

Is there a way to rewrite the loop so that there is only one call to getchar, responsible for reading all the characters? Is there a way to read a character, test it for EOF, and assign it to the variable c, all at the same time?

There is. It relies on the fact that the assignment operator, =, is just another operator in C. An assignment is not (necessarily) a standalone statement; it is an expression, and it has a value (the value that's assigned to the variable on the left-hand side), and it can therefore participate in a larger, surrounding expression. Therefore, most C programmers would write the character-copying loop like this:

```
while((c = getchar()) != EOF)
putchar(c);
```

The function getchar is called, as before, and its return value is assigned to the variable c. Then the value is immediately compared against the value EOF. Finally, the true/false value of the comparison controls the whileloop: as long as the value is not EOF, the loop continues executing, but as soon as an EOF is received, no more trips through the loop are taken, and it exits. The net result is that the call to getchar happens inside the test at the top of the whileloop, and doesn't have to be repeated before the loop and within the loop (more on this in a bit).

Stated another way, the syntax of a while loop is always

```
while(expression)...
```

A comparison (using the != operator) is of course an expression; the syntax is

```
expression != expression
```

And an assignment is an expression; the syntax is

```
expression = expression
```

What we're seeing is just another example of the fact that expressions can be combined with essentially limitless generality and therefore infinite variety. The left-hand side of the != operator (its first *expression*) is the (sub)expression c = getchar(), and the combined expression is the *expression* needed by the while loop.

The extra parentheses around,

```
(c = getchar())
```

are important, and are there because because the *precedence* of the != operator is higher than that of the = operator.

If we (incorrectly) wrote,

```
while(c = getchar() != EOF)  /* WRONG */
```

the compiler would interpret it as

```
while(c = (getchar() != EOF))
```

That is, it would assign the result of the != operator to the variable c, which is *not* what we want. ("Precedence" refers to the rules for which operators are applied to their operands in which order, that is, to the rules controlling the default grouping of expressions and subexpressions. For example, the multiplication operator * has higher precedence than the addition operator +, which means that the expression a + b * c is parsed as a + (b * c). We'll have more to say about precedence later.)

The line,

```
while((c = getchar()) != EOF)
```

epitomizes the cryptic brevity which C is notorious for. You may find this terseness infuriating (and you're not alone!), and it can certainly be carried too far, but bear with me for a moment while I defend it. The simple example we've been discussing illustrates the tradeoffs well.

We have four things to do:

- Call getchar,
- Assign its return value to a variable,
- Test the return value against EOF, and
- Process the character (in this case, print it out again).

We can't eliminate any of these steps. We have to assign getchar's value to a variable because we have to do two different things with it (test, and print).

Therefore, compressing the assignment and test into the same line is the only good way of avoiding two distinct calls to getchar. You may not agree that the compressed idiom is better for being more compact or easier to read, but the fact that there is now only one call to getchar *is* a real virtue. Don't think that you'll have to write compressed lines like,

```
while((c = getchar()) != EOF)
```

right away, or in order to be an "expert C programmer." But, for better or worse, most experienced C programmers do like to use these idioms (whether they're justified or not), so you'll need to be able to at least recognize and understand them when you're reading other peoples' code.

READING LINES

It's often convenient for a program to process its input not a character at a time but rather a line at a time, that is, to read an entire line of input and then act on it all at once. The standard C library has a couple of functions for reading lines, but they have a few awkward features, so we're going to learn more about character input (and about writing functions in general) by writing our own function to read one line.

Here it is:

```
#include <stdio.h>
/* Read one line from standard input, */
/* copying it to line array (but no more than
  max chars). */
/* Does not place terminating \n in line
  array. */
/* Returns line length, or 0 for empty line,
  or EOF for end-of-file.
*/int getline(char line[], int max)
{
int nch = 0;
int c;
max = max - 1; /* leave room for '\0' */
while((c = getchar()) != EOF)
{
if(c == '\n')
```

```
break;
if(nch < max)
{
line[nch] = c;
nch = nch + 1;
}
}
if(c == EOF && nch == 0)
return EOF;
line[nch] = '\0';
return nch;
}
```

As the comment indicates, this function will read one line of input from the standard input, placing it into the line array. The size of the line array is given by the max argument; the function will never write more than max characters into line.

The main body of the function is a getchar loop, much as we used in the character-copying program. In the body of this loop, however, we're storing the characters in an array. Also, we're only reading one line of characters, then stopping and returning.

First of all, the getline function accepts an array as a parameter. As we've said, array parameters are an exception to the rule that functions receive copies of their arguments—in the case of arrays, the function *does* have access to the actual array passed by the caller, and *can* modify it.

Since the function is accessing the caller's array, not creating a new one to hold a copy, the function does not have to declare the argument array's size; it's set by the caller. However, so that we won't overflow the caller's array by reading too long a line into it, we allow the caller to pass along the size of the array, which we promise not to exceed.

Second, we see an example of the break statement. The top of the loop looks like our earlier character-copying loop—it stops when it reaches EOF—but we only want this loop to read one line, so we also stop (that is, break out of the loop) when we see the \n character signifying end-of-line.

An equivalent loop, without the break statement, would be,

```
while((c = getchar()) != EOF && c != '\n')
{
if(nch < max)
{
line[nch] = c;
nch = nch + 1;
}
}
```

We haven't learned about the internal representation of strings yet, but it turns out that strings in C are simply arrays of characters, which is why we are reading the line into an array of characters. The end of a string is marked by the special character, '\0'. To make sure that there's always room for that character, on our way in we subtract 1 from max, the argument that tells us how many characters we may place in the line array. When we're done reading the line, we store the end-of-string character '\0' at the end of the string we've just built in the line array.

Finally, there's one subtlety in the code which isn't too important for our purposes now but which you may wonder about: it's arranged to handle the possibility that a few characters (*i.e.* the apparent beginning of a line) are read, followed immediately by an EOF, without the usual \n end-of-line character.

In any case, the function returns the length (number of characters) of the line it read, not including the \n. (Therefore, it returns 0 for an empty line.) Like getchar, it returns EOF when there are no more lines to read. (It happens that EOF is a negative number, so it will never match the length of a line that getline has read.)

Here is an example of a test program which calls getline, reading the input a line at a time and then printing each line back out:

```
#include <stdio.h>
extern int getline(char [], int);
main()
{
```

```
char line[256];
while(getline(line, 256) != EOF)
printf("you typed \"%s\"\n", line);
return 0;
}
```

The notation char [] in the function prototype for getline says that getline accepts as its first argument an array ofchar. When the program calls getline, it is careful to pass along the actual size of the array. You might notice a potential problem: since the number 256 appears in two places, if we ever decide that 256 is too small, and that we want to be able to read longer lines, we could easily change one of the instances of 256, and forget to change the other one.

READING NUMBERS

The getline function of the previous section reads one line from the user, as a *string*. What if we want to read a number? One straightforward way is to read a string as before, and then immediately convert the string to a number. The standard C library contains a number of functions for doing this. The simplest to use are atoi(), which converts a string to an integer, and atof(), which converts a string to a floating-point number. (Both of these functions are declared in the header<stdlib.h>, so you should #include that header at the top of any file using these functions.)

You could read an integer from the user like this:

```
#include <stdlib.h>
char line[256];
int n;
printf("Type an integer:\n");
getline(line, 256);
n = atoi(line);
```

Now the variable n contains the number typed by the user. (This assumes that the user *did* type a valid number, and thatgetline did not return EOF.)

Reading a floating-point number is similar:

```
#include <stdlib.h>
char line[256];
```

```
double x;
printf("Type a floating-point number:\n");
getline(line, 256);
x = atof(line);
```

(atof is actually declared as returning type double, but you could also use it with a variable of type float, because in general, C automatically converts between float and double as needed.) Another way of reading in numbers, which you're likely to see in other books on C, involves the scanf function, but it has several problems, so we won't discuss it for now. (Superficially, scanf seems simple enough, which is why it's often used, especially in textbooks. The trouble is that to perform input reliably using scanf is not nearly as easy as it looks, especially when you're not sure what the user is going to type.)

FORMATTED I/O

There are a number of related functions used for formatted I/O, each one determining the format of the I/O from a *format string*. For output, the format string consists of plain text, which is output unchanged, and embedded *format specifications* which call for some special processing of one of the remaining arguments to the function. On input, the plain text must match what is seen in the input stream; the format specifications again specify what the meaning of remaining arguments is.

Each format specification is introduced by a % character, followed by the rest of the specification.

OUTPUT: THE PRINTF FAMILY

For those functions performing output, the format specification takes the following form, with optional parts enclosed in brackets:

```
%<flags><field width><precision><length>
 conversion
```

The meaning of *flags*, *field width*, *precision*, *length*, and *conversion* are given below, although tersely. For more detail, it is worth looking at what the Standard says.

Flags

Zero or more of the following:

- Left justify the conversion within its field.

+ A signed conversion will always start with a plus or minus sign.

Space

If the first character of a signed conversion is not a sign, insert a space. Overridden by + if present.

\# Forces an alternative form of output. The first digit of an octal conversion will always be a 0; inserts 0X in front of a non-zero hexadecimal conversion; forces a decimal point in all floating point conversions even if one is not necessary; does not remove trailing zeros from g and G conversions.

0 Pad d, i, o, u, x, X, e, E, f, F and G conversions on the left with zeros up to the field width. Overidden by the - flag. If a precision is specified for the d, i, o, u, x or X conversions, the flag is ignored. The behaviour is undefined for other conversions.

Field width

A decimal integer specifying the minimum output field width. This will be exceeded if necessary. If an asterisk is used here, the next argument is converted to an integer and used for the value of the field width; if the value is negative it is treated as a - flag followed by a positive field width. Output that would be less than the field width is padded with spaces (zeros if the*field width* integer starts with a zero) to fit. The padding is on the left unless the left-adjustment flag is specified.

Precision

This starts with a period '.'. It specifies the minimum number of digits for d,i, o, u, x, or X conversions; the number of digits after the decimal point for e,E, f conversions; the maximum number of digits for g and G conversions; the number of characters to be printed from a string for s conversion.

The amount of padding overrides the field width. If an asterisk is used here, the next argument is converted to an integer and used for the value of the field width. If the value is negative, it is treated as if it were missing. If only the period is present, the precision is taken to be zero.

Length

The preceding a specifier to print an integral type causes it to be treated as if it were a short. (Note that the various sorts of short are always promoted to one of the flavours of int when passed as an argument.) l works like h but applies to a long integral argument.

L is used to indicate that a long doubleargument is to be printed, and only applies to the floating-point specifiers. These are cause undefined behaviour if they are used with the 'wrong' type of conversion.

INPUT SCANF

A number of functions exist analogous to the printf family, but for the purposes of input instead. The most immediate difference between the two families is that thescanf group needs to be passed *pointers* to their arguments, so that the values read can be assigned to the proper destinations. Forgetting to pass a pointer is a very common error, and one which the compiler cannot detect—the variable argument list prevents it.

The format string is used to control interpretation of a stream of input data, which generally contains values to be assigned to the objects pointed to by the remaining arguments to scanf. The contents of the format string may contain:

White Space

This causes the input stream to be read up to the next non-white-space character.

Ordinary Character

Anything except white-space or % characters. The next character in the input stream must match this character.

Conversion Specification

This is a % character, followed by an optional * character (which suppresses the conversion), followed by an optional nonzero decimal integer specifying the maximum field width, an optional h, l or L to control the length of the conversion and finally a non-optional conversion specifier. Note that use ofh, l, or L will affect the type of pointer which must be used. Except for the specifiers c, n and [, a field of input is a sequence of non-space characters starting at the first non-space character in the input. It terminates at the first conflicting character or when the input field width is reached. The result is put into wherever the corresponding argument points, unless the assignment is suppressed using the * mentioned already.

The following conversion specifiers may be used:

`d i o u x`

Convert a signed integer, a signed integer in a form acceptable to strtol, an octal integer, an unsigned integer and a hexadecimal integer respectively.

`e f g`

Convert a float (not a double).

`s`

Read a string, and add a null at the end. The string is terminated by whitespace on input (which is not read as part of the string).

`[`

Read a string. A list of characters, called the *scan set* follows the [. A]delimits the list. Characters are read until (but not including) the first character which is not in the scan set. If the first character in the list is a circumflex ^, then the scan set includes any character not in the list. If the initial sequence is [^] or [], the] is not a delimiter, but part of the list and another] will be needed to end the list. If there is a minus sign (-) in the list, it must be either the first or the last character; otherwise the meaning is implementation defined.

`c`

Read a single character; white space is significant here. To read the first non-white space character, use %1s. A field width indicates that an array of characters is to be read.

`p`

Read a (void *) pointer previously written out using the %p of one of theprintfs.

`%`

A % is expected in the input, no assignment is made.

`n`

Return as an integer the number of characters read by this call so far. The size specifiers have the effect shown in Table.

Table. Size Specifiers

Specifier	Modifies	Converts
l	d i o u x	long int
h	d i o u x	short int
l	e f	double
L	e f	long double

The functions are described below, with the following declarations:

```
#include <stdio.h>
int fscanf(FILE *stream, const char
  *format...);
int sscanf(const char *s, const char
  *format...);
int scanf(const char *format...);
```

Fscanf takes its input from the designated stream, scanf is identical to fscanfwith a first argument of stdin, and sscanf takes its input from the designated character array. If an input failure occurs before any conversion, EOF is returned. Otherwise, the number of successful conversions is returned: this may be zero if no conversions are performed. An input failure is caused by reading EOF or reaching the end of the input string (as appropriate). A conversion failure is caused by a failure to match the proper pattern for a particular conversion.

OPERATORS

`v = v op e`

where *v* is any variable (or anything like a[i]), *op* is any of the binary arithmetic operators we've seen so far, and *e* is any expression, you can replace it with the simplified,

```
v op= e
```

For example, you can replace the expressions,

```
i = i + 1
j = j - 10
k = k * (n + 1)
a[i] = a[i]/b
```

with,

```
i += 1
j -= 10
k *= n + 1
a[i]/= b
```

In an example, we used the assignment,

```
a[d1 + d2] = a[d1 + d2] + 1;
```

to count the rolls of a pair of dice. Using +=, we could simplify this expression to,

```
a[d1 + d2] += 1;
```

As these examples show, you can use the "op=" form with any of the arithmetic operators (and with several other operators that we haven't seen yet). The expression, *e*, does not have to be the constant 1; it can be any expression. You don't always need as many explicit parentheses when using the *op*= operators: the expression

```
k *= n + 1
```

is interpreted as,

```
k = k * (n + 1)
```

INCREMENT AND DECREMENT OPERATORS

The assignment operators of the previous section let us replace *v* = *v op e* with *v op*= *e*, so that we didn't have to mention*v* twice. In the most common cases, namely when we're adding or subtracting the constant 1 (that is, when *op* is + or – and*e* is 1), C provides another set of shortcuts: the *autoincrement* and *autodecrement* operators.

In their simplest forms, they look like this:

```
++i add 1 to i
—j  subtract 1 from j
```

These correspond to the slightly longer i += 1 and j - = 1, respectively, and also to the fully "longhand" forms i = i + 1 and j = j – 1.

The ++ and — operators apply to one operand (they're *unary* operators). The expression ++i adds 1 to i, and stores the incremented result back in i. This means that these operators don't just compute new values; they also modify the value of some variable. (They share this property—modifying some variable—with the assignment operators; we can say that these operators all have *side effects*. That is, they have some effect, on the side, other than just computing a new value.) The incremented (or decremented) result is also made available to the rest of the expression, so an expression like,

```
k = 2 * ++i
```

means "add one to i, store the result back in i, multiply it by 2, and store *that* result in k." (This is a pretty meaningless expression; our actual uses of ++ later will make more sense.)

Both the ++ and — operators have an unusual property: they can be used in two ways, depending on whether they are written to the left or the right of the variable they're operating on. In either case, they increment or decrement the variable they're operating on; the difference concerns whether it's the old or the new value that's "returned" to the surrounding expression. The *prefix* form ++i increments i and returns the incremented value.

The *postfix* form i++ increments i, but returns the *prior*, non-incremented value. Rewriting our previous example slightly, the expression,

```
k = 2 * i++
```

means "take i's old value and multiply it by 2, increment i, store the result of the multiplication in k." The distinction between the prefix and postfix forms of ++ and — will probably seem strained at first, but it will make more sense once we begin using these operators in more realistic situations.

For example, our getline function used the statements,

```
line[nch] = c;
nch = nch + 1;
```

as the body of its inner loop. Using the ++ operator, we could simplify this to,

```
line[nch++] = c;
```

We wanted to increment nch *after* deciding which element of the line array to store into, so the postfix form nch++ is appropriate. Notice that it only makes sense to apply the ++ and – operators to variables (or to other "containers," such as a). It would be meaningless to say something like

```
1++
```

or

```
(2+3)++
```

The ++ operator doesn't just mean "add one"; it means "add one *to a variable*" or "make a variable's value one more than it was before." But (1+2) is not a variable, it's an expression; so there's no place for ++ to store the incremented result.

Another unfortunate example is,

```
i = i++;
```

which some confused programmers sometimes write, presumably because they want to be extra sure that i is incremented by 1. But i++ all by itself is sufficient to increment i by 1; the extra (explicit) assignment to i is unnecessary and in fact counterproductive, meaningless, and incorrect. If you want to increment i (that is, add one to it, and store the result back in i), either use,

```
i = i + 1;
```

or

```
i += 1;
```

or

```
++i;
```

or

```
i++;
```

Don't try to use some bizarre combination. Did it matter whether we used ++i or i++ in this last example? Remember, the difference between the two forms is what value (either the old or the new) is passed on to the surrounding expression. If there is no surrounding expression, if the++i or i++ appears all by itself, to increment i and do nothing else, you can use either form; it makes no difference. (Two ways that an expression can appear "all by itself," with "no surrounding expression," are when it is an expression statement terminated by a semicolon, as above, or when it is one of the controlling expressions of a for loop.) For example, both the loops

```
for(i = 0; i < 10; ++i)
printf("%d\n", i);
and
for(i = 0; i < 10; i++)
printf("%d\n", i);
```

will behave exactly the same way and produce exactly the same results. (In real code, postfix increment is probably more common, though prefix definitely has its uses, too.)

In the preceding section, we simplified the expression

```
a[d1 + d2] = a[d1 + d2] + 1;
```

from previous

```
a[d1 + d2] += 1;
```

Using ++, we could simplify it still further to

```
a[d1 + d2]++;
```

or

```
++a[d1 + d2];
```

(Again, in this case, both are equivalent.)

ORDER OF EVALUATION

When you start using the ++ and – operators in larger expressions, you end up with expressions which do several things at once, *i.e.*, they modify several different variables at more or less the same time. When you write such an expression, you must be careful not to have the expression "pull the rug out from under itself" by assigning two different values to the same variable, or by assigning a new value to a variable at the same time that another part of the expression is trying to use the value of that variable.

Actually, we had already started writing expressions which did several things at once even before we met the ++ and –operators.

The expression,

```
(c = getchar()) != EOF
```

assigns getchar's return value to c, *and* compares it to EOF. The ++ and — operators make it much easier to cram a lot into a small expression: the example

```
line[nch++] = c;
```

from the previous section assigned c to line[nch], *and* incremented nch. We'll eventually meet expressions which do*three* things at once, such as

```
a[i++] = b[j++];
```

which assigns b[j] to a[i], and increments i, *and* increments j.

If you're not careful, though, it's easy for this sort of thing to get out of hand. Can you figure out exactly what the expression

```
a[i++] = b[i++]; /* WRONG */
```

should do? I can't, and here's the important part: *neither can the compiler*. We know that the definition of postfix ++ is that the former value, before the increment, is what goes on to participate in the rest of the expression, but the expressiona[i++] = b[i++] contains *two* ++ operators. Which of them happens first? Does this expression assign the old ith element of b to the new ith element of a, or vice versa? No one knows.

When the order of evaluation matters but is not well-defined (that is, when we can't say for sure which order the compiler will evaluate the various dependent parts in) we say that the meaning of the expression is *undefined*, and if we're smart we won't write the expression in the first place. (Why would anyone ever write an "undefined" expression? Because sometimes, the compiler happens to evaluate it in the order a programmer wanted, and the programmer assumes that since it works, it must be okay.)

For example, suppose we carelessly wrote this loop:

```
int i, a[10];
i = 0;
while(i < 10)
a[i] = i++; /* WRONG */
```

It looks like we're trying to set a[0] to 0, a[1] to 1, etc. But what if the increment i++ happens before the compiler decides which cell of the array a to store the (unincremented) result in? We might end up setting a[1] to 0, a[2] to 1, etc., instead. Since, in this case, we can't be sure which order things would happen in, we simply shouldn't write code like this. In this case, what we're doing matches the pattern of a for loop, anyway, which would be a better choice:

```
for(i = 0; i < 10; i++)
a[i] = i;
```

Now that the increment i++ isn't crammed into the same expression that's setting a[i], the code is perfectly well-defined, and is guaranteed to do what we want.

In general, you should be wary of ever trying to second-guess the order an expression will be evaluated in, with two exceptions:

- You can obviously assume that precedence will dictate the order in which binary operators are applied. This typically says more than just what order things happens in, but also what the expression actually *means*. (In other words, the precedence of * over + says more than that the multiplication "happens first" in 1 + 2 * 3; it says that the answer is 7, not 9.)
- Although we haven't mentioned it yet, it is guaranteed that the logical operators && and || are evaluated left-to-right, and that the right-hand side is not evaluated at all if the left-hand side determines the outcome.

To look at one more example, it might seem that the code:

```
int i = 7;
printf("%d\n", i++ * i++);
```

would have to print 56, because no matter which order the increments happen in, 7*8 is 8*7 is 56. But ++ just says that the increment happens later, not that it happens immediately, so this code could print 49 (if the compiler chose to perform the multiplication first, and both increments later). And, it turns out that ambiguous expressions like this are such a bad idea that the ANSI C Standard does not require compilers to do anything reasonable with them at all. Theoretically, the above code could end up printing 42, or 8923409342, or 0, or crashing your computer. Programmers sometimes mistakenly imagine that they can write an expression which tries to do too much at once and then predict exactly how it will behave based on "order of evaluation." For example, we know that multiplication has higher*precedence* than addition, which means that in the expression

```
i + j * k
```

j will be multiplied by k, and then i will be added to the result. Informally, we often say that the multiplication happens "before" the addition. That's true in this case, but it doesn't say as much as we might think about a more complicated expression, such as,

```
i++ + j++ * k++
```

In this case, besides the addition and multiplication, i, j, and k are all being incremented. We can *not* say which of them will be incremented first; it's the compiler's choice. (In particular, it is *not* necessarily the case that j++ or k++ will happen first; the compiler might choose to save i's value somewhere and increment i first, even though it will have to keep the old value around until after it has done the multiplication.)

In the preceding example, it probably doesn't matter which variable is incremented first. It's not too hard, though, to write an expression where it does matter. In fact, we've seen one already: the ambiguous assignment a[i++] = b[i++]. We still don't know which i++ happens first. (We can *not* assume, based on the right-to-left behaviour of the = operator, that the right-hand i++ will happen first.) But if we had to know what a[i++] = b[i++] really did, we'd have to know whichi++ happened first.

Finally, note that parentheses don't dictate overall evaluation order any more than precedence does. Parentheses override precedence and say which operands go with which operators, and they therefore affect the overall meaning of an expression, but they don't say anything about the order of subexpressions or side effects. We could not "fix" the evaluation order of any of the expressions we've been discussing by adding parentheses. If we wrote

```
i++ + (j++ * k++)
```

we still wouldn't know which of the increments would happen first. (The parentheses would force the multiplication to happen before the addition, but precedence already would have forced that, anyway.)

If we wrote,

```
(i++) * (i++)
```

the parentheses wouldn't force the increments to happen before the multiplication or in any well-defined order; this parenthesized version would be just as undefined as i++ * i++ was.

There's a line from Kernighan & Ritchie, which I am fond of quoting when discussing these issues: The moral is that writing code that depends on order of evaluation is a bad programming practice in any language. Naturally, it is necessary to know what things to avoid, but if you don't know *how* they are done on various machines, you won't be tempted to take advantage of a particular implementation.

The first edition of K&R said...if you don't know *how* they are done on various machines, that innocence may help to protect you.

I actually prefer the first edition wording. Many textbooks encourage you to write small programs to find out how your compiler implements some of these ambiguous expressions, but it's just one step from writing a small program to find out, to writing a real program which makes use of what you've just learned. But you *don't* want to write programs that work only under one particular compiler, that take advantage of the way that one compiler (but perhaps no other) happens to implement the undefined expressions. It's fine to be curious about what goes on "under the hood," and many of you will be curious enough about what's going on with these "forbidden" expressions that you'll want to investigate them, but please keep very firmly in mind that, for real programs, the very easiest way of dealing with ambiguous, undefined expressions (which one compiler interprets one way and another interprets another way and a third crashes on) is not to write them in the first place.

8

Programming Strings

STRING

In fact, C's only truly built-in string-handling is that it allows us to use *string constants* (also called *string literals*) in our code. Whenever we write a string, enclosed in double quotes, C automatically creates an array of characters for us, containing that string, terminated by the \0 character. For example, we can declare and define an array of characters, and initialize it with a string constant:

```
char string[] = "Hello, world!";
```

In this case, we can leave out the dimension of the array, since the compiler can compute it for us based on the size of the initializer (14, including the terminating \0). This is the only case where the compiler sizes a string array for us, however; in other cases, it will be necessary that *we* decide how big the arrays and other data structures we use to hold strings are. To do anything else with strings, we must typically call functions. The C library contains a few basic string manipulation functions, and to learn more about strings, we'll be looking at how these functions might be implemented.

Since C never lets us assign entire arrays, we use the strcpy function to copy one string to another:

```
#include <string.h>
char string1[] = "Hello, world!";
char string2[20];
strcpy(string2, string1);
```

The destination string is strcpy's first argument, so that a call to strcpy mimics an assignment expression (with the destination on the left-hand side). Notice that we had to allocate string2 big enough to hold the string that would be copied to it. Also, at the top of any source file where we're using the standard library's string-handling functions (such as strcpy) we must include the line

```
#include <string.h>
```

which contains external declarations for these functions.

Since C won't let us compare entire arrays, either, we must call a function to do that, too. The standard library's strcmp function compares two strings, and returns 0 if they are identical, or a negative number if the first string is alphabetically "less than" the second string, or a positive number if the first string is "greater." (Roughly speaking, what it means for one string to be "less than" another is that it would come first in a dictionary or telephone book, although there are a few anomalies.)

Here is an example:

```
char string3[] = "this is";
char string4[] = "a test";
if(strcmp(string3, string4) == 0)
printf("strings are equal\n");
else printf("strings are different\n");
```

This code fragment will print "strings are different". Notice that strcmp does *not* return a Boolean, true/false, zero/nonzero answer, so it's not a good idea to write something like,

```
if(strcmp(string3, string4))
...
```

because it will behave backwards from what you might reasonably expect. (Nevertheless, if you start reading other people's code, you're likely to come across conditionals like if(strcmp(a, b)) or even if(!strcmp(a, b)). The first does something if the strings are unequal; the second does something if they're equal. You can read these more easily if you pretend for a moment that strcmp's name were strdiff, instead.)

Another standard library function is strcat, which concatenates strings. It does *not* concatenate two strings together and give you a third, new string; what it really does is append one string onto the end of another. (If it gave you a new string, it would have to allocate memory for it somewhere, and the standard library string functions generally never do that for you automatically.)

Here's an example:

```
char string5[20] = "Hello, ";
char string6[] = "world!";
printf("%s\n", string5);
strcat(string5, string6);
printf("%s\n", string5);
```

The first call to printf prints "Hello, ", and the second one prints "Hello, world!", indicating that the contents of string6 have been tacked on to the end ofstring5. Notice that we declared string5 with extra space, to make room for the appended characters. If you have a string and you want to know its length (perhaps so that you can check whether it will fit in some other array you've allocated for it), you can callstrlen, which returns the length of the string (*i.e.* the number of characters in it), not including the \0:

```
char string7[] = "abc";
int len = strlen(string7);
printf("%d\n", len);
```

Finally, you can print strings out with printf using the %s format specifier, as we've been doing in these examples already (*e.g.* printf("%s\n", string5);).

Since a string is just an array of characters, all of the string-handling functions we've just seen can be written quite simply, using no techniques more complicated than the ones we already know. In fact, it's quite instructive to look at how these functions might be implemented.

Here is a version of strcpy:

```
mystrcpy(char dest[], char src[])
{
int i = 0;
while(src[i] != '\0')
{
dest[i] = src[i];
i++;
```

```
}
dest[i] = '\0';
}
```

We've called it mystrcpy instead of strcpy so that it won't clash with the version that's already in the standard library. Its operation is simple: it looks at characters in the src string one at a time, and as long as they're not \0, assigns them, one by one, to the corresponding positions in the dest string. When it's done, it terminates the dest string by appending a \0. (After exiting the while loop, i is guaranteed to have a value one greater than the subscript of the last character in src.) For comparison, here's a way of writing the same code, using a for loop:

```
for(i = 0; src[i] != '\0'; i++)
dest[i] = src[i];
dest[i] = '\0';
```

Yet a third possibility is to move the test for the terminating \0 character out of the for loop header and into the body of the loop, using an explicit if and breakstatement, so that we can perform the test after the assignment and therefore use the assignment inside the loop to copy the \0 to dest, too:

```
for(i = 0;; i++)
{
dest[i] = src[i];
if(src[i] == '\0')
break;
}
```

Here is a version of strcmp:

```
mystrcmp(char str1[], char str2[])
{
int i = 0;
while(1)
{
if(str1[i] != str2[i])
return str1[i] - str2[i];
if(str1[i] == '\0' || str2[i] == '\0')
return 0;
```

```
i++;
}
}
```

Characters are compared one at a time. If two characters in one position differ, the strings are different, and we are supposed to return a value less than zero if the first string (str1) is alphabetically less than the second string. Since characters in C are represented by their numeric character set values, and since most reasonable character sets assign values to characters in alphabetical order, we can simply subtract the two differing characters from each other: the expression str1[i] - str2[i] will yield a negative result if the i'th character of str1 is less than the corresponding character in str2. (As it turns out, this will behave a bit strangely when comparing upper- and lower-case letters, but it's the traditional approach, which the standard versions of strcmp tend to use.) If the characters are the same, we continue around the loop, *unless* the characters we just compared were (both) \0, in which case we've reached the end of both strings, and they were both equal. Notice that we used what may at first appear to be an infinite loop—the controlling expression is the constant 1, which is always true. What actually happens is that the loop runs until one of the two return statements breaks out of it (and the entire function). Note also that when one string is longer than the other, the first test will notice this (because one string will contain a real character at the [i] location, while the other will contain \0, and these are not equal) and the return value will be computed by subtracting the real character's value from 0, or vice versa. (Thus the shorter string will be treated as "less than" the longer.)

Finally, here is a version of strlen:

```
int mystrlen(char str[])
{
int i;
for(i = 0; str[i] != '\0'; i++)
{}
return i;
}
```

In this case, all we have to do is find the \0 that terminates the string, and it turns out that the three control expressions of the for loop do all the work; there's nothing left to do in the body. Therefore, we use an empty pair of braces {} as the loop body.

Equivalently, we could use a null statement, which is simply a semicolon:

```
for(i = 0; str[i] != '\0'; i++)
;
```

Empty loop bodies can be a bit startling at first, but they're not unheard of. Everything we've looked at so far has come out of C's standard libraries. As one last example, let's write a substr function, for extracting a substring out of a larger string.

We might call it like this:

```
char string8[] = "this is a test";
char string9[10];
substr(string9, string8, 5, 4);
printf("%s\n", string9);
```

The idea is that we'll extract a substring of length 4, starting at character 5 (0-based) of string8, and copy the substring to string9. Just as with strcpy, it's our responsibility to declare the destination string (string9) big enough. Here is an implementation of substr. Not surprisingly, it's quite similar to strcpy:

```
substr(char dest[], char src[], int offset,
  int len)
{
int i;
for(i = 0; i < len && src[offset + i] !=
  '\0'; i++)
dest[i] = src[i + offset];
dest[i] = '\0';
}
```

If you compare this code to the code for mystrcpy, you'll see that the only differences are that characters are fetched from src[offset + i] instead of src[i], and that the loop stops when len characters have been copied (or when the src string runs out of characters, whichever comes first). In this, we've been careless about declaring the return types of the string functions, and (with the exception of mystrlen) they haven't returned values. The real string functions do return values, but they're of type "pointer to character," which we haven't discussed yet.

When working with strings, it's important to keep firmly in mind the differences between characters and strings. We must also occasionally remember the way characters are represented, and about the relation between character values and integers.

As we have had several occasions to mention, a character is represented internally as a small integer, with a value depending on the character set in use. For example, we might find that 'A' had the value 65, that 'a' had the value 97, and that '+' had the value 43.

These are, in fact, the values in the ASCII character set, which most computers use. However, you don't need to learn these values, because the vast majority of the time, you use character constants to refer to characters, and the compiler worries about the values for you. Using character constants in preference to raw numeric values also makes your programs more portable.

As we may also have mentioned, there is a big difference between a character and a string, even a string which contains only one character (other than the \0). For example, 'A' is *not* the same as "A". To drive home this point, let's illustrate it with a few examples.

If you have a string:

```
char string[] = "hello, world!";
```

```
you can modify its first character by saying
```

```
string[0] = 'H';
```

(Of course, there's nothing magic about the first character; you can modify any character in the string in this way. Be aware, though, that it is not always safe to modify strings in-place like this; we'll say more about the modifiability of strings on pointers.) Since you're replacing a character, you want a character constant, 'H'.

It would not be right to write:

```
string[0] = "H"; /* WRONG */
```

because "H" is a string (an array of characters), not a single character. (The destination of the assignment, string[0], is a char, but the right-hand side is a string; these types don't match.) On the other hand, when you need a string, you must use a string.

To print a single newline, you could call,

```
printf("\n");
It would not be correct to call
printf('\n'); /* WRONG */
```

printf always wants a string as its first argument. (As one final example, putchar wants a single character, so putchar ('\n') would be correct, andputchar("\n") would be incorrect.) We must also remember the difference between strings and integers. If we treat the character '1' as an integer, perhaps by saying,

```
int i = '1';
```

we will probably *not* get the value 1 in i; we'll get the value of the character '1' in the machine's character set. (In ASCII, it's 49.) When we do need to find the numeric value of a digit character (or to go the other way, to get the digit character with a particular value) we can make use of the fact that, in any character set used by C, the values for the digit characters, whatever they are, are contiguous. In other words, no matter what values '0' and '1' have, '1' - '0' will be 1 (and, obviously, '0' - '0' will be 0). So, for a variable c holding some digit character, the expression,

```
c - '0'
```

gives us its value. (Similarly, for an integer value i, i + '0' gives us the corresponding digit character, as long as 0 <= i <= 9.)

Just as the character '1' is not the integer 1, the string "123" is not the integer 123. When we have a string of digits, we can convert it to the corresponding integer by calling the standard function atoi:

```
char string[] = "123";
int i = atoi(string);
int j = atoi("456");
```

PREPROCESSOR

Conceptually, the "preprocessor" is a translation phase that is applied to your source code before the compiler proper gets its hands on it. (Once upon a time, the preprocessor was a separate program, much as the compiler and linker may still be separate programs today.) Generally, the preprocessor performs textual substitutions on your source code, in three sorts of ways:

- *File inclusion*: inserting the contents of another file into your source file, as if you had typed it all in there.
- *Macro substitution*: replacing instances of one piece of text with another.
- *Conditional compilation*: Arranging that, depending on various circumstances, certain parts of your source code are seen or not seen by the compiler at all.

The syntax of the preprocessor is different from the syntax of the rest of C in several respects. First of all, the preprocessor is "line based." Each of the preprocessor directives we're going to learn about (all of which begin with the # character) must begin at the beginning of a line, and each ends at the end of the line. (The rest of C treats line ends as just another whitespace character, and doesn't care how your program text is arranged into lines.) Secondly, the preprocessor does not know about the structure of C—about functions, statements, or expressions. It is possible to play strange tricks with the preprocessor to turn something which does not look like C into C (or vice versa).

It's also possible to run into problems when a preprocessor substitution does not do what you expected it to, because the preprocessor does not respect the structure of C statements and expressions (but you expected it to). For the simple uses of the preprocessor we'll be discussing, you shouldn't have any of these problems, but you'll want to be careful before doing anything tricky or outrageous with the preprocessor. (As it happens, playing tricky and outrageous games with the preprocessor is considered sporting in some circles, but it rapidly gets out of hand, and can lead to bewilderingly impenetrable programs.)

WORKING OF PREPROCESSOR

The preprocessor doesn't know about the scope rules of C. Preprocessor directives like #define take effect as soon as they are seen and remain in effect until the end of the file that contains them; the program's block structure is irrelevant. This is one of the reasons why it's a good idea to make sparing use of these directives.

The less you have in your program that doesn't obey the 'normal' scope rules, the less likely you are to make mistakes. This is mainly what gives rise to our comments about the poor level of integration between the preprocessor and the rest of C.

The Standard gives some complicated rules for the syntax of the preprocessor, especially with respect to *tokens*. To understand the operation of the preprocessor you need to know a little about them. The text that is being processed is not considered to be a uniform stream of characters, but is separated into tokens then processed piecemeal.

For a full definition of the process, it is best to refer to the Standard, but an informal description follows. Each of the terms used to head the list below is used later in descriptions of the rules.

- Header-name
  - '<' almost any character '>'
- Preprocessing-token
  - A header-name as above but only when the subject of #include,
  - or an identifier which is any C identifier or keyword,
  - or a constant which is any integral or floating constant,
  - or a string-literal which is a normal C string,
  - or an operator which is one of the C operators,
  - or one of [] () {} * ,: =;... # (punctuators)
  - or any non-white-space character not covered by the list above.

The '*almost any character*' above means any character except '>' or newline.

FILE INCLUSION

A line of the form,

```
#include <filename.h>
```

or

```
#include "filename.h"
```

causes the contents of the file filename.h to be read, parsed, and compiled at that point. (After filename.h is processed, compilation continues on the line following the #include line.)

For example, suppose you got tired of retyping external function prototypes such as

```
extern int getline(char [], int);
```

at the top of each source file. You could instead place the prototype in a header file, perhaps getline.h, and then simply place,

```
#include "getline.h"
```

at the top of each source file where you called getline. (You might not find it worthwhile to create an entire header file for a single function, but if you had a package of several related function, it might be very useful to place all of their declarations in one header file.) As we may have mentioned, that's exactly what the Standard header files such as stdio.hare—collections of declarations (including external function prototype declarations) having to do with various sets of Standard library functions. When you use #include to read in a header file, you automatically get the prototypes and other declarations it contains, and you *should* use header files, precisely so that you will get the prototypes and other declarations they contain.

The difference between the <> and "" forms is where the preprocessor searches for filename.h. As a general rule, it searches for files enclosed in <> in central, standard directories, and it searches for files enclosed in "" in the "current directory," or the directory containing the source file that's doing the including. Therefore, "" is usually used for header files you've written, and <> is usually used for headers which are provided for you (which someone else has written).

The extension ".h", by the way, simply stands for "header," and reflects the fact that #include directives usually sit at the top (head) of your source files, and contain global declarations and definitions which you would otherwise put there. (That extension is not mandatory—you can theoretically name your own header files anything you wish—but .h is traditional, and recommended.)

As we've already begun to see, the reason for putting something in a header file, and then using #include to pull that header file into several different source files, is when the something (whatever it is) must be declared or defined consistently in all of the source files.

If, instead of using a header file, you typed the something in to each of the source files directly, and the something ever changed, you'd have to edit all those source files, and if you missed one, your program could fail in subtle (or serious) ways due to the mismatched declarations (*i.e.* due to the incompatibility between the new declaration in one source file and the old one in a source file you forgot to change). Placing common declarations and definitions into header files means that if they ever change, they only have to be changed in one place, which is a much more workable system.

What should you put in header files?

- External declarations of global variables and functions. We said that a global variable must have exactly one*defining instance*, but that it can have *external declarations* in many places. We said that it was a grave error to issue an external declaration in one place saying that a variable or function has one type, when the defining instance in some other place actually defines it with another type. (If the two places are two source files, separately compiled, the compiler will probably not even catch the discrepancy.) If you put the external declarations in a header file, however, and include the header wherever it's needed, the declarations are virtually guaranteed to be consistent. It's a good idea to include the header in the source file where the defining instance appears, too, so that the compiler can check that the declaration and definition match. (That is, if you ever change the type, you do still have to change it in two places: in the source file where the defining instance occurs, and in the header file where the external declaration appears. But at least you don't have to change it in an arbitrary number of places, and, if you've set things up correctly, the compiler can catch any remaining mistakes.)

- Preprocessor macro definitions (which we'll meet in the next section).
- Structure definitions (which we haven't seen yet).
- Typedef declarations (which we haven't seen yet).

However, there are a few things not to put in header files:

- Defining instances of global variables. If you put these in a header file, and include the header file in more than one source file, the variable will end up multiply defined.
- Function bodies (which are also defining instances). You don't want to put these in headers for the same reason—it's likely that you'll end up with multiple copies of the function and hence "multiply defined" errors. People sometimes put commonly-used functions in header files and then use #include to bring them (once) into each program where they use that function, or use #include to bring together the several source files making up a program, but both of these are poor ideas. It's much better to learn how to use your compiler or linker to combine together separately-compiled object files.

Since header files typically contain only external declarations, and should *not* contain function bodies, you have to understand just what does and doesn't happen when you #include a header file. The header file may provide the declarations for some functions, so that the compiler can generate correct code when you call them (and so that it can make sure that you're calling them correctly), but the header file does *not* give the compiler the functions themselves. The actual functions will be combined into your program at the end of compilation, by the part of the compiler called the *linker*.

The linker may have to get the functions out of libraries, or you may have to tell the compiler/linker where to find them. In particular, if you are trying to use a third-party library containing some useful functions, the library will often come with a header file describing those functions.

Using the library is therefore a two-step process: you must #include the header in the files where you call the library functions, *and* you must tell the linker to read in the functions from the library itself.

FILE INCLUSION

A line of the form,

```
#include <filename.h>
```

or

```
#include "filename.h"
```

causes the contents of the file filename.h to be read, parsed, and compiled at that point. (After filename.h is processed, compilation continues on the line following the #include line.) For example, suppose you got tired of retyping external function prototypes such as,

```
extern int getline(char [], int);
```

at the top of each source file. You could instead place the prototype in a header file, perhaps getline.h, and then simply place,

```
#include "getline.h"
```

at the top of each source file where you called getline. (You might not find it worthwhile to create an entire header file for a single function, but if you had a package of several related function, it might be very useful to place all of their declarations in one header file.) As we may have mentioned, that's exactly what the Standard header files such as stdio.hare—collections of declarations (including external function prototype declarations) having to do with various sets of Standard library functions. When you use #include to read in a header file, you automatically get the prototypes and other declarations it contains, and you *should* use header files, precisely so that you will get the prototypes and other declarations they contain.

The difference between the <> and "" forms is where the preprocessor searches for filename.h. As a general rule, it searches for files enclosed in <> in central, standard directories, and it searches for files enclosed in "" in the "current directory," or the directory containing the source file that's doing the including.

Therefore, "" is usually used for header files you've written, and <> is usually used for headers which are provided for you (which someone else has written).

The extension ".h", by the way, simply stands for "header," and reflects the fact that #include directives usually sit at the top (head) of your source files, and contain global declarations and definitions which you would otherwise put there. (That extension is not mandatory—you can theoretically name your own header files anything you wish—but .h is traditional, and recommended.)

As we've already begun to see, the reason for putting something in a header file, and then using #include to pull that header file into several different source files, is when the something (whatever it is) must be declared or defined consistently in all of the source files. If, instead of using a header file, you typed the something in to each of the source files directly, and the something ever changed, you'd have to edit all those source files, and if you missed one, your program could fail in subtle (or serious) ways due to the mismatched declarations (*i.e.* due to the incompatibility between the new declaration in one source file and the old one in a source file you forgot to change).

Placing common declarations and definitions into header files means that if they ever change, they only have to be changed in one place, which is a much more workable system.

- External declarations of global variables and functions. We said that a global variable must have exactly one*defining instance,* but that it can have *external declarations* in many places. We said that it was a grave error to issue an external declaration in one place saying that a variable or function has one type, when the defining instance in some other place actually defines it with another type. (If the two places are two source files, separately compiled, the compiler will probably not even catch the discrepancy.) If you put the external declarations in a header file, however, and include the header wherever it's needed, the declarations are virtually guaranteed to be consistent. It's a good idea to include the header in the source file where the defining instance appears, too, so that the compiler can check that the declaration and definition match. (That is, if you ever change the type, you do still have to change it in two places: in the source file where the defining instance occurs, and in the header file where the external declaration appears. But at least you don't have to change it in an arbitrary number of places, and, if you've set things up correctly, the compiler can catch any remaining mistakes.)

- Preprocessor macro definitions (which we'll meet in the next section).
- Structure definitions (which we haven't seen yet).
- Typedef declarations (which we haven't seen yet).

However, there are a few things not to put in header files:

- Defining instances of global variables. If you put these in a header file, and include the header file in more than one source file, the variable will end up multiply defined.
- Function bodies (which are also defining instances). You don't want to put these in headers for the same reason—it's likely that you'll end up with multiple copies of the function and hence "multiply defined" errors. People sometimes put commonly-used functions in header files and then use #include to bring them (once) into each program where they use that function, or use #include to bring together the several source files making up a program, but both of these are poor ideas. It's much better to learn how to use your compiler or linker to combine together separately-compiled object files.

Since header files typically contain only external declarations, and should *not* contain function bodies, you have to understand just what does and doesn't happen when you #include a header file. The header file may provide the declarations for some functions, so that the compiler can generate correct code when you call them (and so that it can make sure that you're calling them correctly), but the header file does *not* give the compiler the functions themselves.

The actual functions will be combined into your program at the end of compilation, by the part of the compiler called the *linker*. The linker may have to get the functions out of libraries, or you may have to tell the compiler/linker where to find them.

In particular, if you are trying to use a third-party library containing some useful functions, the library will often come with a header file describing those functions. Using the library is therefore a two-step process: you must #include the header in the files where you call the library functions, *and* you must tell the linker to read in the functions from the library itself.

MACRO AND SUBSTITUTION

A preprocessor line of the form,

```
#define name text
```

defines a *macro* with the given name, having as its *value* the given replacement text. After that (for the rest of the current source file), wherever the preprocessor sees that name, it will replace it with the replacement text. The name follows the same rules as ordinary identifiers (it can contain only letters, digits, and underscores, and may not begin with a digit). Since macros behave quite differently from normal variables (or functions), it is customary to give them names which are all capital letters (or at least which begin with a capital letter). The replacement text can be absolutely anything—it's not restricted to numbers, or simple strings, or anything. The most common use for macros is to propagate various constants around and to make them more self-documenting.

We say:

```
char line[100];
```

```
...
getline(line, 100);
```

but this is neither readable nor reliable; it's not necessarily obvious what all those 100's scattered around the program are, and if we ever decide that 100 is too small for the size of the array to hold lines, we'll have to remember to change the number in two (or more) places. A much better solution is to use a macro:

```
#define MAXLINE 100
char line[MAXLINE];
...
getline(line, MAXLINE);
```

Now, if we ever want to change the size, we only have to do it in one place, and it's more obvious what the wordsMAXLINE sprinkled through the program mean than the magic numbers 100 did. Since the replacement text of a preprocessor macro can be anything, it can also be an expression, although you have to realise that, as always, the text is substituted (and perhaps evaluated) later. No evaluation is performed when the macro is defined. For example, suppose that you write something like,

```
#define A 2
#define B 3
#define C A + B
```

(this is a pretty meaningless example, but the situation does come up in practice).

Then, later, suppose that you write,

```
int x = C * 2;
```

If A, B, and C were ordinary variables, you'd expect x to end up with the value 10. But let's see what happens. The preprocessor always substitutes text for macros exactly as you have written it. So it first substitites the replacement text for the macro C, resulting in,

```
int x = A + B * 2;
```

Then it substitutes the macros A and B, resulting in,

```
int x = 2 + 3 * 2;
```

Only when the preprocessor is done doing all this substituting does the compiler get into the act. But when it evaluates that expression (using the normal precedence of multiplication over addition), it ends up initializing x with the value 8! To guard against this sort of problem, it is always a good idea to include explicit parentheses in the definitions of macros which contain expressions. If we were to define the macro C as

```
#define C (A + B)
```

then the declaration of x would ultimately expand to

```
int x = (2 + 3) * 2;
```

and x would be initialized to 10, as we probably expected.

Notice that there does not have to be (and in fact there usually is *not*) a semicolon at the end of a #define line. (This is just one of the ways that the syntax of the preprocessor is different from the rest of C.) If you type

```
#define MAXLINE 100;   /* WRONG */
```

then when you later declare,

char line[MAXLINE];

the preprocessor will expand it to,

```
char line[100;];      /* WRONG */
```

which is a syntax error. This is what we mean when we say that the preprocessor doesn't know much of anything about the syntax of C—in this last example, the *value* or replacement text for the macro MAXLINE was the 4 characters 1 0 0; , and that's exactly what the preprocessor substituted (even though it didn't make any sense). Simple macros like MAXLINE act sort of like little variables, whose values are constant (or constant expressions). It's also possible to have macros which look like little functions (that is, you invoke them with what looks like function call syntax, and they expand to replacement text which is a function of the actual arguments they are invoked with) but we won't be looking at these yet.

CONDITIONAL COMPILATION

The last preprocessor directive we're going to look at is #ifdef.

If you have the sequence,

```
#ifdef name
```

program text,

```
#else
```

more program text,

```
#endif
```

in your program, the code tnat gets compiled depends on whether a preprocessor macro by that *name* is defined or not. If it is (that is, if there has been a #define line for a macro called *name*), then "*program text*" is compiled and "*more program text*" is ignored. If the macro is not defined, "*more program text*" is compiled and "*program text*" is ignored. This looks a lot like an if statement, but it behaves completely differently: an if statement controls which statements of your program are executed at run time, but #ifdef controls which parts of your program actually get compiled.

Just as for the if statement, the #else in an #ifdef is optional. There is a companion directive #ifndef, which compiles code if the macro is *not* defined (although the "#else clause" of an #ifndef directive will then be compiled if the macro*is* defined). There is also an #if directive which compiles code depending on whether a compile-time expression is true or false. (The expressions which are allowed in an #if directive are somewhat restricted, however, so we won't talk much about #if here.)

Conditional compilation is useful in two general classes of situations:

- You are trying to write a portable program, but the way you do something is different depending on what compiler, operating system, or computer you're using. You place different versions of your code, one for each situation, between suitable #ifdef directives, and when you compile the progam in a particular environment, you arrange to have the macro names defined which select the variants you need in that environment. (For this reason, compilers usually have ways of letting you define macros from the invocation command line or in a configuration file, and many also predefine certain macro names related to the operating system, processor, or compiler in use. That way, you don't have to change the code to change the #define lines each time you compile it in a different environment.)

For example, in ANSI C, the function to delete a file is remove. On older Unix systems, however, the function was called unlink. So if filename is a variable containing the name of a file you want to delete, and if you want to be able to compile the program under these older Unix systems, we write

```
#ifdef unix
unlink(filename);
#else
remove(filename);
#endif
```

Then, you could place the line,

```
#define unix
```

at the top of the file when compiling under an old Unix system. (Since all you're using the macro unix for is to control the #ifdef, you don't need to give it any replacement text at all. *Any* definition for a macro, even if the replacement text is empty, causes an #ifdef to succeed.) (In fact, in this example, you wouldn't even need to define the macro unix at all, because C compilers on old Unix systems tend to predefine it for you, precisely so you can make tests like these.)

- You want to compile several different versions of your program, with different features present in the different versions. You bracket the code for each feature with #ifdef directives, and (as for the previous case) arrange to have the right macros defined or not to build the version you want to build at any given time. This way, you can build the several different versions from the same source code. (One common example is whether you turn debugging statements on or off. You can bracket each debugging printout with #ifdef DEBUG and #endif, and then turn on debugging only when you need it.)

For example, you might use lines like this:

```
#ifdef DEBUG
printf("x is %d\n", x);
#endif
```

to print out the value of the variable x at some point in your program to see if it's what you expect. To enable debugging printouts, you insert the line,

```
#define DEBUG
```

at the top of the file, and to turn them off, you delete that line, but the debugging printouts quietly remain in your code, temporarily deactivated, but ready to reactivate if you find yourself needing them again later. (Also, instead of inserting and deleting the #define line, you might use a compiler flag such as -DDEBUG to define the macro DEBUGfrom the compiler invocatin line.)

Conditional compilation can be very handy, but it can also get out of hand. When large chunks of the program are completely different depending on, say, what operating system the program is being compiled for, it's often better to place the different versions in separate source files, and then only use one of the files (corresponding to one of the versions) to build the program on any given system. Also, if you are using an ANSI Standard compiler and you are writing ANSI-compatible code, you usually won't need so much conditional compilation, because the Standard specifies exactly how the compiler must do certain things, and exactly which library functions it much provide, so you don't have to work so hard to accommodate the old variations among compilers and libraries.

DIRECTIVES

Directives are always introduced by a line that starts with a # character, optionally preceded by white space characters (although it isn't common practice to indent the #). Table below is a list of the directives defined in the Standard.

Table. Preprocessor directives

Directive	Meaning
# include	include a source file
# define	define a macro
# undef	undefine a macro
# if	conditional compilation

# ifdef	conditional compilation
# ifndef	conditional compilation
# elif	conditional compilation
# else	conditional compilation
# endif	conditional compilation
# line	control error reporting
# error	force an error message
# pragma	used for implementation-dependent control
#	null directive; no effect

The meanings and use of these features are described in the following sections. Make a note that the # and the following keyword, if any, are individual items. They may be separated by white space.

DEFINE

There are two ways of defining *macros*, one of which looks like a function and one which does not.

Here is an example of each:

```
#define FMAC(a,b) a here, then b
#define NONFMAC some text here
```

Both definitions define a macro and some *replacement text*, which will be used to replace later occurrences of the macro name in the rest of the program. After those definitions, they can be used as follows, with the effect of the macro replacement shown in comments:

```
NONFMAC
/* some text here */
FMAC(first text, some more)
/* first text here, then some more */
```

For the non-function macro, its name is simply replaced by its replacement text. The function macro is also replaced by its replacement text; wherever the replacement text contains an identifier which is the name of one of the macro's 'formal parameters', the actual text given as the argument is used in place of the identifier in the replacement text. The scope of the names of the formal parameters is limited to the body of the #define directive.

For both forms of macro, leading or trailing white space around the replacement text is discarded. A curious ambiguity arises with macros: how do you define a non-function macro whose replacement text happens to start with the opening parenthesis character (? The answer is simple. If the definition of the macro has a space in front of the (, then it isn't the definition of a function macro, but a simple replacement macro instead. When you use function-like macros, there's no equivalent restriction. The Standard allows either type of macro to be redefined at any time, using another # define, provided that there isn't any attempt to change the type of the macro and that the tokens making up both the original definition and the redefinition are identical in number, ordering, spelling and use of white space. In this context all white space is considered equal, so this would be correct:

```
# define XXX abc/*comment*/def hij
# define XXX abc def hij
```

because comment is a form of white space. The token sequence for both cases (*w-s* stands for a white-space token) is:

```
# w-s define w-s XXX w-s abc w-s def w-s hij
  w-s
```

MACRO SUBSTITUTION

Where will occurrences of the macro name cause the replacement text to be substituted in its place? Practically anywhere in a program that the identifier is recognized as a separate token, except as the identifier following the # of a preprocessor directive.

You can't do this:

```
#define define XXX
#define YYY ZZZ
```

and expect the second #define to be replaced by #XXX, causing an error. When the identifier associated with a non-function macro is seen, it is replaced by the macro replacement tokens, then *rescanned* for further replacements to make.

Function macros can be used like real functions; white space around the macro name, the argument list and so on, may include the newline character:

```
#define FMAC(a, b) printf("%s %s\n", a, b)
FMAC ("hello",
"sailor"
);
/* results in */
printf("%s %s\n", "hello", "sailor")
```

The 'arguments' of a function macro can be almost any arbitrary token sequence. Commas are used to separate the arguments from each other but can be hidden by enclosing them within parentheses, (and) Matched pairs of (and) inside the argument list balance each other out, so a) only ends the invocation of the macro if the corresponding (is the one that started the macro invocation.

```
#define CALL(a, b) a b
CALL(printf, ("%d %d %s\n",1, 24, "urgh"));
/* results in */
printf ("%d %d %s\n",1, 24, "urgh");
```

Note very carefully that the parentheses around the second argument to CALL were preserved in the replacement: they were not stripped from the text. If you want to use macros like printt, taking a variable number of arguments, the Standard is no help to you. They are not supported. If any argument contains no preprocessor tokens then the behaviour is undefined. The same is true if the sequence of preprocessor tokens that forms the argument would otherwise have been another preprocessor directive:

```
#define CALL(a, b) a b
/* undefined behaviour in each case.... */
CALL(,hello)
CALL(xyz,
#define abc def)
```

In our opinion, the second of the erroneous uses of CALL should result in defined behaviour—anyone capable of writing that would clearly benefit from the attentions of a champion weightlifter wielding a heavy leather bullwhip.

When a function macro is being processed, the steps are as follows:

- All of its arguments are identified.

- Except in the cases listed in item 3 below, if any of the tokens in an argument are themselves candidates for macro replacement, the replacement is done until no further replacement is possible. If this introduces commas into the argument list, there is no danger of the macro suddenly seeming to have a different number of arguments; the arguments are *only* determined in the step above.
- In the macro replacement text, identifiers naming one of the macro formal arguments are replaced by the (by now expanded) token sequence supplied as the actual argument. The replacement is suppressed only if the identifier is preceded by one of # or ##, or followed by ##.

STRINGIZING

There is special treatment for places in the macro replacement text where one of the macro formal parameters is found preceded by #. The token list for the actual argument has any leading or trailing white space discarded, then the # and the token list are turned into a single string literal. Spaces between the tokens are treated as space characters in the string. To prevent 'unexpected' results, any "or \ characters within the new string literal are preceded by \.

This example demonstrates the feature:

```
#define MESSAGE(x) printf("Message: %s\n", #x)
MESSAGE (Text with "quotes");
/*
* Result is
* printf("Message: %s\n", "Text with
  \"quotes\"");
*/
```

RESCANNING

Once the processing described above has occurred, the replacement text plus the following tokens of the source file is rescanned, looking for more macro names to replace. The one exception is that, within a macro's replacement text, the name of the macro itself is not expanded. Because maci ɔ replacement can be nested, it is possible for several macros to be in the process of being replaced at any one point: none of their names is a candidate for further replacement in the 'inner' levels of this process.

This allows redefinition of existing functions as macros:

```
#define exit(x) exit((x)+1)
```

These macro names which were not replaced now become tokens which are immune from future replacement, even if later processing might have meant that they had become available for replacement. This prevents the danger of infinite recursion occurring in the preprocessor. The suppression of replacement is only if the macro name results directly from *replacement* text, not the other source text of the program.

Here we mean:

```
#define m(x) m((x)+1)
/* so */
m(abc);
/* expands to */
m((abc)+1);
/*
* even though the m((abc)+1) above looks like
  a macro,
* the rules say it is not to be re-replaced
*/
m(m(abc));
/*
* the outer m(starts a macro invocation,
* but the inner one is replaced first (as
  above)
* with m((abc)+1), which becomes the argument
  to the outer call,
* giving us effectively
*/
m(m((abc+1));
/*
* which expands to
*/
m((m((abc+1))+1);
```

If that doesn't make your brain hurt, then go and read what the Standard says about it, which will.

NOTES

There is a subtle problem when using arguments to function macros.

```
/* warning - subtle problem in this example
  */
#define SQR(x) (x * x)
/*
* Wherever the formal parameters occur in
* the replacement text, they are replaced
* by the actual parameters to the macro.
*/
printf("sqr of %d is %d\n", 2, SQR(2));
```

The formal parameter of SQR is x; the actual argument is 2. The replacement text results in,

```
printf("sqr of %d is %d\n", 2, (2 * 2));
```

The use of the parentheses should be noticed.

The following example is likely to give trouble:

```
/* bad example */
#define DOUBLE(y) y+y
printf("twice %d is %d\n", 2, DOUBLE(2));
printf("six times %d is %d\n", 2, 3*DOUBLE(2));
```

The problem is that the last expression in the second printf is replaced by,

```
3*2+2
```

which results in 8, not 12! The rule is that when using macros to build expressions, careful parenthesizing is necessary.

Here's another example:

```
SQR(3+4)
/* expands to */
(3+4 * 3+4)
/* oh dear, still wrong! */
```

so, when formal parameters occur in the replacement text, you should look carefully at them too

Correct versions of SQR and DOUBLE are these:

```
#define SQR(x) ((x)*(x))
```

```
#define DOUBLE(x) ((x)+(x))
```

Macros have a last little trick to surprise you with, as this shows.

```
#include <stdio.h>
#include <stdlib.h>
#define DOUBLE(x) ((x)+(x))
main(){
int a[20], *ip;
ip = a;
a[0] = 1;
a[1] = 2;
printf("%d\n", DOUBLE(*ip++));
exit(EXIT_SUCCESS);
}
```

Example: Why is this going to cause problems? Because the replacement text of the macro refers to *ip++ twice, so ip gets incremented twice. Macros should never be used with expressions that involve side effects, unless you check very carefully that they are safe. Despite these warnings, they provide a very useful feature, and one which will be used a lot from now on.

UNDEF

The name of any #defined identifier can be forcibly forgotten by saying

```
#undef NAME
```

It isn't an error to #undef a name which isn't currently defined.

INCLUDE

This comes in two flavours:

```
#include <filename>
#include "filename"
```

both of which cause a new file to be read at the point where they occur. It's as if the single line containing the directive is replaced by the contents of the specified file. If that file contains erroneous statements, you can reasonably expect that the errors will be reported with a correct file name and line number.

It's the compiler writer's job to get that right. The Standard specifies that at least eight nested levels of # include must be supported. The effect of using brackets <> or quotes " " around the filename is to change the places searched to find the specified file. The brackets cause a search of a number of implementation defined places, the quotes cause a search of somewhere associated with the original source file. Your implementation notes must tell you the specific details of what is meant by 'place'. If the form using quotes can't find the file, it tries again as if you had used brackets.

In general, brackets are used when you specify standard library header files, quotes are used for private header files—often specific to one program only.

Although the Standard doesn't define what constitutes a valid file name, it does specify that there must be an implementation-defined unique way of translating file names of the form xxx.x (where x represents a 'letter'), into source file names. Distinctions of upper and lower case may be ignored and the implementation may choose only to use six significant characters before the '.' character.

You can also write this:

```
# define NAME <stdio.h>
# include NAME
```

to get the same effect as

```
# include <stdio.h>
```

but it's a rather roundabout way of doing it, and unfortunately it's subject to implementation defined rules about how the text between < and > is treated. It's simpler if the replacement text for NAME comes out to be a string, for example,

```
#define NAME "stdio.h"
#include NAME
```

There is no problem with implementation defined behaviour here, but the paths searched are different, as explained above. For the first case, what happens is that the token sequence which replaces NAME is (by the rules already given),

```
<
stdio
```

```
.
h
>
```

and for the second case

```
"stdio.h"
```

The second case is easy, since it's just a *string-literal* which is a legal token for a# include directive. It is implementation defined how the first case is treated, and whether or not the sequence of tokens forms a legal *header-name*. Finally, the last character of a file which is being included must be a plain newline. Failure to include a file successfully is treated as an error.

PREDEFINED NAMES

The following names are predefined within the preprocessor:

`__LINE__`

The current source file line number, a decimal integer constant.

`__FILE__`

The 'name' of the current source code file, a string literal.

`__DATE__`

The current date, a string literal. The form is Apr 21 1990 where the month name is as defined in the library function asctime and the first digit of the date is a space if the date is less than 10.

`__TIME__`

The time of the translation; again a string literal in the form produced by asctime, which has the form "hh:mm:ss".

`__STDC__`

The integer constant 1. This is used to test if the compiler is Standard-conforming, the intention being that it will have different values for different releases of the Standard. A common way of using these predefined names is the following:

```
#define TEST(x) if(!(x))\
printf("test failed, line %d file %s\n",\
__LINE__, __FILE__)
/**/
TEST(a != 23);
```

```
/**/
```

Example: If the argument to TEST gives a false result, the message is printed, including the filename and line number in the message.

There's only one minor caveat: the use of the if statement can cause confusion in a case like this:

```
if(expression)
TEST(expr2);
else
statement_n;
```

The else will get associated with the hidden if generated by expanding the TESTmacro. This is most unlikely to happen in practice, but will be a thorough pain to track down if it ever does sneak up on you. It's good style to make the bodies of every control of flow statement compound anyway; then the problem goes away.

None of the names __LINE__, __FILE__, __DATE__, __TIME__, __STDC__ or defined may be used in #define or # undef directives. The Standard specifies that any other reserved names will either start with an underscore followed by an upper case letter or another underscore, so you know that you are free to use any other names for your own purposes (but watch out for additional names reserved in Library header files that you may have included).

#LINE

This is used to set the value of the built in names __LINE__ and __FILE__. Why do this? Because a lot of tools nowadays actually generate C as their output. This directive allows them to control the current line number. It is of very limited interest to the 'ordinary' C programmer.

Its form is,

```
# line number optional-string-literal newline
```

The number sets the value of __LINE__, the string literal, if present, sets the value of __FILE__. In fact, the sequence of tokens following #line will be macro expanded. After expansion, they are expected to provide a valid directive of the right form.

CONDITIONAL COMPILATION

A number of the directives control conditional compilation, which allows certain portions of a program to be selectively compiled or ignored depending upon specified conditions.

The directives concerned are: #if, #ifdef, #ifndef, #elif,#else, #endif together with the preprocessor unary operator defined.

The way that they are used is like this:

```
#ifdef NAME
/* compile these lines if NAME is defined */
#endif
#ifndef NAME
/* compile these lines if NAME is not defined
*/
#else
/* compile these lines if NAME is defined */
#endif
```

So, #ifdef and #endif can be used to test the definition or otherwise of a given macro name. Of course the #else can be used with #ifdef (and #if or #elif) too. There is no ambiguity about what a given #else binds to, because the use of#endif to delimit the scope of these directives eliminates any possible ambiguity. The Standard specifies that at least eight levels of nesting of conditional directives must be supported, but in practice there is not likely to be any real limit. These directives are most commonly used to select small fragments of C that are machine specific (when it is not possible to make the whole program completely machine independent), or sometimes to select different algorithms depending on the need to make trade-offs.

The #if and #elif constructs take a single integral constant expression as their arguments. Preprocessor integral constant expressions are the same as other integral constant expressions except that they must not contain cast operators. The token sequence that makes up the constant expression undergoes macro replacement, except that names prefixed by defined are not expanded. In this context, the expression defined NAME or defined (NAME) evaluates to 1 if NAMEis currently defined, 0 if it is not. Any other identifiers in the expression *including those that are C keywords* are replaced with the value 0. Then the expression is evaluated. The replacement even of keywords means that sizeof can't be used in these expressions to get the result that you would normally expect.

As with the other conditional statements in C, a resulting value of zero is used to represent 'false', anything else is 'true'. The preprocessor always must use arithmetic with at least the ranges defined in the <limits.h> file and treats int expressions as long int and unsigned int as unsigned long int. Character constants do not necessarily have the same values as they do at execution time, so for highly portable programs, it's best to avoid using them in preprocessor expressions. Overall, the rules mean that it is possible to get arithmetic results from the preprocessor which are different from the results at run time; although presumably only if the translation and execution are done on different machines.

Here's an example:

```
#include <limits.h>
#if ULONG_MAX+1 != 0
printf("Preprocessor: ULONG_MAX+1 != 0\n");
#endif
if(ULONG_MAX+1 != 0)
printf("Runtime: ULONG_MAX+1 != 0\n");
```

Example: It is conceivable that the preprocessor might perform arithmetic with a greater range than that used in the target environment. In that case, the preprocessor expression ULONG_MAX+1 might not 'overflow' to give the result of 0, whereas in the execution environment, it must.

The following skeleton example illustrates the use of such constants and also the 'conditional else', #elif.

```
#define NAME 100
#if ((NAME > 50) && (defined __STDC__))
/* do something */
#elif NAME > 25
/* do something else*/
#elif NAME > 10
/* do something else */
```

```
#else
/* last possibility */
#endif
```

These conditional compilation directives do not obey the same scope rules as the rest of C. They should be used sparingly, unless your program is rapidly to become unreadable. It is impossible to read C when it is laced with these things every few lines. The urge to maim the author of a piece of code becomes very strong when you suddenly come across,

```
#else
}
#endif
```

with no #if or whatever immediately visible above. They should be treated like chilli sauce; essential at times, but more than a tiny sprinkle is too much.

#PRAGMA

This was the Standard Committee's way of 'opening the back door'. It allows implementation-defined things to take place. If the implementation was not expecting what you wrote (*i.e.* doesn't recognize it), it is ignored.

Here is a possible example:

```
#pragma byte_align
```

which could be used to tell the implementation that all structure members should be aligned on byte addresses - some processor architectures are able to cope with word-sized structure members aligned on byte addresses, but with a penalty in access speed being incurred.

It could, of course, mean anything else that the implementation chooses it to mean. If your implementation doesn't have any special meaning for this, then it will have no effect. It will not count as an error.

#ERROR

This directive is followed by one or more tokens at the end of the line. A diagnostic message is produced by the compiler, which includes those tokens, but no further detail is given in the Standard.

It might be used like this to abort a compilation on unsuitable hardware:

```
#include <limits.h>
#if CHAR_MIN > -128
#error character range smaller than required
#endif
```

which would be expected to produce some sort of meaningful compilation error and message.

9

Programming Language

INTRODUCTION

The best way to start learning a programming language is by writing a program.

Therefore, here is our first program:

```
//my first program in C++
#include <iostream>
using namespace std;
int main ()
{
  cout << "Hello World!";
  return 0;
} Hello World!
```

The first panel shows the source code for our first program. The second one shows the result of the program once compiled and executed. The way to edit and compile a program depends on the compiler you are using. Depending on whether it has a Development Interface or not and on its version. Consult the compilers section and the manual or help included with your compiler if you have doubts on how to compile a C++ console program. The previous program is the typical program that programmer apprentices write for the first time, and its result is the printing on screen of the "Hello World!" sentence. It is one of the simplest programs that can be written in C++, but it already contains the fundamental components that every C++ program has. We are going to look line by line at the code we have just written:

```
//my first program in C++
```

This is a comment line. All lines beginning with two slash signs (//) are considered comments and do not have any effect on the behaviour of the program. The programmer can use them to include short explanations or observations within the source code itself. In this case, the line is a brief description of what our program is.

```
#include <iostream>
```

Lines beginning with a pound sign (#) are directives for the preprocessor. They are not regular code lines with expressions but indications for the compiler's preprocessor. In this case the directive #include <iostream> tells the preprocessor to include the iostream standard file. This specific file (iostream) includes the declarations of the basic standard input-output library in C++, and it is included because its functionality is going to be used later in the program.

```
using namespace std;
```

All the elements of the standard C++ library are declared within what is called a namespace, the namespace with the name *std*. So in order to access its functionality we declare with this expression that we will be using these entities. This line is very frequent in C++ programs that use the standard library, and in fact it will be included in most of the source codes included in these tutorials.

```
int main ()
```

This line corresponds to the beginning of the definition of the main function. The main function is the point by where all C++ programs start their execution, independently of its location within the source code. It does not matter whether there are other functions with other names defined before or after it - the instructions contained within this function's definition will always be the first ones to be executed in any C++ program. For that same reason, it is essential that all C++ programs have a main function.

The word main is followed in the code by a pair of parentheses (()). That is because it is a function declaration: In C++, what differentiates a function declaration from other types of expressions are these parentheses that follow its name. Optionally, these parentheses may enclose a list of parameters within them. Right after these parentheses we can find the body of the main function enclosed in braces ({}). What is contained within these braces is what the function does when it is executed.

```
cout << "Hello World";
```

This line is a C++ statement. A statement is a simple or compound expression that can actually produce some effect. In fact, this statement performs the only action that generates a visible effect in our first program. cout represents the standard output stream in C++, and the meaning of the entire statement is to insert a sequence of characters (in this case the Hello World sequence of characters) into the standard output stream (which usually is the screen). cout is declared in the iostream standard file within the std namespace, so that's why we needed to include that specific file and to declare that we were going to use this specific namespace earlier in our code.

Notice that the statement ends with a semicolon character (;). This character is used to mark the end of the statement and in fact it must be included at the end of all expression statements in all C++ programs (one of the most common syntax errors is indeed to forget to include some semicolon after a statement).

```
return 0;
```

The return statement causes the main function to finish. return may be followed by a return code (in our example is followed by the return code 0). A return code of 0 for the main function is generally interpreted as the program worked as expected without any errors during its execution. This is the most usual way to end a C++ console program.

You may have noticed that not all the lines of this program perform actions when the code is executed. There were lines containing only comments (those beginning by//). There were lines with directives for the compiler's preprocessor (those beginning by #). Then there were lines that began the declaration of a function (in this case, the main function) and, finally lines with statements (like the insertion into cout), which were all included within the block delimited by the braces ({}) of the main function.

The program has been structured in different lines in order to be more readable, but in C++, we do not have strict rules on how to separate instructions in different lines. For example, instead of

```
int main ()
{
  cout << " Hello World ";
  return 0;
}
```

We could have written:

```
int main () {cout << "Hello World"; return
0;}
```

All in just one line and this would have had exactly the same meaning as the previous code. In C++, the separation between statements is specified with an ending semicolon (;) at the end of each one, so the separation in different code lines does not matter at all for this purpose. We can write many statements per line or write a single statement that takes many code lines. The division of code in different lines serves only to make it more legible and schematic for the humans that may read it.

Let us add an additional instruction to our first program:

```
//my second program in C++
#include <iostream>
using namespace std;
int main ()
{
  cout << "Hello World! ";
  cout << "I'm a C++ program";
  return 0;
}
```

Hello World! I'm a C++ program

In this case, we performed two insertions into cout in two different statements. Once again, the separation in different lines of code has been done just to give greater readability to the program, since main could have been perfectly valid defined this way:

```
int main () {cout << " Hello World! "; cout
  << " I'm a C++ program "; return 0;}
```

We were also free to divide the code into more lines if we considered it more convenient:

```
int main ()
{
  cout <<
    "Hello World!";
  cout
    << "I'm a C++ program";
  return 0;
}
```

And the result would again have been exactly the same as in the previous examples. Preprocessor directives (those that begin by #) are out of this general rule since they are not statements. They are lines read and processed by the preprocessor and do not produce any code by themselves. Preprocessor directives must be specified in their own line and do not have to end with a semicolon (;).

COMMENTS

Comments are parts of the source code disregarded by the compiler. They simply do nothing. Their purpose is only to allow the programmer to insert notes or descriptions embedded within the source code.

C++ supports two ways to insert comments:

```
//line comment
/* block comment */
```

The first of them, known as line comment, discards everything from where the pair of slash signs (//) is found up to the end of that same line. The second one, known as block comment, discards everything between the/* characters and the first appearance of the */characters, with the possibility of including more than one line.

We are going to add comments to our second program:

```
/* my second program in C++
with more comments */
#include <iostream>
using namespace std;
int main ()
```

```
{
  cout << "Hello World! ";//prints Hello World!
  cout << "I'm a C++ program";//prints I'm a
    C++ program
  return 0;
} Hello World! I'm a C++ program
```

If you include comments within the source code of your programs without using the comment characters combinations//,/* or */, the compiler will take them as if they were C++ expressions, most likely causing one or several error messages when you compile it.

VARIABLES. DATA TYPES.

The usefulness of the "Hello World" programs shown in the previous section is quite questionable. We had to write several lines of code, compile them, and then execute the resulting program just to obtain a simple sentence written on the screen as result. It certainly would have been much faster to type the output sentence by ourselves. However, programming is not limited only to printing simple texts on the screen. In order to go a little further on and to become able to write programs that perform useful tasks that really save us work we need to introduce the concept of variable.

The whole process that you have just done with your mental memory is a simile of what a computer can do with two variables.

The same process can be expressed in C++ with the following instruction set:

```
a = 5;
b = 2;
a = a + 1;
result = a - b;
```

Obviously, this is a very simple example since we have only used two small integer values, but consider that your computer can store millions of numbers like these at the same time and conduct sophisticated mathematical operations with them. Therefore, we can define a variable as a portion of memory to store a determined value. Each variable needs an identifier that distinguishes it from the others, for example, in the previous code the variable identifiers were a, b and result, but we could have called the variables any names we wanted to invent, as long as they were valid identifiers.

IDENTIFIERS

A valid identifier is a sequence of one or more letters, digits or underscore characters (_). Neither spaces nor punctuation marks or symbols can be part of an identifier. Only letters, digits and single underscore characters are valid. In addition, variable identifiers always have to begin with a letter. They can also begin with an underline character (_), but in some cases these may be reserved for compiler specific keywords or external identifiers, as well as identifiers containing two successive underscore characters anywhere. In no case they can begin with a digit.

Another rule that you have to consider when inventing your own identifiers is that they cannot match any keyword of the C++ language nor your compiler's specific ones, which are *reserved keywords*.

The standard reserved keywords are: asm, auto, bool, break, case, catch, char, class, const, const_cast, continue, default, delete, do, double, dynamic_cast, else, enum, explicit, export, extern, false, float, for, friend, goto, if, inline, int, long, mutable, namespace, new, operator, private, protected, public, register, reinterpret_cast, return, short, signed, sizeof, static, static_cast, struct, switch, template, this, throw, true, try, typedef, typeid, typename, union, unsigned, using, virtual, void, volatile, wchar_t, while

Additionally, alternative representations for some operators cannot be used as identifiers since they are reserved words under some circumstances: and, and_eq, bitand, bitor, compl, not, not_eq, or, or_eq, xor, xor_eq. Your compiler may also include some additional specific reserved keywords.

Very important: The C++ language is a "case sensitive" language. That means that an identifier written in capital letters is not equivalent to another one with the same name but written in small letters. Thus, for example, the RESULT variable is not the same as the result variable or the Result variable. These are three different variable identifiers.

FUNDAMENTAL DATA TYPES

When programming, we store the variables in our computer's memory, but the computer has to know what kind of data we want to store in them, since it is not going to occupy the same amount of memory to store a simple number than to store a single letter or a large number, and they are not going to be interpreted the same way.

The memory in our computers is organized in bytes. A byte is the minimum amount of memory that we can manage in C++.

A byte can store a relatively small amount of data: one single character or a small integer (generally an integer between 0 and 255). In addition, the computer can manipulate more complex data types that come from grouping several bytes, such as long numbers or non-integer numbers.

DECLARATION OF VARIABLES

In order to use a variable in C++, we must first declare it specifying which data type we want it to be. The syntax to declare a new variable is to write the specifier of the desired data type (like int, bool, float...) followed by a valid variable identifier.

For example:

```
int a;b
float mynumber;
```

These are two valid declarations of variables. The first one declares a variable of type int with the identifier a. The second one declares a variable of type float with the identifier mynumber. Once declared, the variables a and mynumber can be used within the rest of their scope in the program. If you are going to declare more than one variable of the same type, you can declare all of them in a single statement by separating their identifiers with commas.

For example:

```
int a, b, c;
```

This declares three variables (a, b and c), all of them of type int, and has exactly the same meaning as:

```
int a;
int b;
int c;
```

The integer data types char, short, long and int can be either signed or unsigned depending on the range of numbers needed to be represented. Signed types can represent both positive and negative values, whereas unsigned types can only represent positive values (and zero). This can be specified by using either the specifier signed or the specifier unsigned before the type name.

For example:

```
unsigned short int NumberOfSisters;
signed int MyAccountBalance;
```

By default, if we do not specify either signed or unsigned most compiler settings will assume the type to be signed, therefore instead of the second declaration above we could have written:

```
int MyAccountBalance;
```

with exactly the same meaning (with or without the keyword signed) An exception to this general rule is the char type, which exists by itself and is considered a different fundamental data type from signed char and unsigned char, thought to store characters. You should use either signed or unsigned if you intend to store numerical values in a char-sized variable. short and long can be used alone as type specifiers. In this case, they refer to their respective integer fundamental types: short is equivalent to short int and long is equivalent to long int.

The following two variable declarations are equivalent:

```
short Year;
short int Year;
```

Finally, signed and unsigned may also be used as standalone type specifiers, meaning the same as signed int and unsigned int respectively.

The following two declarations are equivalent:

```
unsigned NextYear;
unsigned int NextYear;
```

To see what variable declarations look like in action within a program, we are going to see the C++ code of the example about your mental memory proposed at the beginning of this section:

```
//operating with variables
#include <iostream>
using namespace std;
int main ()
{
  //declaring variables:
  int a, b;
  int result;
  //process:
  a = 5;
  b = 2;
  a = a + 1;
  result = a - b;
  //print out the result:
  cout << result;
  //terminate the program:
  return 0;
} 4
```

Do not worry if something else than the variable declarations themselves looks a bit strange to you. You will see the rest in detail in coming sections.

INITIALIZATION OF VARIABLES

When declaring a regular local variable, its value is by default undetermined. But you may want a variable to store a concrete value at the same moment that it is declared. In order to do that, you can initialize the variable.

There are two ways to do this in C++: The first one, known as c-like, is done by appending an equal sign followed by the value to which the variable will be initialized:

```
type identifier = initial_value;
```

For example, if we want to declare an int variable called a initialized with a value of 0 at the moment in which it is declared, we could write:

```
int a = 0;
```

The other way to initialize variables, known as constructor initialization, is done by enclosing the initial value between parentheses (()):

```
type identifier (initial_value);
For example:
int a (0);
Both ways of initializing variables are valid
  and equivalent in C++.
//initialization of variables
#include <iostream>
using namespace std;
int main ()
{
  int a=5;//initial value = 5
  int b(2);//initial value = 2
  int result;//initial value undetermined
  a = a + 3;
  result = a - b;
  cout << result;
  return 0;
} 6
```

STRINGS

Variables that can store non-numerical values that are longer than one single character are known as strings. The C++ language library provides support for strings through the standard string class. This is not a fundamental type, but it behaves in a similar way as fundamental types do in its most basic usage. A first difference with fundamental data types is that in order to declare and use objects (variables) of this type we need to include an additional header file in our source code: <string> and have access to the std namespace (which we already had in all our previous programs thanks to the using namespace statement).

```
//my first string
  #include <iostream>
  #include <string>
  using namespace std;
```

```
  int main ()
{
  string mystring = "This is a string";
  cout << mystring;
  return 0;
}
  output
  This is a string
```

As you may see in the previous example, strings can be initialized with any valid string literal just like numerical type variables can be initialized to any valid numerical literal. Both initialization formats are valid with strings:

```
string mystring = "This is a string";
string mystring ("This is a string");
```

Strings can also perform all the other basic operations that fundamental data types can, like being declared without an initial value and being assigned values during execution:

```
//my first string
  #include <iostream>
  #include <string>
  using namespace std;
int main ()
{
  string mystring;
  mystring = "This is the initial string
    content";
  cout << mystring << endl;
  mystring = "This is a different string
    content";
  cout << mystring << endl;
  sreturn 0;
}
output
  This is the initial string content
  This is a different string content
```

For more details on C++ strings, you can have a look at the string class reference.

Constants: Constants are expressions with a fixed value.

LITERALS

Literals are used to express particular values within the source code of a program. We have already used these previously to give concrete values to variables or to express messages we wanted our programs to print out, for example, when we wrote:

```
a = 5;
```

the 5 in this piece of code was a literal constant. Literal constants can be divided in Integer Numerals, Floating-Point Numerals, Characters, Strings and Boolean Values.

INTEGER NUMERALS

```
1776
707
-273
```

They are numerical constants that identify integer decimal values. Notice that to express a numerical constant we do not have to write quotes (") nor any special character. There is no doubt that it is a constant: whenever we write 1776 in a program, we will be referring to the value 1776.

In addition to decimal numbers (those that all of us are used to use every day) C++ allows the use as literal constants of octal numbers (base 8) and hexadecimal numbers (base 16). If we want to express an octal number we have to precede it with a 0 (zero character). And in order to express a hexadecimal number we have to precede it with the characters 0x (zero, x).

For example, the following literal constants are all equivalent to each other:

```
75//decimal
0113//octal
0x4b//hexadecimal
```

All of these represent the same number: 75 (seventy-five) expressed as a base-10 numeral, octal numeral and hexadecimal numeral, respectively. Literal constants, like variables, are considered to have a specific data type. By default, integer literals are of type int. However, we can force them to either be unsigned by appending the u character to it, or long by appending l:

```
75//int
```

```
75u//unsigned int
75l//long
75ul//unsigned long
```

In both cases, the suffix can be specified using either upper or lowercase letters.

Floating Point Numbers: They express numbers with decimals and/or exponents. They can include either a decimal point, an e character (that expresses "by ten at the Xth height", where X is an integer value that follows the e character), or both a decimal point and an e character:

```
3.14159//3.14159
6.02e23//6.02 x 10^23
1.6e-19//1.6 x 10-19
3.0//3.0
```

These are four valid numbers with decimals expressed in C++. The first number is PI, the second one is the number of Avogadro, the third is the electric charge of an electron (an extremely small number) -all of them approximated- and the last one is the number three expressed as a floating-point numeric literal.

The default type for floating point literals is double. If you explicitly want to express a float or long double numerical literal, you can use the f or l suffixes respectively:

```
3.14159L//long double
6.02e23f//float
```

Any of the letters than can be part of a floating-point numerical constant (e, f, l) can be written using either lower or uppercase letters without any difference in their meanings.

Character and String Literals

There also exist non-numerical constants, like:

```
'z'
'p'
"Hello world"
"How do you do?"
```

The first two expressions represent single character constants, and the following two represent string literals composed of several characters. Notice that to represent a single character we enclose it between single quotes (') and to express a string (which generally consists of more than one character) we enclose it between double quotes ("). When writing both single character and string literals, it is necessary to put the quotation marks surrounding them to distinguish them from possible variable identifiers or reserved keywords.

Notice the difference between these two expressions:

```
x
'x'
```

x alone would refer to a variable whose identifier is x, whereas 'x' (enclosed within single quotation marks) would refer to the character constant 'x'.

Character and string literals have certain peculiarities, like the escape codes. These are special characters that are difficult or impossible to express otherwise in the source code of a program, like newline (\n) or tab (\t). All of them are preceded by a backslash (\).

Here you have a list of some of such escape codes:

```
\n newline
\r carriage return
\t tab
\v vertical tab
\b backspace
\f form feed (page feed)
\a alert (beep)
\' single quote (')
\" double quote (")
\? question mark (?)
\\ backslash (\)
```

For example:

```
'\n'
'\t'
"Left \t Right"
"one\ntwo\nthree"
```

Additionally, you can express any character by its numerical ASCII code by writing a backslash character (\) followed by the ASCII code expressed as an octal (base-8) or hexadecimal (base-16) number. In the first case (octal) the digits must immediately follow the backslash (for example \23 or \40), in the second case (hexadecimal), an x character must be written before the digits themselves (for example \x20 or \x4A). String literals can extend to more than a single line of code by putting a backslash sign (\) at the end of each unfinished line.

```
"string expressed in \
two lines"
```

You can also concatenate several string constants separating them by one or several blank spaces, tabulators, newline or any other valid blank character:

```
"this forms" "a single" "string" "of
 characters"
```

Finally, if we want the string literal to be explicitly made of wide characters (wchar_t), instead of narrow characters (char), we can precede the constant with the L prefix:

```
L"This is a wide character string"
```

Wide characters are used mainly to represent non-English or exotic character sets.

BOOLEAN LITERALS

There are only two valid Boolean values: true and false. These can be expressed in C++ as values of type bool by using the Boolean literals true and false.

Defined constants (#define): You can define your own names for constants that you use very often without having to resort to memory-consuming variables, simply by using the #define preprocessor directive.

Its format is:

```
#define identifier value
```

For example:

```
#define PI 3.14159265
#define NEWLINE '\n'
```

This defines two new constants: PI and NEWLINE. Once they are defined, you can use them in the rest of the code as if they were any other regular constant, for example:

```
//defined constants: calculate circumference
#include <iostream>
```

```
using namespace std;
#define PI 3.14159
#define NEWLINE '\n'
int main ()
{
  double r=5.0;//radius
  double circle;
  circle = 2 * PI * r;
  cout << circle;
  cout << NEWLINE;
  return 0;
}
output
31.4159
```

In fact the only thing that the compiler preprocessor does when it encounters #define directives is to literally replace any occurrence of their identifier (in the previous example, these were PI and NEWLINE) by the code to which they have been defined (3.14159265 and '\n' respectively).

The #define directive is not a C++ statement but a directive for the preprocessor; therefore it assumes the entire line as the directive and does not require a semicolon (;) at its end. If you append a semicolon character (;) at the end, it will also be appended in all occurrences within the body of the program that the preprocessor replaces.

DECLARED CONSTANTS (CONST)

With the const prefix you can declare constants with a specific type in the same way as you would do with a variable:

```
const int pathwidth = 100;
const char tabulator = '\t';
```

Here, pathwidth and tabulator are two typed constants. They are treated just like regular variables except that their values cannot be modified after their definition.

OPERATORS

Once we know of the existence of variables and constants, we can begin to operate with them. For that purpose, C++

integrates operators. Unlike other languages whose operators are mainly keywords, operators in C++ are mostly made of signs that are not part of the alphabet but are available in all keyboards. This makes C++ code shorter and more international, since it relies less on English words, but requires a little of learning effort in the beginning.

Assignment (=)

The assignment operator assigns a value to a variable.

```
a = 5;
```

This statement assigns the integer value 5 to the variable a. The part at the left of the assignment operator (=) is known as the *lvalue* (left value) and the right one as the *rvalue* (right value). The lvalue has to be a variable whereas the rvalue can be either a constant, a variable, the result of an operation or any combination of these.

The most important rule when assigning is the *right-to-left* rule: The assignment operation always takes place from right to left, and never the other way:

```
a = b;
```

This statement assigns to variable a (the lvalue) the value contained in variable b (the rvalue). The value that was stored until this moment in a is not considered at all in this operation, and in fact that value is lost. Consider also that we are only assigning the value of b to a at the moment of the assignment operation. Therefore a later change of b will not affect the new value of a. For example, let us have a look at the following code - I have included the evolution of the content stored in the variables as comments:

```
//assignment operator
#include <iostream>
using namespace std;
int main ()
{
  int a, b;//a:?, b:?
  a = 10;//a:10, b:?
  b = 4;//a:10, b:4
  a = b;//a:4, b:4
```

```
    b = 7;//a:4, b:7
    cout << "a:";
    cout << a;
    cout << " b:";
    cout << b;
    return 0;
}
output
a:4 b:7
```

This code will give us as result that the value contained in a is 4 and the one contained in b is 7. Notice how a was not affected by the final modification of b, even though we declared a = b earlier (that is because of the *right-to-left rule*).

A property that C++ has over other programming languages is that the assignment operation can be used as the rvalue (or part of an rvalue) for another assignment operation.

For example:

```
a = 2 + (b = 5);
```

is equivalent to:

```
b = 5;
a = 2 + b;
```

that means: First assign 5 to variable b and then assign to a the value 2 plus the result of the previous assignment of b (*i.e.* 5), leaving a with a final value of 7.

The following expression is also valid in C++:

```
a = b = c = 5;
```

It assigns 5 to the all the three variables: a, b and c.

Arithmetic operators (+, -, *,/, %)

The five arithmetical operations supported by the C++ *language are*:

```
+ addition
- subtraction
* multiplication
/division
% modulo
```

Operations of addition, subtraction, multiplication and division literally correspond with their respective mathematical operators. The only one that you might not be so used to see may be *modulo*; whose operator is the percentage sign (%). Modulo is the operation that gives the remainder of a division of two values.

For example, if we write:

```
a = 11 % 3;
```

the variable a will contain the value 2, since 2 is the remainder from dividing 11 between 3.

Compound assignment (+=, -=, *=,/=, %=, >>=, <<=, &=, ^=, |=)

When we want to modify the value of a variable by performing an operation on the value currently stored in that variable we can use compound assignment operators:

Expression	Is equivalent to
value += increase;	value = value + increase;
a -= 5;	a = a - 5;
a/= b;	a = a/b;
price *= units + 1;	price = price * (units + 1);

and the same for all other operators. For example:

```
//compound assignment operators
#include <iostream>
using namespace std;
int main ()
{
  int a, b=3;
  a = b;
  a+=2;//equivalent to a=a+2
  cout << a;
  return 0;
} 5
```

Increase and decrease (++, —)

Shortening even more some expressions, the increase operator (++) and the decrease operator (—) increase or reduce by one the value stored in a variable. They are equivalent to +=1 and to -=1, respectively.

Thus:

```
c++;
c+=1;
c=c+1;
```

are all equivalent in its functionality: the three of them increase by one the value of c. In the early C compilers, the three previous expressions probably produced different executable code depending on which one was used. Nowadays, this type of code optimization is generally done automatically by the compiler, thus the three expressions should produce exactly the same executable code.

CONTROL STRUCTURES

A program is usually not limited to a linear sequence of instructions. During its process it may bifurcate, repeat code or take decisions. For that purpose, C++ provides control structures that serve to specify what has to be done by our program, when and under which circumstances.

With the introduction of control structures we are going to have to introduce a new concept: the *compound-statement* or *block*. A block is a group of statements which are separated by semicolons (;) like all C++ statements, but grouped together in a block enclosed in braces: {}:

```
{statement1; statement2; statement3;}
```

Most of the control structures that we will see in this section require a generic statement as part of its syntax. A statement can be either a simple statement (a simple instruction ending with a semicolon) or a compound statement (several instructions grouped in a block), like the one just described. In the case that we want the statement to be a simple statement, we do not need to enclose it in braces ({}). But in the case that we want the statement to be a compound statement it must be enclosed between braces ({}), forming a block.

Conditional Structure: If and Else

The if keyword is used to execute a statement or block only if a condition is fulfilled. Its form is:

```
if (condition) statement
```

Where condition is the expression that is being evaluated. If this condition is true, statement is executed. If it is false, statement is ignored (not executed) and the program continues right after this conditional structure.

For example, the following code fragment prints x is 100 only if the value stored in the x variable is indeed 100:

```
if (x == 100)
  cout << "x is 100";
```

If we want more than a single statement to be executed in case that the condition is true we can specify a block using braces {}:

```
if (x == 100)
{
  cout << "x is ";
  cout << x;
}
```

We can additionally specify what we want to happen if the condition is not fulfilled by using the keyword else. Its form used in conjunction with if is: if (condition) statement1 else statement2.

For example:

```
if (x == 100)
  cout << "x is 100";
else
  cout << "x is not 100";
```

prints on the screen x is 100 if indeed x has a value of 100, but if it has not -and only if not- it prints out x is not 100.

The if + else structures can be concatenated with the intention of verifying a range of values. The following example shows its use telling if the value currently stored in x is positive, negative or none of them (*i.e.* zero):

```
if (x > 0)
  cout << "x is positive";
else if (x < 0)
  cout << "x is negative";
else
  cout << "x is 0";
```

Remember that in case that we want more than a single statement to be executed, we must group them in a block by enclosing them in braces {}.

Iteration Structures (Loops)

Loops have as purpose to repeat a statement a certain number of times or while a condition is fulfilled.

The while loop

Its format is: While (expression) statement and its functionality is simply to repeat statement while the condition set in expression is true.

For example, we are going to make a program to countdown using a while-loop:

```
// custom countdown using while
#include <iostream>
using namespace std;
int main ()
{
  int n;
  cout << "Enter the starting number > ";
  cin >> n;
  while (n>0) {
  cout << n << ", ";
  —n;
}
   cout << "FIRE!\n";
   return 0;
}
  Output
  Enter the starting number > 8
  8, 7, 6, 5, 4, 3, 2, 1, FIRE!
```

When the program starts the user is prompted to insert a starting number for the countdown. Then the while loop begins, if the value entered by the user fulfills the condition n>0 (that n is greater than zero) the block that follows the condition will be executed and repeated while the condition (n>0) remains being true. The whole process of the previous program can be interpreted according to the following script (beginning in main):

1. User assigns a value to n
2. The while condition is checked (n>0). At this point there are two posibilities:
   * condition is true: statement is executed (to step 3)
   * condition is false: ignore statement and continue after it (to step 5)

3. *Execute statement*:
   cout << n << ", "; —n;
   (prints the value of n on the screen and decreases n by 1)
4. End of block. Return automatically to step 2
5. Continue the program right after the block: print FIRE! and end program.

Bibliography

Bass, L.: *Software Architecture in Practice*, Philippines: Oxford University Press, 2008.

Beringer, D.: *Scenario Modelling: Modelling Global Behaviour with Scenarios in Object Oriented Analysis*, Hyderabad: Perspectives Publishers, 2007.

Cheng, J. H.: *Acta Informatica*, Princeton: Princeton University Press, 2005.

Cockburn, A.: *Surviving Object Oriented Projects: A Manager's Guide*, Guwahati: United Publishers, 2003.

Coleman, D.: *Object Oriented Development: The Fusion Method*, Mumbai: Sabrang Publications, 2000.

Cook, S.: *Designing Object Systems: Object Oriented Modeling with Syntrophy*, New Jersey: Prentice Hall, 2003.

Jones. C.B.: *Mural: A Formal Development Support System*, New York: Springer, 2005.

Luckham, D. C.: *Specification and Analysis of System Architecture*, New Delhi: Three Essays, 2002.

Manna, Z.: *The Temporal Logic of Reactive and Concurrent Systems: Specification*, New York: Springer-Verlag, 2002

Martin, R.: *Designing Object Oriented Applications Using the Booch Method*, New Jersey: Prentice Hall, 2005.

McConnell, S.: *Rapid Development: Taming Wild Software Schedules*, London: Picador, 2004.

Mellor, S.: *Object Life Cycles: Modeling the World in States*, New Jersey: Prentice Hall, 2006.

Meyer, B.: *Object Oriented Software Construction*, New Jersey: Prentice Hall, 2003.

Nerson, J.: *Seamless Object Oriented Architecture: Analysis and Design of Reliable Systems*, New Jersey: Prentice Hall, 2007.

Odell, J. J.: *Object Oriented Analysis and Design*, New Jersey: Prentice Hall, 2008.

Rumbaugh, J.: *Object Oriented Modeling and Design.* New Jersey: Prentice Hall, 2001.

Selic, B.: *Real-Time Object Oriented Modeling*, New York: John Wiley and Sons, 2000.

Shaw, A.: *Formulations and Formalisms in Software Architecture*, New York: Springer-Verlag, 1998.

Shaw, M.: *Software Architecture: Perspectives on an Emerging Discipline*, New Jersey: Prentice Hall, 1999.

Shlaer, S.: *Object Oriented Systems Analysis: Modeling the World of Data*, New Jersey: Prentice Hall, 2005.

Index

I

L

M

P

R

S

T

V

W